D0948115

Fundamentals of

Day Camping

Fundamentals of

Day Camping

by Grace Mitchell
with
Irwin Rhodes and Robert Rhodes

American Camping Association
Martinsville, Indiana

Library of Congress Cataloging in Publication Data

Mitchell, Grace L.
Fundamentals of Day Camping

Reprint. Originally published: New York: Association
Press, 1961.
1. Day Camp—Management.   I. Title.
[GV197.D3M5   19811   796.54'068   81-8088
                                                        AACR2

ISBN No. 0-87603-067-X

Dedication

This book is dedicated to the memory of Waldo Stone. The radiance of his love for God's world and its children reached out to all who knew him.

Contents

A Word from the Authors ... ix

Preface xi

Acknowledgements xiii

Introduction xv

1   The Day Camp Story 1

2   First Steps in Establishing a Day Camp 7

3   The Day Camp Site 13

4   Buildings and Equipment 23

5   Enrolling the Campers 33

6   Administration 41

7   Finance 53

8   Insurance 61

9   Transportation 69

10   Health and Safety 79

11   Food in the Day Camp 97

12   The Day Camp Staff 103

13 Staff Training and Supervision 119

14 Discipline in the Day Camp 137

15 The Day Camp Program............................. 147

16 Arts and Crafts 163

17 Making the Most of Natural Resources................... 177

18 Adventures in Camping 187

19 Athletics and Camp Life 199

20 Musical Experience in the Day Camp 207

21 A Bag of Tricks 217

22 Rainy Days Can Be the Best 231

23 Day Camping Is for Everyone 239

24 Reflections 247

A Word from the Authors

When I wrote *Fundamentals of Day Camping* in 1960 I was riding on a cause—a conviction that there was only one way to conduct a day camp, and that having discovered that way, I had an obligation to tell the rest of the world about it.

In the intervening years my mind has stretched beyond the limits of personal bias. I have visited day camps which were not at all like the image I had described, and they were doing very well, not just in a business sense but in what they were offering to children. When I was asked to revise my book, the first step was to go back and read the original. One thing became quite clear. If my first attempt had been so exclusively "right" the rest of the world would have jumped on my bandwagon and emulated my fine example.

Thus in a more humble spirit I welcomed Irwin and Bob Rhodes as partners in this revision and went to visit Deerkill, their day camp in Suffern, New York. In preparation for my visit, they had found a copy (now out of print) of *Fundamentals* and read it. During my visit we discovered that while we may have approached our commitment to day care from different directions, we met and converged on all of the important issues.

We want to give happy experiences and joyful memories to our campers. We want to open up new interests that will enrich their lives and teach them new skills. We want to help them become physically and emotionally strong, capable human beings. We both believe that camp can accomplish some of these lofty goals in a unique way that school, with its pressures and strains, seldom attains.

Having affirmed our common beliefs, it was not hard to establish a plan for expressing our differences in methods and approach, which we believe greatly enhances the value of this book. The reader can glean from it that which best suits his purpose, and if our efforts have been worthwhile day campers in many parts of the country will benefit.

Preface

In the twenty years that have passed since I wrote *Fundamentals of Day Camping* there have been some who have openly suggested, others who have implied, that the philosophies and practices were "very nice but unrealistic." "Idealistic but not practical."

From a strictly business point of view I can now answer, "When, over the years, you can have more business than you can accommodate without spending money on advertising and brochures, you must have something worthy of consideration. When parents send their children, summer after summer, and ask you to "up" the age limits; when campers beg to stay on as C.I.T.'s and junior counselors, and when more than half of the staff return each year, this surely is proof that those idealistic ideas are very practical, indeed."

The spirit that keynotes Green Acres comes from setting idealistic goals and working to achieve them.

The camp director or owner who sets his expectations too low, who is willing to settle for less than excellence, underrates his own capacity for leadership. What is worse—he works harder.

Everything written here has been tested—experienced. It is plain, ordinary common sense. I offer it with the hope that it can be used for the benefit of others—my legacy to future generations of children.

Acknowledgements

The authors wish to express their appreciation to Monte Melemud and Allen Beavers for their contributions; to Margo Childs who, in addition to many patient hours of typing, served as a sounding board, and to Lois Dewsnap for editing the final manuscript.

Introduction

This book was developed because of an expressed need. Each year there are many new day camps launched by individuals or groups of individuals who are sincerely interested in offering a good camping experience to children. In addition, there are many other summertime groupings of children which are more rightly classified as day care programs, play schools, or summer playground excursions. The Day Camp Standards of the American Camping Association provide a measure for determining what "is" and what "is not" a day camp, but standards alone are but a skeleton—a frame without life or vitality. The material presented here attempts to put meat on the bones of that skeleton and to breathe life into the spirit of day camping.

Day camps are operated by so many different agencies and sponsors that an attempt to describe procedures appropriate for all would be impossible. Each reader will have to look at his own organizational structure to determine where and how the various functions of planning, policy making, coordinating, operating, and evaluating are best carried out. It is hoped that the suggestions offered will serve as a guide toward creating a safe and happy environment in which children can learn and grow.

It is what the campers do in that environment which determines success. Program is the "product" of the day camp, and so in the second part of the book we have shared some of the ideas and activities which have left our campers with a host of good memories.

The reader will find frequent references to two resources which are "musts."

The first, *Basic Camp Management* by Armand and Beverly Ball, ACA, 1979, contains essential information and forms which we saw no reason to duplicate.

The second, *The Day Camp Program Book* by Virginia Musselman, Follett, 1980, was first printed in 1960 and was considered a companion piece to *Fundamentals of Day Camping*. It is a "goldmine" of program ideas that practically guarantee exciting, fun-filled days for campers. This and the ACA Song Book should be purchased in quantity so that each unit or group can have frequent access to them.

Since the Standards of the American Camping Association are referred to frequently throughout the text, a copy of the present Standards are they apply to day camping will be found at the end of the book.

For the sake of convenience we have interspersed the masculine and feminine pronouns indiscriminately throughout this book . . .

chapter 1

The Day Camp Story

What is day camping? The answer is found . . .

. . . in the faces of eager, bright-eyed children; climbing into buses or station wagons, with an expression that says, "I have somewhere important to go—and I can't wait to get there."

. . . in the light in the camper's eyes when he is greeted by his counselor and his friends—a light that says, "I belong. Someone likes me—and wants me!"

. . . in the look of complete absorption on a small boy's face as he watches the activities of a colony of ants through a magnifying glass.

. . . in the "I did it myself" expression of satisfaction as he eats the meal he prepared and cooked over an open fire.

. . . in the glow of pride and success when he hits his first home run, or swims for the first time; or the almost fearful surprise and delight when he sees and feels his first fish on a hook.

. . . in the intense determination with which he applies himself to the "real work" of a camp project, or in the "good" tiredness that follows a day of balanced activity and rest.

. . . in a child's world of fun, friendship, adventure, satisfaction, and success—all in an outdoor setting.

This is day camping!

The Origins of Day Camping

The development of day camping as a natural outgrowth of resident camping was so gradual that the date of the initial venture is indeterminable. In some cases a small number of campers who lived in close proximity to overnight camps were allowed to participate in daily activities and go home at night. One of the first day camps of which there are written records was established in Chicago in 1921 by the Girl Scouts, with the encouragement and assistance of Mrs. Herbert Hoover. Its objective was to get the girls off the city streets and to provide a genuine camping experience for many girls who could not go to a resident camp. At about the same time, other youth service organizations embarked on similar ventures, and a few private day camps came into existence.

The depression of the thirties gave impetus to the day camp movement. Times were hard; parents were working or searching for work, and the need for day care for children increased. Few parents or agencies, however, could afford to send children to resident camps. Much credit belongs to Mrs. Maude Dryden, who developed and supervised the day camp program of the Works Project Administration in New York City from 1934 to 1940, a program which was adopted by many other cities and states. Mrs. Dryden, whose book served as a guide for many day camps that followed, has often been called the "godmother" of day camping. When the need for public service abated she devoted her wisdom and experience to establishing a private day camp which was known as one of the finest in the entire country.

Another national crisis in the forties, World War II, again made day care for children a necessity, and again public and private day camping came to the fore. A lasting contribution was made at the time by Mrs. Mabel Jobe, who helped to initiate and administer the Day Camp Program of the Recreation Department of the District of Columbia. Through her program and her book, *Handbook of Day Camping*, she presented convincing evidence that good day camping is contingent on competent leadership, imagination, and the will to make the best use of available outdoor facilities, rather than on expensive equipment or elaborate surroundings. Her philosophy was expressed in the definition of day camping that appears in the preface of her book: "Day camp is not a place; it is a way of living that stimulates mind and body, enriches life, and builds the habits of happy, cooperative living."

With the rapid growth of day camping, some clarification was needed as to what actually constituted a day camp, as distinguished from supervised recreation. In 1945, at the request of the American Camping Association, the Chicago Section of the organization set up a committee to define the term "day camp" and to formulate Standards. The report of this committee was printed in *Camping Magazine* in 1945 in an article by Reynold Carlson, chairman of the committee, and Professor of Recreation at Indiana University. Reprints of this article have been used as guidelines for many day camp leaders since then.

In 1949 a National Day Camp Committee was established by the American Camping Association. The first task of the committee was to develop Standards which would be acceptable to day camp leaders throughout the country. This effort culminated in February of 1956, when Day camp Standards were adopted by the American Camping Association and a program to implement them was set in motion. Since then, as more and more day camps have come into being, improving and upgrading these Standards has been an ongoing process. Day camp director have been able to use them as a yardstick for improving their own camps and as a means for providing better camping for all children.

During the years of recovery following the war, day camping continued to receive its greatest impetus through the efforts of public and private agencies to provide care for children. The most rapid growth took place in the fifties. This was made evident by National Recreation Association studies of Parks and Recreation. In 1950 its yearbook reported a figure of 747 day camps in 285 cities. Total attendance figures were not reported but 173 of the cities reporting on 389 camps cited an attendance of 638,116 campers. In 1955 the number of day camps had jumped to 971 in 327 communities, and 157 of these cities' reporting on 350 camps cited an attendance of 831,622 children. These figures represent day camps administered by public recreation and do not include day camps sponsored by youth-serving agencies, churches, social agencies, or private individuals.

Figures released in 1960 by the American Camping Association gave an actual card count of 1,336 day camps with an enrollment of 1,036,068 campers per season. It was estimated that there were at least 1,000 more day camps which were not counted in this survey due to lack of sufficient information.

The American Camping Association estimates that in 1980 there were over 3,000 day camps across the country. State economic impact studies in Maine, New York, Wisconsin, Michigan, and Connecticut indicate day camps are a highly significant economic force in those states with investments in facilities and land often larger than resident camps.

Reasons for Growth

The most obvious reason for this tremendous expansion is based on the reality that there is less space and more children. Children who live in the inner city, whether it be the crowded ghetto or the high-rise apartment, share the same basic needs to express their natural exuberance through physical activity and their desire for adventure through healthy dramatic play. Watching sports events and the adventures of James Bond on the television are poor substitutes for real life experiences that allow the child to be involved rather than to be a passive observer.

To some extent the state of the economy has brought abut the proliferation of day camping. During the fifties and sixties, when the country was recovering from the effects of the war and replacing luxuries which had been displaced for military needs, the life-style of the average citizen improved. More people could afford to give their children the advantages of a day camp experience. Private day camps flourished and many agency camps became more self-supporting.

Another phenomenon occurred as a result of the war. Women who had been called away from their homes to replace men in the workplace discovered a new world out there, one which brought them personal satisfaction as well as financial benefits, and many of them opted not to go back to their diapers and dishpans. In 1960, 30 percent of all mothers with children under eighteen were working. In 1980, that number had jumped to better than 50 percent and it is predicted that by 1990 three mothers out of four will be working outside the home. The increase in the divorce rate, and the subsequent number of single parents, male and female, who are responsible for the upbringing of one or more children, has also increased the need for child-care services. Day care and day camping, once looked upon as totally separate services, have gradually been coming closer together as more and more day camps have been extending their hours and services to meet the needs of working parents. The image of a "working parent" as a woman standing over a machine has also changed; working parents are also executives in large companies, doctors, lawyers, teachers, and scientists. They want the best for their children and day camp offers them an interesting, exciting summer combined with good care.

In this same period of time day camping has gained the respect of the camping community. Colleges offer courses in camping, academic credits can be earned for supervised experiences in camp counseling, and some private schools have extended their program to include day camping in the summer months. Camping, once categorized as recreation, has been emerging as another discipline in the field of education.

Has the quality of the day camp experience kept pace with the increase in the number of camps? Zoning, licensing, regulatory procedures, and the Standards of the American Camping Association, now nationally recognized as a yardstick by which quality can be measured, have all played a part in the accountability process. But some of the most important aspects of day camping, those intangible features which may have a lasting effect on the child's attitude toward himself as a confident, competent human being, cannot be regulated. They rest on the integrity of the individuals who direct the process, and if those individuals are truly committed to excellence, they will constantly be seeking new ways to improve their services, to discover more efficient methods, and develop more exciting programs.

It is for them that we have dug into the files and into the recesses of our minds for those bits of information which have worked for us. In sharing our own successes we ask only that the reader who finds an idea useful will feel an obligation to pass it on. We do not write about our failures, but the knowledge we have acquired as we suffered through them is reflected here. On the foundations laid down by Dryden, Jobe, and Carlson we shall attempt to strengthen the structure of day camping for the future and to make it an adventure in cooperative living rather than a sterile extension of the school year.

The first half of this book is directed to the multitudinous details of administration—the oil that lubricates the wheels.

In the second half we offer help to directors and counselors in understanding the needs of campers and how to use program to meet those needs.

| chapter 2 | # First Steps to Establishing a Day Camp |

"Let's start a day camp!" Judging by the rapid growth of day camping in recent years, it becomes evident that this idea has occurred to a vast number of people. Mentally envisioning happy campers engaged in wholesome activities under summer skies, the novice frequently does not realize how much careful planning must take place before that dream becomes a reality. If the needs of children, parents, and staff are to be meshed, there are logical steps to be taken. It is our intent to place markers along the road that starts with an idea and ends with a reality.

Who Can Start a Day Camp?

It is customary to speak of "organization" camps and "private" camps as if they were two separate operations. That the line between the two is not distinct will be seen from the following descriptions.

Agency Camps

This widely inclusive term is used to describe nonprofit camps operated or supported by national youth-serving agencies, religious groups, service clubs, welfare agencies, and public recreation services. Enrollment is usually restricted by capacity rather than other considerations, although it may be limited to members of the sponsoring group. Fees may be nonexistent, or based on ability to pay. They may constitute a small fraction of the total cost of the program, or cover most of the running expenses. The management is handled by a local board or committee, but when the supporting agency is national in scope, policies and procedures may be determined by the parent organization. Frequently such an organization will also have a set of written standards that are used in conjunction with the Standards of the American Camping Association.

Private, Nonprofit Day Camps

The term nonprofit is somewhat misleading in this case because this type of camp may realize as great a profit as one owned and operated by an individual. The difference is that in a camp of this type, no individual or group of individuals makes any financial gain, other than a salary which is commensurate with the responsibility involved. The profits are turned back to the sponsor, which may be a private school or similar institution, a church, a club, or a parent cooperative. Administrative duties are usually handled by a paid director who is responsible to a camp committee or governing board. Enrollment can be limited to the children of employees or patrons of the institution, but this is not the usual practice.

Private Day Camps

Day camps which are completely private in structure are similar in nature to other types of businesses. They may be owned and operated by a corporation, a partnership, or by an individual. A single owner will in many cases by supported by an advisory board or backed by businessmen who have invested in the camp. It is desirable in every case to seek competent legal advice; but if the plan calls for a business corporation, an attorney with experience in corporate work should be employed.

Determine the Need

The first logical step in planning is to explore the need or potential for a day camp in the area being considered. Some of the questions to be asked are these:

—How many day camps are already established in the area? Are they similar in type to the one being contemplated, or do they take care of a limited group? Is there room for one more?

—What other recreation facilities are available? Does the community provide supervised public playgrounds, and/or free instruction in swimming, crafts, or other skills? If so, will the parents recognize the advantages of a day camp program? Will they be willing to pay for this specialized service?

—What is the socio-economic background of the anticipated camper clientele? Will the children come from homes where mothers are working, from crowded city settlements, from a middle-class business and professional group, from the country club set, or from summer resort residents? Will they be fee-paying customers who will be able to pay the cost of the service you intend to offer?

—What problems will be encountered in transportation? Will there be enough campers within a reasonable radius, or will they cover such a wide area that the cost of transporting them will be prohibitive? Can the Standard that "no camper should ride more than one hour each way" be met?

What Kind of Camp Will It Be?

If, after a careful study of the situation, the need or potential for a day camp is apparent, the second step is to consider the purposes. What kind of camp will best meet this need? The overall objectives of day camping are stated in the American Camping Association Standards, but these are intentionally generalized so they will not limit or restrict the unique characteristics of each camp. In addition to these Standards, the board or committee may have written objectives determined by the sponsoring agency; but these also should be considered in relation to the particular situation. The private camp director will need to examine and evaluate his personal philosophy and goals, for he will be called upon to explain them to parents. It is not enough to have these objectives in mind: Standards require that they be in writing. This may seem superfluous to the busy individual who is involved in the practical aspects of setting up a camp, but these very procedures will move with greater ease and precision when they are based on clear-cut, well-defined written objectives.

Who Will Come to the Day Camp?

The third step is to decide who will come to the day camp. Is there to be a special program emphasis which will limit enrollment? There are riding camps, sailing camps, baseball camps, and camps for overweight children. There are health camps for children with special physical or emotional needs. There are nursery camps, camps for teenagers, and day camps for senior citizens. Whenever it is possible to combine several of these various groups, the end product will be richer and contribute more to the child's knowledge of the real world.

When Will the Day Camp Operate?

The length of the day, of the camping period, and of the season should be decided next. ACA Standards state that there must be a minimum of six days in two consecutive weeks, to provide continuity of experience. This is admittedly a very short time, but it is based on the theory of quality over quantity. Thus, six days of real camping in an outdoor setting may serve as an introduction to an experience which will develop into a lifetime interest; whereas a longer period of marginal day camping bordering on supervised play may serve only as a temporary child care convenience.

Agency camps often limit the period of attendance to two weeks for any camper in order that the maximum number of children can benefit. For the same reason some camps will operate for six days a week with two separate groups, each attending three days a week. In general, day camps operate from two to ten weeks with camping periods broken down into any fraction thereof. Some private camps accept only full-season campers, and quite a few limit enrollment to a four-week period. There are a few day camps that conduct programs on a year-round basis, operating after school hours, on weekends, and through school vacations.

The usual camp day is from nine or nine-thirty in the morning to four or four-thirty in the afternoon. However, with the rapid increase of working parents, extended hours are becoming a necessary addition. Some children may arrive as early as seven in the morning and some will not be picked up by their parents until six at night. In such cases, special attention should be given to programming for those hours, and staff employed who can create a home-like, pleasant environment. The goal should be for children to say, "Good! Now that the rest have gone WE can . . ." rather than gazing wistfully after their friends as they leave. A camp director should not accept this kind of responsibility without adequate preparation.

Support Systems

While the initial exploration and planning is going on, it is suggested that the prospective owner or director become a member of the American Camping Association. Their headquarters staff is an invaluable resource center. Their many publications, written by experienced camping people, will save novices from reinventing the wheel, and members of each local or state group can offer more immediate support.

The ACA Standards are guidelines which will point out things new camp directors or owners might never think of, and make them aware of the many facets of camp operation. They provide a skeleton—the task, then, will be to add the unique features which will make the camp different from any other: to put meat on the bones. In camp something happens which is seldom seen in public schools—something called spirit for lack of a better word. It is that which brings campers back year after year, which stores away memories which will last a lifetime.

Where Will the Day Camp Be?

Sometimes the idea for a day camp grows out of the availability of a desirable site. Someone has said, "This is a lovely spot. It should be used for children."

More often, though, the project starts with a need, and in that case the next step is to find a suitable location. When searching for a day camp site, it is important to know what to look for, and equally important to know what to avoid. In the next chapter, site selection will be explored.

| chapter 3 | # The Day Camp Site |

The word "camp" usually calls forth a mental image of whispering pines, sunlight sparkling on a lake, wooded trails, a lodge, tents, or cabins. In the case of a resident camp, at least part of this description will apply, but day camps will of necessity be found in a greater variety of locations, ranging from local parks and playgrounds to privately owned or rented property. Individuals in search of a site may start out with some preconceived ideal, but should leave their minds open to all kinds of possibilities. As an initial step the need for a site should be made known to as many people as possible through friends, parents, and board and committee members. A carefully worded advertisement in a newspaper may bring results, and the real estate columns should be regularly scanned for places worth investigating. City, county, and state recreation personnel may be consulted about public properties available for such use, and a reliable real estate agent who will take a genuine interest in the project should be consulted.

Where to Look

A description of some of the properties on which day camps are presently operating may open up some new possibilities to the reader.

Schools, Colleges, and Institutions

In most cases day camps conducted on such sites will have a fairly formalized setting. Lawns, tennis and badminton courts, archery and rifle ranges, and rooms in buildings may be supplemented by large shade trees, pine groves, a pond, or a brook. In the absence of wooded areas appropriate for campcraft activities, the resourceful director will search for an area within easy driving distance where such activities may be conducted on a part-time basis.

Public Parks

Thousands of children every year enjoy a real camping experience in city, county, or state parks and reservations. In many cases they come closer to learning the real meaning of camping than those who attend day camps with elaborate facilities. In one of our largest cities a youth-serving agency accommodates as many as 3,000 girls in one summer in a city park. A specific area is reserved for the camps's exclusive use on specified camp dates, as well as for their precamp training sessions. The park department is cooperative in preserving privacy for the camp activities, but the park is large enough so that all of the usual public activities can go on at the same time. Water, rest rooms, and a telephone are available. Individual groups make their own arrangements to use nearby churches or other buildings on rainy days.

When public parks are used, the camp should work out rules and policies with park officials with both groups cooperating to achieve the long-range public welfare.

Roof Camping

The greatest need for day camping is in the city where facilities are most limited. When public parks can be utilized, the problem becomes largely one of transportation. Roof camping has been tried as a next-best substitute in some crowded instances. In one city the roof of a skyscraper was made as camp-like as possible by use of potted plants and trees, a fence made of saplings, a fireplace for outdoor cooking, tents, and totem poles. The pool in the building was used for swimming. These day campers had one advantage over their suburbanite contemporaries: when they were on an overnight campout, they slept closer to the stars!

Ranches

In sharp contrast to the day camp located on the roof of a city sky-scraper is the one located on a Western ranch, where the problems are quite different. Enrollment is difficult because of the distances which have to be covered to transport the campers; but even more startling is the difference in the basic needs of the children who attend. More than anything else, the city child needs a chance to stretch without touching another human being, a chance to occasionally isolate his mind and body from the multitude by which he is surrounded. On the other hand, the child in the West needs companionship and a chance to rub elbows with his peers. The common denominator in these two widely differing situations would be the program objectives. Children's needs are the same—they need an environment in which social, physical, spiritual, and intellectual development can take place. While the social and physical growth may be emphasized in a summer program, none of these important developmental needs can be overlooked.

Farms

Several of the oldest day camps in the country are located on farm property. In some, the campers have opportunities for real farming experiences as they work in gardens, pick berries or fruit, care for the animals, or help bring in the hay. In others, the farm-like atmosphere has been maintained though no actual farming goes on. Usually there are some wooded areas which are appropriate for camping activities.

Seashore

In most parts of the country, seaside property is so expensive that unless the day camp is already established, such land is not likely to be available. When such a site is used, two factors to be considered are the proximity of neighbors and a beach with sufficient privacy to maintain the safe supervision of campers.

Lakes

There are many day camps in settings much like the one described in the beginning of this chapter, with frontage on the shore of a pond or lake which can be used for swimming and boating. Their fortunate owners should be mindful of the relentless spread of urban development and acquire as much surrounding land as possible.

Estates

A large, old estate may be the answer for those who seek a day camp site. In some cases there will be buildings which can be utilized; often there is a pool or tennis court which can be restored for use. Such property may be loaned, leased, or purchased. In any case, it is good to enlist legal advice to determine the terms and conditions for use.

What to Look For

Before the search is begun for a day camp site, consideration needs to be given to a number of important features, the presence or absence of which boost or kill the success of the venture.

Acreage

Since land is becoming more scarce every day, particularly in the area where day camps are needed, there is a definite trend for agencies and individuals to invest in land and utilities, rather than in expensive equipment or buildings. Where space is limited, the number of campers should be proportionately limited, and every effort made to arrange for part-time use of wooded areas within the limits of transportation. Minimum requirements for the amount of indoor and outdoor space per camper will usually be specified by local ordinance. This should be checked at the outset.

When property is being purchased, the farsighted camp director will ascertain whether there is adjacent land which may be available with an option to purchase, or whether he is likely to be hemmed in by business or industry.

Accessibility

This factor makes the search for acreage doubly difficult, since land increases in value with proximity to the city. Standards recommend that riding time for the camper should not exceed one hour each way. In addition, the beginning camp director must carefully consider the time and expense involved in transportation if the campers live in a widely scattered area. A car may be able to travel thirty miles to pick up seven campers within the prescribed time limit, but the cost of making such a trip may be prohibitive.

Varied Topography

Trees for shade; sunny fields or meadows; woods for campcraft or nature lore; hills and trails for hiking; a brook, lake, or pond; areas where unit sites can be developed and fires may be built for outdoor cooking; open spaces large enough for physical activities and all-camp gatherings; land for gardening; and, last but not least, a parking area—few day camps will be able to boast of all these advantages, but they are goals worth seeking.

Water

Water for drinking and sanitation is a *must*. Water to be used for drinking or swimming must be tested for health requirements. If the campsite is in a public park and the campers are expected to carry water, it is important to note the distance to the nearest source. Campers should be able to have a drink of cold water as often as they may want it throughout the day, and to this end the director might persuade the park commissioner to have an additional pipe and faucet installed. Standards also require that handwashing facilities be available in close proximity to toilets.

A lake or pond for swimming and boating is an asset worth hunting for, but the purchaser should not be deceived by its appearance in the spring of the year. Unless fed by natural springs, a pond may dry up into an unsightly mud hole before the summer is over. Another serious mistake, which might be made by novices, is that of underestimating the work and expense involved in making a pond or lake with a muddy bottom into a swimming area with clear water and a sandy beach.

If public beaches are to be used, the following conditions should be investigated:

—Are there any restrictions? Will there be objections to use of the beach or of its approaches by a day camp group?
—How crowded will it be? Will it be possible to maintain adequate supervision? Which hours will be most desirable?
—What about toilet facilities? Drinking water? Dressing rooms?
—How far is it from the parking area to the beach?
—Is the beach on a protected cove or inlet, or is it open to the dangers of high surf and undertow?

Pools are used by a great many day camps. In some cases, as in schools or colleges, they are a part of the facilities. In one such camp the school hockey rink was constructed so that it could be filled for swimming in summer.

Some day camps may build one large pool and others find it advantageous to build several smaller pools. There are many new types of materials for pools, including asphalt, aluminum, plastic, canvas, cement, and steel. Magazines and newspapers are filled with advertisements, and a telephone call will bring eager salesmen to the door of a prospective buyer. Local and state regulations for chlorination, filters, and testing must be explored before a pool is installed. Even though there may not be any immediate plans for building a pool, it might be wise to investigate the possibility before purchasing a site. Important considerations would be a suitable location close to electricity (for the filter systems), sources for water, and the type of soil. In one case it was possible to exchange valuable loam for some of the cost of excavation, but if ledge or rock were encountered the expense might be out of reason. Many day camps transport their campers by bus to indoor pools once or twice a week.

Hazards

When inspecting a prospective site, it is important to look for natural hazards. Good drainage is important, and swampy areas or stagnant pools should be avoided; they breed mosquitoes. There may be pits or quarries covered with undergrowth, or an old, unused well which is not adequately covered. Ravines, jagged rocks, or old cellar holes may cause future concern. Dilapidated buildings which are unfit for repair and unsafe for use may be an expensive nuisance. One or two cases are known where flood damage from the ocean or a river has been a menace which was not discernible when the site was purchased. Stumps, fallen trees, brush piles which create a fire hazard, and poisonous weeds can all be eliminated, but the expense and trouble should be taken into account. Unless the site is extremely desirable in every other respect, such effort may not be worthwhile.

Seashore

When looking at an oceanside site, either as a permanent location or just for swimming, it is advisable to view it at high tide and low tide. A gradual decline in depth at low tide may become a hazardous drop-off at high water.

Rocks which are ideal for climbing and hold fascinating salt water pools at low tide may be bordered with dangerously deep or rough water.

Proximity to highways should be considered. Fencing is very expensive; if it is going to be necessary, its costs should be considered in the original planning.

A prospective buyer should take a long look at the neighbors, from the angle of possible expansion and future relations. A personal call on the abutters to explain the purposes of the camp is not only a gracious gesture but a necessary precaution. Many people have a very hazy idea of what day camping is, and immediately picture their property as being invaded by hordes of noisy, unrestricted, unsupervised children. The time to correct these impressions is before irate neighbors register their objections to the town fathers. On the other hand, there is always the possibility that a very attractive site could be spoiled for the camp by undesirable neighbors.

Close proximity to an airfield, especially if the site is in a direct flight path, may be looked upon with anxiety by parents. Futhermore, it is not conducive to good programming to have planes overhead all day.

When You Find It

Finding a satisfactory campsite is not the end of the road. There are regulatory relationships with town or state to be checked and legal formalities of ownership to be met.

Licensing and Zoning

When a desirable campsite has been found, the next step is to look into the licensing and zoning regulations of the state and local community. Where this important point has been overlooked, day camps already established have had to move and others have lost valuable time, effort, and money because they have gone too far in planning before they realized there were restrictions. If a variance is necessary, petition to a local board of appeals may be delayed for months, particularly if there are strong objectors. In one case the owner of a private day camp had to postpone operations for a whole year, and another obtained the final approval only three weeks before the opening date.

In most instances a license will be issued by the local board of health. If a license is not required, the director should use the American Camping Association Standards as a guide in setting up his own minimum requirements.

Proprietorship

Whenever possible, outright ownership of property is best. There is greater incentive to make improvements when the security of ownership makes long-range planning possible. Camp spirit, built on sentiment and tradition, has a chance to flower when continuity is assured.

More often than not, a new camp owner finds it necessary to rent property until he can accumulate some capital with which to buy. If the spot is very desirable, he should make every effort to get a lease with an option to buy. Otherwise, the terms of the lease should include a provision (called a restrictive covenant) whereby the landlord cannot start or permit anyone else to operate a day camp on the premises for a stated length of time after the expiration of the lease. More than one camp director has built up a name and reputation only to have to move and to find someone else capitalizing on his efforts.

Agencies or religious groups are sometimes offered a piece of property as a gift. Strangely enough, the warning here is to have the courage to "look a gift horse in the mouth" if necessary. A site which is unsuitable may become more of a liability than an asset.

It is not unusual for public-spirited citizens to lend a piece of property for day camp use, or lease it for one dollar.

For the good of both parties, such arrangements should always include a written agreement drawn up with legal advice. This would include such terms as:

—Purposes for which the site will be used
—Ways in which the site will be used in regard to shelters, firebuilding, cutting trees, and so on
—Hours and days when the site will be used
—Approximate number of campers and adults who will use the site
—Use of the site and camp equipment by the owner's family and friends
—A statement of the camp's responsibility for the conduct of campers and staff
—Responsibility for personal liability, utilities, and insurance

Whether the property is to be purchased, loaned, or leased, it is always advisable to employ legal and realtor advice, in order to assure clear titles, proper lease, and compliance with local requirements, such as ordinances, zoning, registering of deed, easements, and right-of-way.

Master Plan

When property is purchased it is well worth the expense to employ professional advice in drawing up a master plan for future development. The usual "hit or miss" procedure, adding a building here and a program area there as the need arises, is often wasteful in the long run; and in many cases space which may be badly needed at a later date has thus been irreparable damaged.

Property Management

When a satisfactory site for the day camp has been found, it is necessary to plan for maintenance and supervision. This is an area in which campers can take an active part. In the program section of the Standards of the American Camping Association, it states that "campers should be given an opportunity to share in the care and improvement of the camp." Strangely enough this has been a controversial issue, mainly because of misunderstanding. It was not intended that campers should be exploited or expected to work beyond their abilities or physical strength. The provision was included because if our natural resources are to be preserved, it is necessary for the youth of our nation to learn the basic rules of conservation, and camp is a logical place in which to impart this knowledge. We do our campers a real service when we help them to acquire good habits for the care of camp facilities and respect for the property of others.

Responsibility of Camper, Counselor, and Director

The satisfaction which accompanies pride of achievement is one of the greatest rewards of a camping experience. Witness the sparkle in a camper's eye as he points with pride to the small tree he helped to plant, or the serious tone with which he explains the project his unit is conducting to combat erosion.

The camper who has made a contribution to the development of a campsite will come back long after his camping years are over to view the results with sentiment. This pride and interest is the essence of camp spirit and tradition, which is the greatest asset of camp promotion.

A counselor also has a responsibility for camp maintenance. His first obligation is to the camper, for whom he is the model; for if he is careless about dropping papers, or if he leaves untidy cooking areas or cuts firewood indiscriminately, he defeats the true purpose of a camping program.

The counselor's second obligation is to the camp management. He should watch for faulty equipment and report promptly to the director any hazard such as a loose board, an exposed nail, or a weakened or dead tree branch.

Although campers and staff may share in the care and improvement of property, the final responsibility rests squarely on the shoulders of the camp director. By persuasion, education, and example, he will encourage campers and staff to take pride in maintaining and improving the camp. No matter how busy a director may be when he is approached, he should always acknowledge reports of hazardous situations with thanks and give them prompt attention, thus encouraging further attention to safety. He should watch for signs of erosion, consulting experts if his own knowledge is inadequate, and when it is necessary he should convince the employer, board, or camp committee of a need for a plan of prevention. He must give constant attention to the preservation of buildings and equipment. Finally, the director should encourage staff and campers to plan for some major improvement in the campsite each year. It may be a row of trees, a natural amphitheater, rustic accoutrements for an outdoor chapel, or terraced steps where a path has eroded. The camp director with vision will always see more projects ahead than can be accomplished in any given year.

Although most of the foregoing seems to apply to the day camp with a permanent site, those using public property are by no means exempt from responsibility. On the contrary, they have an obligation to return "that which they have borrowed" in as good or better condition than they found it. Campers and staff should include camp maintenance as an integral part of the daily program, but the director must take the final responsibility for seeing that plans are carried through.

Maintenance Manual

A maintenance manual is an indispensable aid in keeping track of the routine chores. Contents should include such information as the following:

—A yearly calendar of maintenance chores
—Job descriptions for maintenance workers
—Specific instructions for opening and closing camp
—The storage locations of all equipment
—Inventory lists
—Building and layout plans, including electrical shutoffs
—Plans of water and sewage systems, including locations of springs, pipes, shutoffs, filter systems, clean-out traps, septic tanks, and cesspools
—Manufacturers' instructions for care of equipment
—Names and telephone numbers of plumber, electrician, and other service representatives.

chapter 4 | Buildings and Equipment

Any attempt to say which of the properties herein described are actually essential to day camping would invite controversy. Some will think buildings are necessary, but excellent day camp programs are carried on without buildings. One day camp will think sports equipment important, and another will ask only for tools for campcraft. Certainly all day camps will not need boats, and others would find archery equipment superfluous. The age of the campers is a deciding factor. If early adolescents are enrolled, the day camp program may offer such specialized activities as sailing, riding, or one-day trips, which would make the purchase of appropriate equipment necessary. The challenge is to make the best possible use of that which is available, to leave some room for children and staff to develop their own imaginations and resourcefulness, and "to cut the cloth" to fit the budget.

Shelters for Small Groups

The day camp plan of organization usually calls for some division of campers into small groups. (See American Camping Association Standards.) In the interest of group solidarity, a "home base" is needed for each small unit where its members can meet with each other and their leader. In one day camp, which is located in the woods, each camper group chooses a site at the beginning of the season and develops it in accordance with a particular theme. Some are Indians, others may be frontiersmen or pirates. The counselor stimulates ideas with stories, pictures, and artifacts, but the campers are encouraged to develop their own originality as they work together to create their camp home. Extra clothing and personal belongings are kept in lockers in a main lodge.

Another camp uses tents for small-group shelters. They are set up in units with four tents to a unit. Each tent accommodates eight to ten

campers and a counselor. A unit leader completes that branch of the camp family. Tents can seldom be used exclusively to house campers on rainy days. They may be adequate for a few hours; but after that they tend to be cold, dark, and damp, and additional accommodations are necessary. When tents are used, the newest features such as high side walls, windows, and screens should be investigated.

In still another situation, a large barn has been adapted to day camp use. The stalls had been converted to small-group headquarters and the hay loft to a combined office and balcony overlooking a stage. The central area is used for plays, games, and dancing.

When day camps are conducted on school or college campuses, it is a temptation to use indoor facilities more than is necessary. One visit disclosed campers having nature classes in an indoor science room when they could have been exploring a meadow and a pond outside. The arts and crafts room was busy, but the activity could have been carried on better outdoors. Rehearsals were going on in the gym for a dramatic production, and yet there was a lovely natural amphitheater in a pine grove on the campus. The director was blissfully unaware of the wasted potential as he proudly conducted his visitors about his so-called day camp.

By way of contrast, in another school with limited outdoor facilities classrooms were used for small groups, and the leader had been resourceful in developing an Indian theme. Each camper made his own tepee using schoolroom furniture and blankets. When the Indian braves met with their chief, they sat in a council ring in the center of the room, encircled by their tepees. The imaginative powers of the children easily enabled them to feel that they were sitting on a carpet of pine needles.

Covered wagons, Indian hogans, and tree houses are all possibilities for unusual shelters. But however valuable it may be to combine housing with the glamour of adventure, the basic rules for health and safety must always be observed.

Since the matter of property supervision after camp hours is often a problem in the day camp, many directors are looking into the advantages of portable steel, aluminum, and plywood buildings. These can be locked up on nights and weekends and can be moved with other camp property if the site is changed.

Housing for Large Groups

Though a lodge or building which will house all the campers at one time may seem desirable, camp directors often feel that the stimulation engendered by too many children under one roof is contrary to the objectives of health, safety, and a good program. This is particularly true on a rainy day.

The director of one day camp, who had first leased property that included a lodge, chose a different plan when he purchased and developed his own site. He started with two buildings and added several more as his camp grew. These buildings were twenty by thirty feet and were covered with rough siding for the first three feet from the bottom. The sides were screened for the remaining five feet, and the ends had V-shaped screened openings near the roof for ventilation. A wide overhang protected the occupants from all but a driving rain; and plexiglass shutters, hinged at the top and hooked to the crossbeams when not in use, were swung down to provide protection on cold, windy, or wet days.

Aluminum roofs were used because they are easy to install, require little maintenance, and are cool in the summer. In a very heavy rainstorm, however, they tend to be noisy.

At Green Acres, rustic buildings, thirty feet by thirty feet, have been used as shelters for units of forty campers. Over the years vandalism

has increased and they have become attractive as clubhouses for marauders who have not only left the building and grounds littered with bottles and cans but have scribbled, painted, even gouged obscenities on the walls. On five occasions buildings were razed by fire within a month of camp opening.

Finally, out of desperation and frustration, new shelters were designed which were aesthetically ugly, but fireproof. (The designers describe them as modern Greek ruins.)

Cement block pillars on a thirty-foot square cement slab are topped by steel roofing joists and a corrugated metal roof. Walls of plywood are set between the cement columns and have plywood doors on two sides. There are three-foot openings between the tops of the walls and the overhanging roof to let in light and air.

In the fall the portable wooden walls are disassembled and stored in a safer area, leaving only the bare columns and roof to weather the winter. Because these structures are open to the elements, they are less attractive for use as clubhouses.

Toilet Facilities

The section on sanitation in the American Camping Association Standards states explicitly the requirements for toilets and handwashing facilities.

It is also necessary to consult local and state regulations concerning toilet facilities, not only in regard to number, but for construction and maintenance. For example, in one day camp when a simple wooden building was contemplated for additional toilets, the owners found that if urinals were used, the most expensive tile floors were required. Although in appearance they seem quite out of line with the rest of the building, time proved that for sanitation and facility of cleaning they were worthwhile, and the ordinance was not as unreasonable as it first seemed.

If toilets in a public park must be shared with others using the park, the day camp director should make certain that standards for cleanliness are maintained.

Infirmary

If a building is not available for an infirmary, Standards require that a quiet resting place apart from the center of activity be set aside, and that a place be available for storage of minimum first aid supplies. (See Chapter 11 on "Health and Safety.")

Storage

A place for storing equipment is essential both during the season and through the winter. Where day camps are operated in public parks, sometimes a little space can be found in the caretaker's office, in closets, in restroom facilities, or in shared storage buildings. Equipment with no monetary value, such as orange crates and tin cans for cooking, may be packed in boxes and left at the site. Sometimes service-minded companies interested in the welfare of children will lend a

truck, trailer, or portable building which can be locked and left on the site for the season. If mobile units are used, they should be carefully planned and arranged so that all equipment can be transported daily with minimum effort. Agency personnel, both paid and volunteer, frequently help to transport equipment in their own cars and store it through the winter months in their cellars or garages.

The best planning will contemplate buildings on the site where equipment can be stored. Since many day camps are troubled with marauders at night and on weekends when the property is unattended, facilities which can be locked should be considered. Also for this reason, shutters may offer better protection than windows.

Office

The major business details for some day camps will be carried on in an in-town office or in the home of the director, but Standards require that certain records be available on the campsite. (See Chapter 10 on "Health and Safety.") For these, and for the director's use, some facility should be available, even if it is only a tent. It is conceivable that where a day camp uses a public park or reservation and all equipment is carried to and from the site each day, the director's office may be a station wagon, bus, or trailer.

Other Buildings

Other buildings which might be included in a master plan are a nature house, an arts and crafts and/or woodworking shop, dressing rooms

near the swimming area, a boathouse, a room or building where counselors can keep their belongings and relax during time off, and a stable. If the latter is included, it should be located at a reasonable distance from eating and program areas.

It would be futile to attempt to list equipment which might be considered essential for the many different day camps described in this book. Some suggestions will be found in the chapters on program, but the discussion here will be limited to a few generalizations.

Campcraft

The most exciting feature of a campcraft program for children is the discovery that they can learn to survive without the conveniences they had thought were necessities. In one day camp the most sought-after honor is to be chosen for an overnight survival hike which is patterned after those used in army training. Basic materials for campcraft will include axes, a shovel, knives, nails and a hammer, rope and twine for lashing, and some simple cooking utensils.

Nature

No equipment is so essential to a nature program as the enthusiasm and "let's find out" attitude of a good counselor. A few resource books are important. Bulletin boards, butterfly nets, a beehive with a glass front where the activities of the bees can be observed, magnifying glasses, and a pair of binoculars for bird watching are luxuries which will enrich a nature program.

Sports

Sports equipment may include everything from croquet to lacrosse, but the really essential equipment will be balls of varying types and sizes.

Swimming

This is one of the most important camp activities. It will be observed time and again that when a camper learns to swim, he gains a new self-confidence which carries over into every other activity in the day camp program. When the construction of a swimming pool is contemplated, the relative advantages of two or more small pools rather than one large one might well be considered. In a small pool where the number of campers will be limited, a minimum of confusion and a maximum of safe supervision and individual instruction can be attained. This contributes greatly to the security of the timid camper.

Equipment for the swimming program should be related to safety and instructional aid. Fancy gadgets, such as flippers, goggles, and snorkels, are better left to the realm of family excursions and excluded from the day camp. Flutter boards, floats for marking off sections of the pool for beginners, a rope around the sides of the pool which can be easily grasped, and ladders for safe egress are important. Diving boards may be dangerous in a pool which has not sufficient depth, and slides are fun but require very careful supervision. The Standard which requires that pools must be enclosed by fences with gates which can be kept locked when the pool is not in use is one which protects the camp as well as the campers. Supposedly, supervision in a day camp would preclude the possibility of a camper straying near enough to a pool to fall in and drown, but there is always a danger that some child who does not attend camp might be attracted to the area, and the result would be just as tragic.

Equipment for Dramatic Play

Children in a day camp need equipment which encourages dramatic play, calls for cooperative effort, and stimulates imagination. The most interesting and valuable equipment may be the least expensive and can often be improvised.

Boats that are beyond repair for normal use have years of service left for dry land sailing. A rowboat, sailboat, or derelict cabin cruiser can be repaired, painted, and made into an exciting addition to camp play. The paint on these, however, should be checked for lead content.

Farm wagons, buggies, sleighs, and hay wagons, some that can be pulled around and some made immobile, are also delightful to campers.

Real automobiles, trucks, or buses are great fun, especially a small foreign car. They should be stripped of all doors which can pinch fingers, and glass which might break. Hoods must be fastened down before they fall on investigating hands or heads, but plenty of things should be left which can be pushed, pulled, twisted, turned, or manipulated.

The Deerkill Day Camp has a beautiful fire engine which was donated by the local fire department. Needless to say it is the scene of many dramatic episodes.

A carpenter or handyman can build a train, fire engine, submarine, plane, or spaceship which will provide far greater satisfaction than the slides and swings found on playgrounds. Fathers of campers will often help design or build this type of equipment.

A climbing pole, a cedar post set firmly in cement with wooden wedges inserted at intervals on the sides, offers limitless ideas for dramatic play. It may be a lookout post for Indians, whaling ships, pirates, or moon rockets. One startled counselor discovered that five-year-old boys were "ascending to heaven" assisted by a band of angels and supervised by a "supreme being" ensconced at the top of the pole.

Barns, cellars, attics, dumps, and secondhand shops are storehouses for such treasures as old bicycle pumps, pieces of hose, and pulleys.

Tree houses, ladders, logs, barrels, and sections of pipe satisfy a youngster's need to climb up, over, around, and through.

Funds for equipment in agency-sponsored day camps are usually limited. This is an advantage when it places the emphasis on creative use of imagination. The beginning day camp director, who may think a heavy investment in equipment is essential, will also do well to consider the benefit to campers and counselors who learn to utilize native materials found within the environment for an indigenous program.

At this point the reader is probably saying to himself, "This is all very fine, but when do we get the campers?" In theory it is better to wait until there is something tangible to show before camper solicitation begins, but in actual practice enrollment is usually carried on concurrently with the steps heretofore described.

| chapter 5 | **Enrolling the Campers** |

After a day camp has established a good reputation, publicity may become a matter of maintaining good public relations, but until that enviable state is reached, some promotional work will be necessary. Private camp directors are prone to think this problem is unique with them, but nonprofit camps do not always find campers flocking to their doors. Moreover, the agency, church, or public day camps must justify budgetary needs with evidence of attendance.

Even the older, well-known day camps need to make special efforts to recruit campers from year to year. Some of the many methods of promotion and the necessary records for the enrollment of campers are described in the following pages.

Prospect Lists

Names of prospective campers will come first from friends, acquantances, and parents of campers. Sometimes lists can be obtained from schools, churches, PTAs, and youth organizations.

For a mass mailing, one day camp uses the list of registered voters. The ages of the voters and their residential locations are used to estimate those who might have children eligible for camp.

Referrals

In some American Camping Association Section offices, camper referrals will be sent to members. In many large cities there are school and camp placement agencies which serve the same function as an employment agency. The fee for referrals is a percentage of tuition fees and is normally paid by the camp. A line on the camper application asking for names of friends who might be interested has, in many cases, brought good results. Day camps frequently receive referrals from such sources as schools, social service agencies, and clinics.

Brochures

Probably the most common medium used for selling a camp is the brochure. First impressions are lasting ones, and parents often see a camp first as it is described in print and pictures. A well-designed, well-written brochure will not necessarily sell every prospect, but one which is carelessly prepared may easily discourage enrollment. The relative advantages of various kinds of format, type, and size can best be determined by one who has specialized in this form of advertising. Copy writing is also an art, and consultation should be solicited.

The most effective brochures will be simple, explicit, and accurate. Though camp directors seldom intend to print deliberate misrepresentations, there may be a tendency to exaggerate. Acres of sloping, grassy meadows turn out to be a roughly cleared hillside, a lodge is an oversized cabin, and wooded areas consist of a few trees. Too much verbiage may give an impression of straining to overjustify a weak program. The director who deliberately appropriates pictures, sentences, or whole paragraphs from the brochure of another camp without permission is more likely to bring discredit on himself than campers to his fold.

Some directors include all necessary information in the brochure; others feel that pictures accompanied by a simple statement of aims and objectives will do more to interest campers and parents. Contents of a brochure may include any or all of the following items:

—Brief history of the camp—years of operation
—Aims and objectives
—Description of staff and qualifications
—Description of activities
—Location, with directions and/or map
—Enrollment procedures and methods of payment (may be on separate application form)
—Pictures
—Names of campers, staff, or parents

It is good economy to "mass produce" an expensive brochure, in which case, dates and pertinent information can be printed on a slip sheet and inserted each year. If such a slip sheet is used, it could include this information:

—Number of years camp has operated
—Dates of current season
—Dates and length of periods for current season

—Required or suggested clothing and equipment
—Transportation information
—Fees and extra charges
—Policy on refunds
—Insurance.

When the brochure is an inexpensive leaflet, this information would be included in the original.

Another method is to limit the brochure to strictly promotional material, and to send other necessary information to the parents after a camper has been accepted.

Consult the local post office on bulk mailing rates.

Personal Calls

Very few good things come without hard work, and the beginning camp director, regardless of his background, reputation, or contacts, will still have to sell himself and his camp. It is easy for the teacher, coach, or recreational leader, who is surrounded by children throughout the school year, to assume that his campers will be enrolled with little effort, but parents are often reluctant to have their children attend a day camp in the first year of operation.

There is no substitute for face-to-face contact. The enthusiasm which a director has for camping in general, and his camp in particular, cannot be expressed in words alone; facial expressions and tone of voice play an important part.

A telephone call requesting an appointment will lift such home visits out of the realm of door-to-door selling. Unless the name of a mutual acquaintance can be mentioned with permission, it is wise to send a brochure in advance of the telephone call.

If slides or movies of camp facilities and activities are to be used for promotion, plenty of time should be devoted to the selection, sequence, and accompanying comments. Some directors prefer to use a carefully prepared album of photographs which tell the story of a complete day in camp.

Advertising

The most valuable and effective form of advertising is "word of mouth." When satisfied parents tell their friends about your camp, advertising will not be a heavy item on your budget.

Newspaper, radio, magazine, or television advertising is effective if enough money is available for repetition. It is a common failing for camp operators to underestimate the cost of such promotional expense. If there is money in the budget for this kind of advertising, it may be worthwhile to spend a little more for the services of a professional publicity person who will have the contacts and the "know how."

When one is advertising in newspapers it is important to check the circulation and find out whether the paper is read by parents who will be interested in this particular type of day camp. If advertisements are placed in several papers at the same time, it is a good idea to "code" the advertisements to help determine which advertisement brought the best results.

Feature stories are more likely to be accepted by newspapers if the camp offers special services such as enrollment of exceptional children, handicapped youngsters, or children from a low economic level, and if they are accompanied by good pictures.

News Bulletins

Strategically timed news letters addressed to campers are another means of renewing enthusiasm. The information they contain should provoke memories of past experiences and arouse anticipation of good times to come.

"We have two little baby lambs with black noses and black feet. What shall we name them?"

"Miss Susie will not be with us this summer. She has been chosen to go to India as a foreign exchange student. She will be back before camp is over and has promised to come and tell us about the children she sees on her trip."

"The red-winged blackbirds have a nest down by the swamp."

"Sandy Jones is in the hospital. Let's all send him a card to cheer him up."

"The trees in the row we planted last summer have new little green tips on their branches."

"King has a new red front on his stable."

Greeting Cards

A friendly greeting on his birthday or for special holidays, especially one with a picture of a camp scene, gives the camper a pleasant feeling of being remembered as a person—not just another camper.

Open House

Most parents will want to see the campsite. The best time to do this is obviously while camp is in session, but few parents have the fore-sight to make such visits a full year in advance. Many camp directors spend Saturday or Sunday afternoons at the campsite in May and June and encourage parents to visit. It is wise to have several experienced staff members available to help answer questions and show guests around.

Camp Reunions

Many day camps have a reunion during one of the school vacations or on a Saturday. Arrangements vary from a simple party with all expenses paid by the camp to an elaborate luncheon or dinner with expenses charged to the guests. Some offer a program of professional entertainment; others prefer to rely on camp songs, impromptu skits, and camp movies or slides to build up the desired enthusiasm. Campers are usually urged to bring friends who may be interested in going to the camp.

Enrollment Procedures

Clear-cut, efficient procedures for enrolling campers are indicative of businesslike management and will invoke the confidence of parents.

Application Blanks

In some day camps the application is a simple form requesting admission to the camp, and all other necessary data is obtained after the child is accepted. In many cases the original application contains all the information required for the permanent records.

The application may be a tear-off slip attached to the brochure; it may be on the permanent record card; or it may be in the form of a contract with terms of agreement on one-half which can be detached and kept by the parent. Some day camps send duplicate forms: one on white paper for the office files and one in color which is kept by the parent. It is most important for parents to be thoroughly familiar with all terms for payment of fees, notice in case of withdrawal, return of deposits, and tuition refunds or insurance. They should have a copy of these terms in their possession for reference if some question arises during the season.

Immediate acknowledgement of the receipt of an application is a matter of courtesy. In large camps a form letter is often used which states whether the camper has been accepted, rejected, or put on a waiting list.

Camp directors usually prefer to develop their own forms, but the following information might be included:

APPLICATION BLANK

Camper's Name _____ Date _____

Age _____ Birthdate _____ Phone _____

Address _____

City _____ State _____ Zip _____

Name of Parent/Guardian _____

Address _____

City _____ State _____ Zip _____

Phone _____ Occupation _____

Business Address _____

City _____ State _____ Zip _____

Name of friend/relative to be called in case of emergency if parent

cannot be reached _____

Phone _____ Address _____

City _____ State _____ Zip _____

Names and ages of other children in family:

_____

_____

_____

Previous camp and school experience:

_____

_____

_____

Additional Mailings

After a child has been accepted, and especially in cases where this may be at the close of the previous season or early in the winter, further details can be sent, spaced at intervals that will maintain contact and interest. Even though it entails more postal expense, communications sent separately will be read with greater interest. If several enclosures go in one mailing, they are more likely to receive attention if each one is printed on papers of different colors. All bulletins should be dated and numbered. These might include such items as the following:

—Camper personality sheet (to be filled out by parent)
—Activity choice sheet (camper and parent to check)
—Notice of precamp visiting days, or invitation to open house
—Rules for parents' visits, including time, parking, registering in office
—Lists of required and desirable clothing and equipment
—Description of "Rainy Days" with suggested clothing (See Chapter 18)
—Information on camp uniforms and name tapes
—Information on meals
—Insurance information
—Description of overnights with schedule of dates
—Names of other campers in group or unit
—Health form, to be filled out by doctor within one month of opening date (See Chapter 11)
—Description of system to be used for notifying parents if camp is cancelled for a day because of weather or some other emergency
—Transportation details (driver, time, and so on)
—Identification tags to be worn on first few days of camp
—Who's Who on the staff
—An explanation of American Camping Association and what membership means
—Description of procedures to be used if a parent wishes a child to be dismissed from camp during the day
—Policy on telephone calls from parents to camp and from counselors or director to parents
—Advance information on trips or special excursions
—Description of special services such as riding or tutoring.

While a day camp director is busy selling his camp to parents and enrolling campers, he is at the same time performing many other administrative functions which are spread over the entire year. The problems are somewhat different with camps operated by youth-serving agencies because they maintain continuous contact with their patrons.

chapter 6 | Administration

Administration is a subject of many facets, touching on every phase of camping. Illustrative of this fact is a brief anecdote told by Carol Hulbert, a camp director of renown who was stopped as she hurried across the campgrounds with a million things on her mind by a younger camper who had a new camera. He asked to take her picture so she paused briefly. "It was not until several days later when I saw the print," she related with a chuckle, "that I realized I had been carrying the Bible in my right hand and a toilet plunger in the left." How typical of the scope of a camp director's work!

In a multiple day camp situation sponsored by an agency or recreation department, many functions such as promotion, enrollment, policy-making, and purchasing may be handled through a central office. As long as a camp is small, the owner or director may be able to plan, manage, and supervise the entire project; but as it grows, some division of responsibility must normally take place. Many private day camps are run by husband-wife teams. But wherever there is a partner or co-director, a logical point for this division is between those duties that relate to people (campers, staff, parents), and those which are chiefly concerned with material things such as business management and property maintenance.

It is a popular misconception that day camping is a summertime project. On the contrary, in a camp of any considerable size the administrative functions will be spread out over the entire year. Some directors will start at the end of one camp season to get ready for the next year, and others may wait until spring, but administration will be more efficient if a long-range plan is adopted with tentative dates set for each phase of operation. The following checklist will aid the new camp director in making such a plan.

Precamp Administration

Naturally the first job in precamp to be launched is promotion. There are various steps, and their timing is important and logical.

Promotion

Here are seven suggestions for camp promotion:

1. Prepare brochures.
2. Set up a calendar schedule for all probable mailings up to the opening of camp, listing enclosures for each one. Keep a loose-leaf notebook with a copy of every communication. This will save time in preparing letters in succeeding years and avoid repetition and duplication of exact wording.
3. Send applications and brochures to former campers with a letter inviting them to return. One or two follow-up letters may be necessary.
4. Send applications and brochures to prospective campers with appropriate follow-up letters.
5. As applications are received, send acceptance letters and other necessary forms and communications. (See Chapter 6.)
6. Determine the amount, type, and strategic timing for paid advertising.
7. Arrange for group promotion meetings. Some agencies have spring "Mothers' Meetings" where camp is described with pictures and slides. Church groups, mothers' clubs, PTA organizations, and neighborhood social clubs often have such programs in the spring as a service to members. A private camp director, soliciting such an engagement, might invite several other day camp directors in the vicinity to make this a cooperative project.

Satisfied parents of former campers will often invite groups of friends to their homes to see pictures of the camp and talk with the director, thus enabling him to capitalize on the contagion of their enthusiasm.

Public Relations

This is the age of dissent. Whether it is on a national issue or the simple addition of a new building or adding a few feet to the property line of a day camp, there always seems to be someone ready to draw up the battle lines and start an offensive. The best defense against such negative opposition is to develop a positive image in the community. There are a number of ways to do this. All will involve some effort on the part of the camp director, but the energy expended may be minimal compared to that required when a simple situation is magnified into a major confrontation. In one camp a neighbor's objection was legitimate and a compromise could easily have been reached; but instead a few harsh ill-chosen words ignited a fire that quickly spilled into the areas of religion, politics, and ethnicity. A molehill grew into a mountain of ridiculous heights.

What specifically can a director do?

1. Be a good neighbor, not just during the camp season but throughout the year.
2. Maintain friendly communication with your immediate neighbors. Invite them to visit your camp, to see a program, to share a meal, or just walk around the grounds.
3. You may want to offer them the use of your facilities on evenings or weekends. If you do, it is important to set up the ground rules and have them in writing, with such terms as:

   The invitation is limited to immediate families, not their friends and relatives: Children must be accompanied by adults.

   A signed statement absolving the camp of liability in case of accident might not hold up in court, but it would impress the signer with the need for caution.
4. If it is possible to involve a neighbor in the camp program, such as sharing a hobby or a talent, he is more likely to be understanding if a problem arises.
5. Consult your neighbors before you make changes. In one case when a new fence was contemplated, the neighbor was asked: "Do you prefer chain link so you can watch the children or a solid fence to shut out noise?" It made no difference to the camp owner and the courtesy was appreciated.
6. If a neighbor calls with a complaint follow through immediately— and in person. He is a VIP to you!
7. Get involved in community activities. Your camp is taking up space. If you are nonprofit and do not pay real estate taxes there may be some resentment. If you do pay taxes you have a vested interest in the affairs of the town or city. Join the Chamber of Commerce, a service club, or charitable organization; offer your services for programs or committees. Attend all major functions such as annual banquets, testimonials to retiring officials, etc. You will meet people on a social basis, and their doors will open to you more freely if you have reason to call on them to help solve a problem.

You will want to make financial contributions to local affairs (the Policemen's Ball, Firemen's Fund, etc.) But that is not enough. A good public image is like love; you can't buy it. You have to earn it!

Staff

A good staff is one of your most important assets. Here are some points to consider in staffing your camp:

—Check on number of former staff members who plan to return
—Determine staff needs
—Notify agencies and placement bureaus of staff needs
—As applications are received send for references
—Interview prospective staff members
—As staff are engaged send contracts and additional information (See Chapter 14.)
—Notify staff of training opportunities and courses available

Office Work

Set up a chart for group placements and keep it up to date as enrollment applications are received. In day camps where early enrollment is a practice, it is necessary to (a) number and date applications as they are received; (b) keep a check on group placement if the size of the group is limited by age, sex, or experience; (c) keep a constant check on waiting lists.

Set up books with ledger cards for campers and business accounts.

If camper record cards are used as suggested in the section on records and reports, the information can be typed on these from the applications as they are received.

Get out mailings to campers, parents, and staff.

In a camp where children are enrolled for a minimum of four weeks, it may be advisable to prepare an alphabetical master list of campers for use by key people. This list will not be made up until the last possible moment before camp begins so that it will be reasonably complete. It should be triple-spaced to allow for additions and may contain the following information:

Name of Camper _____ Address _____ Phone No. _____

Name of Parent or Guardian_____

Business Address _____ Phone No. _____

Group _____ Driver_____

Prepare unit lists, group lists, and staff lists according to anticipated uses.

Order supplies.

Set up service contracts for such things as food, towels, and pool maintenance.

Transportation

As campers are accepted, keep track of their location on maps. If these are tacked to bulletin boards, colored pins can be used for each vehicle. Although it is usually impractical to plan routes until shortly before the opening date, the pins will help the director avoid accepting one isolated camper who may be so far out of the way that it would be wiser to refuse the application.

When you contract for hired transportation, be sure to check Standards.

Maintenance

Many camp directors devote all possible time during the spring to the preparation of the campsite by clearing the land, repairing winter damage, and making improvements. Even though the campsite may be located on a school campus or on publicly owned property, there is usually some need for specific preparation for the day camp.

If major repairs or improvements, such as new buildings or pools, are contemplated, plans must get under way very early. Looking up sources, studying advertising literature, talking to salesmen, comparing costs, checking references of suppliers, and preparing and approving bids are time-consuming details that should not be dealt with hastily. American Camping Association members attending Sectional, Regional, or National Conventions are given an opportunity to explore the relative advantages of supplies and equipment as exhibitors solicit their business.

Administration During Camp

Parent contacts, supervision, the purchase and care of supplies, and the upkeep of the camp property are important features of administration. The degree of importance attached to parent-camp relationships varies greatly, and so we shall enumerate in the paragraphs that follow a number of methods used in making contacts with parents.

Parent Contacts

Many of the public and agency-sponsored day camps hold some sort of open house before, during, or at the conclusion of a camping period for parents and members of community groups that have helped the camp in some way. Some of these camps invite parents or whole families to come for a cookout supper or picnic. Exhibitions of work, demonstrations of camper activities, parent participation in camper events, or a planned program are among the methods used to entertain them.

Many day camps limit parent visits to certain designated times, but others feel that a clearer impression of the daily program will be gained if parents are free to drop in at any time. Some camps exclude visitors only during lunch and rest periods.

One day camp director invites the parents from each unit or group for lunch on different days. He discusses with them the overall program and invites their suggestions. After that, parents observe their children at various activities and have an opportunity to talk with counselors.

In still another, parents meet one night a week for a cookout supper and hold discussions that are led by the director or an occasional outside speaker.

Evening and weekend use of camp facilities is offered in a few instances, but insurance restrictions, supervision problems, and safety factors usually prohibit this gesture. (Some privately owned camps with unusually good facilities sell family memberships for weekend privileges. This is operated as a separate business with its own administrative structure.)

It would seem that one of the advantages of a day camp lies in the fact that there is an opportunity for parents and camp leaders to work as a team for the mutual benefit of the child. The value of a day camping experience will be increased when it can be shared in some way with other members of the family.

Supervision

Supervision of staff, campers, and program should be the function of one person who is free at all times to move about the camp. It may be the owner, the director, a head counselor, or a program leader. The title is unimportant; what is essential is that one individual holds the reins, however lightly. Moreover, this one person cannot be tied to single responsibilities in a given area. Such a person should be familiar with the overall picture, for he will constantly need to interpret camp philosophy to campers, staff, parents, and visitors. He will see and appreciate what the campers are doing, he will nourish good program with a word to the counselors, and he will forestall mistakes before they are serious. This person, who has his finger on the pulse of the whole camp, will see where program is lagging or where enthusiasm is dipping too heavily into the resources of energy. He will be constantly on the move for this is a function which cannot be properly administered from behind an office desk.

Supplies

Establishing procedures for ordering, purchasing, and distributing supplies and equipment during the camp season is a very important administrative function. A system for preventing unnecessary waste must be devised. This is a task that calls for much forethought, tact, and the ability to enlist staff cooperation. In a large camp a central depot may be needed for all supplies. In this case an efficient method for recording supplies taken and returned is necessary.

Maintenance

In any day camp, large or small, there will be a constant daily need for minor repairs. In addition, there will be frequent requests for such items as "a frame for our puppet stage," "a cage for the bunny," "a storage box in the woods where campcraft tools can be locked up," or "another sandbox in the nursery camp." Prompt attention to such needs and requests will engender an atmosphere of trust in staff.

The conservation program can never be neglected. Paths become worn, heavy rainstorms take their toll, dust must be kept down, and watering may save a tree or bit of grass.

Maintenance, like housework, is never done; if it is neglected even for a short period, the effect will be felt by the entire camping family.

Additional Duties

Library—Among other responsibilities which may fall into the category of administration is the provision for a camp library. Books to be read by campers should be chosen carefully. The library should be available for counselor use and easily accessible. There will be need of a book checkout system that will make them available at all times and reduce lost books.

Camp Store—Some day camps have a canteen or store, where such items as T-shirts, post cards, equipment, and craft supplies are sold.

Camp Pictures—Frequently a professional photographer is engaged to take camp pictures. If so, a system must be established for displaying the proofs, taking orders, collecting money, and delivering.

Visitors—A method for checking on the identity, purpose, and actions of all outsiders who enter the camp is essential. It is not proper even for parents to be in camp without the knowledge of the director. Some provision must be made for registering visitors. Some camps keep a guest book to register visitors upon arrival.

Camp Newspaper—The camp newspaper is a medium through which the fun and flavor of the day camp program can be shared with parents and friends and, as such, is an indirect method of promotion. When the paper is produced by the campers, it may be a truly creative activity or it can be just a collection of childish impressions. Accounts of activities that mention the names of campers and give credit for achievement provide a psychological lift, both for the camper and the parent.

When teenagers are enrolled, the operation of the newspaper may be a challenging and worthwhile activity for them. (See Teenagers).

The creative effort involved in writing and the discipline necessary to complete the task offer a challenge.

Benefit Performances—A fair, circus, carnival, or benefit performance for charitable purposes is another means of gaining publicity for the camp. Such a project may help to extend the camper's awareness of people and problems outside his own small sphere; but, unless it is carefully planned, the tension and strain imposed on counselors and campers may be out of proportion to the contribution to charity. If long hours are devoted to rehearsals, the value to the campers is questionable.

After-Camp Duties

The season may end for campers and counselors on the final day of camp. Administrative duties, however, will usually extend well beyond the closing date.

Review all records and evaluation reports and use information to make written proposals for next year. A prudent director will review them again in January, too, but it is best to pull together information while details are still fresh.

Office

In addition to closing the books and making necessary financial reports, this is a good time to analyze costs of special services such as food, transportation, riding trips, and overnights. If recommendations for changes in tuition and other charges are made, the board, committee, or owner will have ample time to take action before a new brochure is printed.

Staff manuals may need to be restored and replenished. Pages which have been reviewed and rewritten during the season can be mimeographed and inserted.

Records and Reports

During the camp season the director, though occupied with many details of immediate concern, should not overlook the importance of recording and keeping information which may be needed at a later date. It is not easy for the beginner to anticipate these needs, so we are offering this advice based on long experience:

☐ A careful record of campers' attendance will be helpful another year in determining when peak enrollment can be expected. When a tuition plan is offered the accuracy of such records is essential.

☐ Staff attendance and performance records could be a determining factor for future employment or references for schools, colleges, or employers and references for government security.
☐ Information for health or guidance specialists.
☐ Names and addresses of staff and alumnae for reunions, anniversary celebrations, or solicitations for funds.

The decision as to what is important may be helped by these questions:

☐ Who will use the information?
☐ How will it be used?
☐ How often will it be used?
☐ How long will it be kept? (Consult state and federal laws.)
☐ Who is going to record the information?
    a. Director?
    b. Unit leader?
    c. Counselor?
    d. Nurse?
    e. Office staff?

☐ How long will it take to record information?
☐ When will it be recorded?
    a. During the camp day?
    b. After hours?

For convenience of storage it is best to set up a system at the outset that will be consistently practical and compact. It is suggested that much of the following information can be recorded on five-by-eight cards. Files for these do not take up much space and can be added as needed. A different color for each card will simplify their uses. The cards can be used for these purposes:

☐ Camper registration
    a. Side (A)—personal data
    b. Side (B)—developmental and progress records
☐ Camper physical examination
☐ Record of first aid or treatments by nurse
☐ Staff physical examination
☐ Permanent record of staff
    a. Side (A)—personal data
    b. Side (B)—positions held
    Evaluation of performance of duties
    Reason for leaving
    Details which might be helpful in writing a reference
    Physical characteristics which would help to recall other factors
    A picture would serve the same purpose.

Health and Safety

- ☐ Staff examinations
- ☐ Special tests (such as tubercular) or licenses
- ☐ Camper examinations (Medical history may be separate.)
- ☐ Daily treatment records
- ☐ Report of accidents with names of witnesses

Maintenance

- ☐ Records of major purchases or improvements (including names of persons involved in transaction, date, instructions, guarantees, etc.)
- ☐ Inventory lists filed where they can be consulted for stock replacement

Real Estate

- ☐ Deeds and mortgages
- ☐ Tax receipts

Insurance

- ☐ See Chapter 8

Organizational

- ☐ Minutes of corporation meetings, meetings of trustees, board of directors, etc.
- ☐ Annual reports
- ☐ End-of-season reports
- ☐ Statistical records and analysis

For day camps operated by public recreation departments, or by nonprofit agencies or other groups in which day camping is only one phase of the program, elaborate systems of records and reports as outlined above may not be necessary or may be adapted to the local agency's policies. Usually, however, a day camp director or committee will find that time and effort expended on a well-kept system of records on campers, counselors, and camp program will be invaluable in setting up the day camp program for the next year.

The day camp director, with his camp safely "tucked in" for the winter, will usually find his administrative duties lightest at this point.

He may then find time to review pictures, slides, and movies taken during the summer; select those suitable for promotion or staffing training; and write appropriate talks or captions to go with them.

A discussion of the whole subject of finance in the day camp including the necessity for accurate records, follows in the next chapter.

chapter 7	# Finance

In its simplest form, financial management is a matter of income and expense; every day camp, whether it be large or small, philanthropic or operated for profit, will be obliged to give an account on both sides of the ledger. It goes without saying that the camp supported by public funds must maintain an adequate bookkeeping system to account for these funds; it is the individual owner who may inadvertently get into difficulties. A day camp that starts in a small way may grow rapidly, and before the founder realizes what is happening he finds himself overwhelmed by the intricacies of taxes and business management. The result may be a fine for delinquent tax payments.

Income

This chapter seeks to point out sources of income in a day camp and to provide a check list for expenditures.

Tuition

Tuition fees in day camps vary greatly. In the public or nonprofit camp they may be nonexistent or a token fee, which does little more than to testify to the genuine interest of the parent or camper. More and more agencies are moving in the direction of covering major operating costs through fees.

One of the first problems to be solved is that of determining what constitutes a fair charge. The type of sponsorship, the social and economic level of the community, and the prevailing tuition rates of other day camps in the locale will guide management in arriving at an appropriate figure.

Over and above the basic tuition, additional fees may be charged for the following items:

Transportation

In some camps, including most private camps, transportation is included in tuition. In camps where transportation charges are based on distance, rates may be determined by zones.

Many camps employ counselors who will use their own private cars for transportation of campers. The various methods for compensating them for this service are described in Chapter 9 on "Transportation."

Some camps avoid many problems by turning the entire business over to a transportation firm—in which case the charges may be paid by the camp, the agency, or by the parents directly to the bus or taxi company.

Food Service

Some camps provide a noon meal for all campers with the charge included as part of the camp fee. In other camps the noon meal is optional, and the charges levied only against those who are actually fed. A third system commonly used is that of including the cost of snacks such as hot soup, milk, fruit, or ice cream in the basic fee. In an agency or public camp, such items are often provided without extra charge. (See Chapter 11.)

"Overnights"

In most day camps "overnights" are conducted on an optional basis. If campers bring their own food and the counselors are not given extra pay for supervision, there may not be an extra charge. If the camp pays for food and supervision, charges may be based on actual cost.

Trips

When trips are made to pools, beaches, parks or reservations, riding stables, and so forth, as part of the regular day camp program and to supplement facilities, the fees for transportation are usually included in tuition. If trips are made on an optional basis, there may be an extra charge.

Camp Store

Some private day camps carry quite a variety of miscellaneous items which may be purchased through the office or through a camp store. The money campers spend for such items is separate from and in addition to regular camp fees. There is a growing tendency to eliminate camp stores completely as they add an undesirable commercial element to camp life and are unnecessary in day camps.

Towels

In some day camps fresh towels are provided daily by a linen service company. The charge may be included in tuition or may be an extra. In most agency or public day camps the children bring their own towels.

Insurance

In many camps accident and medical insurance are included in the basic charge since blanket coverage extending to all campers will reduce the overall expense and will greatly simplify bookkeeping procedures. Another method is to offer insurance to campers and staff on an optional basis. In public camps the recreation department usually carries such coverage.

Tutoring

In private camps the charge is usually extra.

Registration Fees

These vary from none to a token fee that accompanies the application as an indication of good faith. In most private camps a deposit is required when the camper is accepted. This deposit may be applied to tuition but not returned in case of cancellations, or it may be a separate fee that is neither returned nor deducted from tuition. In some day camps where enrollments are accepted at the end of the season for the following year, the deposit is refunded up to, but not after, a given date if the camper is not able to attend.

Discounts

In many day camps discounts are allowed for children of staff members. Discounts are also allowed in some cases where a family is sending more than one child to the camp. Also, some camps provide for a graduated reduction in tuition charges proportioned to the length of the enrollment; thus, the weekly tuition fee would be somewhat less for an eight-week enrollment than that for a two-week enrollment. Professional discounts are sometimes allowed for educators and members of the clergy.

Refunds

The failure of fee-charging camps to establish a firm policy regarding refunds can cause the financial downfall of a day camp. This is a problem that private camp directors frequently fail to anticipate.

Many camps furnish adequate notice that "no refunds" will be made for withdrawal for any reason." Other camps refund tuition only when the vacancy caused by the withdrawal has been filled. If refunds are to be made, previous notice of withdrawal is normally required from the parent, varying from five days to four weeks before the camper actually leaves. This may permit the camp to fill the vacancy. In any case the camp's policy should be clearly stated on the registration form.

EXPENSES

Salaries
Owner/Director (to be included in budget even if not paid)
Supervisory Staff
General and Specialty Counselors
Health Staff (Nurse, etc.)
Office Staff
Food Handlers
Drivers (if employed by camp)
Caretaker and Maintenance Staff

Payroll Taxes

Food, Kitchen, and Dining Supplies

Transportation
Chartered or rented vehicles, auto expenses paid to counselors.

Maintenance and Repair Supplies
Toilet paper, paper towels, cleaning and safety supplies, chemicals for pool, repair materials

Program Expense
Athletic, creative and performing arts, nature, games, library, trips

Office Expense
Bookkeeping records, stationery, printing, paper and ink for forms and manuals, postage. (Large items such as duplicators or typewriters are to be amortized.)

Promotion
  Advertising, brochures, postage, movies, slides, travel, and entertainment

Laundry and/or Linen Service

Camper Materials
  T-shirts, tote bags, photographs, etc.

Insurance (See Chapter 8.)

Utilities
  Water, electricity, gas, telephone

Real Estate Taxes

Interest
  Mortgage and line of credit

Depreciation
  Real estate, furniture and fixtures (including vehicles)

Dues, Subscriptions, Conventions and Expense in Work for Professional Organizations

Legal and Accounting Fees

Rentals and/or Contract Services

Budget Control

The control of expenses is one of the most important facets of day camp management. When business failures occur, the most frequent causes are likely to be the result of: (1) lack of sufficient funds; (2) inexperienced management; (3) Failure to anticipate expenditures.

A periodic check of expenses against the anticipated budget will help the day camp management to see where adjustments are needed. Analyses of costs of special services (such as food or transportation) often reveal a need for revision of methods. It should be remembered that gross income must always equal or exceed expenses. A safe working budget usually includes an item for contingencies.

Purchasing

Items purchased in haste because of a pressing need frequently cost more than if efficient planning had "stocked the shelves" well in advance. It is good economy to have the buying power delegated to a single, competent individual who will

    investigate items that will be required,

    compare specifications and prices,

    prepare purchase order,

    receive goods and compare with order and invoices.

After goods are received, this person should maintain constant supervision over supplies and devise methods for dispensing materials to staff, which will eliminate carelessness and waste.

Renting Equipment

A private day camp may want to investigate the possibilities of renting such things as cars, boats, furniture, office equipment, or horses. The advantages are these:

    It avoids heavy capital investment.

    It eliminates the details of working out depreciation schedules for tax purposes.

    It provides up-to-date equipment.

Professional Services

The day camp committee will need to employ the professional services of some of the following experts:

    Realtors

    Insurance consultants

    Legal advisors

    Business management consultants

    Accountants

    Public relations consultants

    Professional cleaning services

    Planning consultants (building and landscape architects)

Cash Flow

Almost as important as planning and adhering to a realistic budget is an understanding of cash flow. As most small businesses and associations grow larger, they are often surprised that, although they are handling a larger volume, they find it more difficult to pay their bills. Then they learn about "Cash Flow" through bitter experience.

After making as certain as you can that your receipts will exceed your expenses, take a little time to analyze when you will receive the income and when your obligations will fall due. This analysis may affect your planning and certainly will help you to sleep at night.

For example, your study may show that with a minimal deposit and very little tuition coming in until the camp is about to open you will have expenses that cannot be paid when due. Therefore you will need a larger investment to begin with, a larger line of credit (which of course will add to your interest cost) or a better tuition payment plan. Perhaps you should increase the initial deposit and require full or partial payment of the tuition at an earlier date? Perhaps you should give a small reduction to those who register early? Of course you must always keep in mind that a larger deposit may discourage or postpone registrations. These are the kind of business decisions that must be made, but the important thing is that you are aware of what is happening and do not drift into financial difficulty.

To prepare a Cash Flow list the twelve months of the year and for each month note your best estimate of income and disbursements. A negative difference will have to be made up by borrowing or from your initial investment. This will give you a rough cash picture of where you expect to be at any time and will help you to plan for the coming year.

Maintenance and Improvements

The expression "penny-wise and pound-foolish" is never more true than in the upkeep and replacement of property. In a day camp where so much of the equipment is exposed to wind and weather, the paint-brush will seldom be idle. Aside from the practical aspects of preservation, the day camp director cannot afford from a promotion standpoint to let his camp look seedy, run down, or drab.

Insurance

The most zealous and conscientious administrator cannot prevent disasters that are classified as "acts of God," but he should have a risk management plan and insurance as described in the following chapter.

chapter 8 | Insurance

by Irwin Rhodes

Risk Management

The longest sustained period of inflation in American history, combined with an increasingly litigious society and rising court awards, have pushed insurance premiums so high that insurance has become a major day camp cost. Camp directors can no longer afford just to sigh deeply each year and set aside a larger percentage of their budget for this vital need. There *are* things they can do to keep premiums down without taking undue risks. Each camp has different problems, but we will outline the elements of a *risk management plan* that applies generally to all.

The camp directors must identify and list all the personal safety and financial risks that their camp may incur. They must then seriously examine the best methods of handling each risk and make a plan to cover each of them.

It is not adequate merely to call one's insurance broker and ask for professional advice about the necessary coverage. Of course the broker should be consulted and the director will have to depend on the broker's expert advice as to rates, etc., but the directors themselves—with all the specific information on hand—should personally make the necessary risk management plan. Insurance forms are but a part of this plan. Directors will find that careful analysis will more than repay their time and trouble.

There are four basic methods to be applied in combination for handling risks most economically.

1. *Avoidance of Risk.* Never be exposed to an unnecessary risk in the first place. For example, if trampolines are so dangerous as to call for a special high-liability premium, think again about their use. You can probably find a safer substitute.

61

2. *Reduction of Risk.* Directors should carefully examine the camp's property and program to discover any conditions that increase the chance of peril. Whenever possible they should make all necessary corrections. They should educate their staff both before and during the season as to the best safety practices. Such education will cut down both the frequency of accidents and the severity of injuries. The in-service training should include an understanding of the camper's capabilities, safe conduct of activities, first aid, emergency procedures, and proper recording. A continuing program of preventive and remedial maintenance of areas, facilities, and equipment should be everyone's responsibility.

3. *Retention of Risk.* Sometimes called self-insurance. Here we mean the retaining of certain risks, either in whole or in part, and payment of these losses rather than insurance against them.

   a. *Non-Insurance.* Low-severity, low-frequency losses such as plate-glass insurance or low-severity, high-frequency losses such as limited medical expense insurance could well come out of one's current budget. Another example would be the common "deductible" insurance, where the first part of the loss is paid by the insured with a substantial reduction in the premium. Still another example would be the elimination of small buildings from the camp's fire-insurance coverage, thus avoiding a premium where one can afford the loss.

   b. *Funded Reserve.* When there is a low-frequency, high-severity risk such as the burning of a major building or liability for a serious personal injury, almost every camp operator, except large institutions such as the Boy Scouts or the YMCA, should have adequate insurance. If such insurance is not obtainable, then a reserve fund approximately equal to the insurance premium that would have been paid should be set aside each year to build a reserve so that in the event of a serious loss the funds will be available. In recent years many municipalities have used a funded reserve most successfully, saving substantial costs.

4. *Transfer of Risk*

   a. *Contractors and Purchases.* When a camp enters into an agreement with a contractor, the liability exposures should be borne by the contractor. Thus a bus company providing transportation should provide the camp with full insurance, giving the camp a certificate for it. Similarly a contractor doing any work for the camp should provide it with both liability and workmen's compensation policies. This principle of transfer of risk should also be applied to important purchases. Where possible the purchase order should spell out that goods are to be shipped F.O.B. destination in order to have the seller "at risk" during transit.

   b. *Insurance.* After we have identified our risks, avoided the ones we could, reduced others, retained minor risks, and, wherever practical, transferred risks to contractors and suppliers, we will *transfer through insurance* the balance of our risks. For a comparatively small certain cost known as a premium, the risk of a larger loss called the face amount or limit of liability is transferred to an insurance company.

There are insurance policies available for virtually all risks. However, every policy has some exclusions and one must remember that the coverage is *only* for listed items *less* exclusions. *If an item is not mentioned it is not covered.* One can now obtain "all risk" coverage for day camps. While these policies are well-designed and avoid the need for many separate policies they are not truly "all risk" for, as noted above, they cover *only* listed items less exclusions.

Let us now proceed to an examination of the various types of insurance generally considered for day camps. But keep in mind that you should not proceed to insure until you have *first* eliminated items as listed above in 1, 2, 3, and 4a, or have decided on some combination of these various methods of saving on insurance premiums. The National Standards Board of the American Camping Association has recommended that all camps accredited by the ACA have a Risk Management Plan.

There are many kinds of insurance available to day camps, some of which are required by law. It is impractical to describe completely in this chapter the coverages required or advisable for day camping in other than general terms because practices and regulations tend to vary from company to company and from state to state. Any day camp director will be wise to deal with an insurance agent who is familiar with his type of day camping and who will take the time to explain the terms and conditions of the policies his companies can offer.

"Proper protection" relates not only to the kind of insurance written, but to the amount of each kind. Some camps have never increased their coverage to keep pace with today's rising costs and increasing judgements, despite casualty experience which indicates how inadequate such coverage is for today's needs. This is particularly true in the field of liability insurance, where large awards are frequently made for serious or permanent injuries.

Camper Medical and Accident Insurance

Such insurance covers the camper to the policy limits for injuries sustained while traveling to, attending, and returning from camp, and also for the expense of treatment received within a specified number of weeks after the time of the accident. Coverage usually includes X-ray and hospital bills; nurses', physicians', and surgeons' fees; laboratory costs, and the like.

Many insurance companies allow counselors to take out accident coverage under the same policy as the campers. This service is not necessary since employees are covered by Workmen's Compensation. Payment for injuries incurred in minor accidents, whether payment is made by the camp or a special accident insurance policy, substantially reduces liability claims and is well worthwhile.

Workmen's Compensation and Sickness Disability

Workmen's Compensation varies in requirements and in benefits among the states. Subject to the requirements of the state, the act has the effect of being compulsory. Therefore, it is wise to check with an insurance company or agent as to the statutory requirements.

All employees, including cooks, maintenance men, carpenters, mechanics, office staff, nurse, and counselors, generally must be included. When counselors-in-training do not pay tuition, the camp owner should check state laws to see whether they are to be covered by Workmen's Compensation.

It may be advisable that the same insurance agency handle Workmen's Compensation, liability, and sickness and accident insurance. This usually eliminates indecision between insurance companies as to which should pay a claim.

Fire Insurance

Construction costs have increased enormously, but many property owners have not increased their insurance coverage proportionately. It is advised that camp directors have a reappraisal of fire insurance coverage every three years.

It is generally considered best, in states which permit, to write fire insurance on a blanket basis with 80 or 90 percent of the sound value of all buildings and contents covered. Should one or two buildings burn completely, the coverage provides 100 percent replacement of these buildings although only 80 or 90 percent of the total values are insured.

If the camp budget or state laws will not allow for 80 or 90 percent coverage as described above, it is possible to have property insurance written on a schedule, with a definite amount applying to each building. If the property has been appraised, one way to set the amount of insurance is to take a straight percentage of each building appraised in order to get some coverage on each piece of property. Some camp owners, however, try to put proper coverage on the most valuable building and allow some of the less valuable buildings to remain underinsured or uninsured. This is not as flexible a plan as the blanket policy since insurance cannot be borrowed, from one building to cover a severe loss on another. If possible, contents, since they are apt to be moved, should not be insured in each building, but on a blanket basis throughout the camp.

In most states, tents, rowboats, canoes, and camp equipment can be lumped as one item on a blanket basis at a slightly lower rate. However, these items may be included in a single broad-form camp-owner's policy which is explained later in this chapter.

An "extended coverage" endorsement including windstorm coverage should probably be carried on camp buildings. Snow collapse, leaking and water damage, and damage from falling trees are among other types of protection now available.

Liability Other than Automobile

Many insurance companies still shy away from summer camps for liability coverage and some still issue only the limited owner's, landlord's, and tenant's form. However, when it is possible to obtain it, the safest liability coverage for a camp is the *comprehensive* liability contract. With this, it is necessary for the camp owner or director to fill out a questionnaire that discloses all hazards involved in camp operation, including those pertaining to boats, canoes, saddle horses, products of the premises, malpractice, persons, area, and other items. If all known hazards are properly covered with the estimated charge for them, the camp is insured against all these known hazards. The final premium charge is determined by an annual audit.

The properly insured camp will show in its comprehensive liability contract year-round premise coverage and any off-premise property specifically mentioned, such as an office in a home or office building, a camping site, and any other property owned, leased or rented, such as laundries and beaches. All canoes, sailboats, rowboats, inboards, and outboards should be declared in the contract; also the total number of saddle animals, whether owned or hired.

One of the most frequent omissions in liability contracts is the uncovered hazard of sending children to riding academies. Riding schools often do not have insurance and, even if they do, the responsibility of the camp does not cease when the director delivers a camper to a riding academy. This hazard should be specifically covered in the liability contract.

Products liability covering food handling and consumption on and off the premises should be mentioned, and contingent malpractice coverage should also be shown. Every doctor and nurse should carry a malpractice policy, but some do not. If they should make a mistake in treating a camper, the camp might be sued.

There are special contracts available for certain public and nonprofit organizations which operate day or establish camps whereby camping activities and meetings at camps not owned by the users can have liability coverage on a daily basis. Local attorneys and insurance agencies should be consulted.

Autombile Liability

The laws of virtually all states require car owners to be insured for damage to people or property. The limits required by the states are not adequate and the camp operator will want to insure for a greater amount. He also will need special insurance for liability due to the operation of cars owned by his employees. The cost of this special blanket coverage is quite moderate.

There is now available to the day camp director insurance that covers counselors while they are transporting campers. Each employee and vehicle used for transporting campers will have to be listed on the policy. This type of insurance is most valuable as many counselors are properly concerned about their own liability, which probably is not properly covered by the regular auto insurance they carry.

Automobile Fire and Theft

Camp-owned vehicles should be covered for comprehensive fire and theft; for, even though stored on the premises during the winter, they can burn or be stolen. If reasonably new, they also should have collision coverage. If the camp owns five or more cars and trucks, fleet rates may be available. However, this is a field in which "self-insurance" as outlined in 3 above is often desirable.

Miscellaneous Coverage

Besides the foregoing types of insurance described, there are several other kinds of coverage that the day camp management may find worth considering.

Burglary and Theft

This can now be written in blanket form on all contents throughout a camp except the owner's residence. Protection covering that building can be written on the regular residence-burglary policy or endorsement.

Interior or Exterior Robbery Insurance and Fidelity Bonds

Some of the larger day camps may wish to protect themselves by carrying interior or exterior robbery insurance. In addition, employees handling money may be covered by some form of fidelity bond.

Business Life Insurance

This type of insurance is worthy of consideration, particularly in the case of a partnership. In the event of the death of one partner, suitable provisions can be made for taking over his share so that the surviving partner does not find himself in business with the deceased partner's widow or other heirs.

Tuition Refund

Tuition Refund insurance in case of a camper's withdrawal due to illness or other reason is available for resident camps and often not available for day camps. Even if this insurance is available for a day camp, it is one of the types of insurance that can be omitted and covered in the camp's budget.

Business Interruption

Under the tuition or camping fees form of contract, coverage may be available for the loss of income occasioned by fire or any of the perils of the extended coverage endorsement, which, of course, includes windstorm and tornado. Under this particular form the wording is such that should a fire occur in the spring or just before the camp opens, the insurance would cover the drop in income even though the camp was repaired in time to open on its regular scheduled date. The premium is not too expensive in proportion to the coverage offered, and can be taken out on various percentages of the total camping income.

Some insurance companies offer a modified tuition refund program to insure only expenses. The coverage protects the camp against total closure due to epidemic and also includes coverage for quarantine. Such expenses would include staff salaries, food products not of a salvageable nature, taxes, bank principal and interest, insurance, printing, and some other necessary continuing expenses. The premium is determined for each camp separately on the basis of a survey.

Broad-Form Camp Owner's Policy

The trend toward the packaging of all camp coverages under one policy is increasing. This type of policy offers many advantages. It eliminates much clerical expense and work, and the cost may be no greater than the total cost of individual policies. In addition it offers some types of coverage not otherwise obtainable, such as building collapse, weight of ice and snow, and trees falling on buildings.

Accredited Camp Insurance Plan

Many companies have stopped writing camp insurance. This trend has continued to such an extent that in many areas only one or two insurers remain and insurance brokers may have difficulty placing camp insurance. The American Camping Association, in order to protect its members from the loss of the availability of insurance at fair rates, developed an insurance program for ACA Accredited camps. It is believed that because of the high standards of ACA camps, the losses are lower than for the average camp and after an initial period the rates would also be lower than that of standard insurers.

chapter
9

Transportation

.

Of the many responsibilities that rest on the shoulders of the day camp director or sponsor, probably the heaviest is transportation. Between the safety of the home and the safety of the campsite lies the danger of the public way, over which the camper must be carried twice daily. Although the director can exert reasonable control over the activities and premises of his camp, he has very little control over the external hazards of the road. He can, however, control the operation of his own vehicles. Carefully planned procedures with minute attention to details are essential. The conscientious director will want to be familiar with every known precaution and to anticipate every possible contingency.

Vehicles

Passenger cars and station wagons used for transporting children may be owned by the public recreation department, by the nonprofit agency, by the camp, by the counselors, by the parents, or may be hired, but in every case the camp sponsor or director should assume personal responsibility for seeing that the condition of the vehicle is carefully checked. In some cases this is done by a mechanic employed by the agency or camp. Surprising deficiences are often discovered in cars that appear to be in excellent condition.

When buses are provided by independent carriers, problems of driver qualification, vehicle inspection, and maintenance are assumed by the firms supplying the buses. However, it is necessary for the director to satisfy himself that he is dealing with a responsible and reputable concern. He will be wise to ascertain personally that the carrier, in addition to meeting the requirements of the standards, is financially secure and adequately insured, and that the drivers meet qualifications. In the event of a serious accident resulting in lawsuits, the camp could be forced to accept liability for judgments the carrier is unable to pay. Contracts for all hired transportation should be in writing, set forth in clear and comprehensive terms.

Since transporting children is an expensive proposition, there is often a strong temptation to overcrowd vehicles. In some states the number of passengers will be determined by law; but, if it is not, it should be remembered that when vehicles transporting children are conspicuous because of poor practices, this not only hurts the camp involved, but also brings discredit on all who are involved with day camping.

Adding to the seating arrangements provided by automobile manufacturers may violate some law or insurance regulation; therefore, this possibility should be carefully scrutinized before any money is expended.

It is suggested that the following items be kept in each car and that periodic checks be made by a responsible person to see that they are there. Since one of them is a first aid kit, the nurse might be asked to do this checking:

1. Envelope containing:

    a. Car registration
    b. Two report blanks to use in case of accident (See Appendix)
    c. Money for emergency phone call taped to card with important numbers listed

2. Recent map of locality covered
3. Up-to-date route list with detailed directions, which could be followed if a substitute driver had to be used
4. A small notebook or pad for messages
5. A box of tissues
6. Paper bag for used tissues (May be attached to dashboard with tape.)
7. Waxed paper bags to use in case of car sickness
8. First aid kit containing:

Bandaids	Gauze bandage
Scissors	Package of gauze squares
Adhesive	Antiseptic
Burn ointment	Spirits of ammonia

8. Book to be read to children in case of delay due to mechanical breakdown

Drivers

A car is only as safe as the human being who operates it. A counselor lacking in judgment will be observed and supervised by experienced staff on the campgrounds; but drivers are strictly on their own, and a substandard driver is often not discovered until too late.

A separate application for drivers (see Appendix) is advisable. A written record of any accidents he may have had can sometimes be procured from the state registry of motor vehicles for a small fee. If this does not corroborate his own application, the employer will want to do some thorough checking.

In addition to the qualifications outlined in the standards, it is most important that drivers like children. Many otherwise excellent drivers have neither the temperament nor the patience for the work.

Drivers should be acquainted with the policies and philosophy of the camp. They should be expected to maintain the same high standards of appearance and deportment required of other staff members.

All requirements for physical examination of counselors should be applied to drivers as well.

A written description of the duties and responsibilities of a driver should be given to each applicant at the time of employment.

Drivers should be given ample time to learn their routes before camp opens. The first day of camp can be ruined for a new camper by a driver who loses his way.

A set of rules and regulations compiled by individuals who are thoroughly familiar with the situation should be in the possession of each driver, and should be referred to frequently at conferences and meetings, with revisions as often as necessary.

In many private day camps, counselors are employed with the understanding that they will use their cars for transportation. In some cases, remuneration is included in their total salary; in others, mileage or a fee per camper is paid. The recommended practice is to make separate arrangements for payment for transporting campers. Then, if for some reason either party chooses to terminate that part of the contract, less confusion or misunderstanding will result.

Sometimes parents are glad to earn all or part of the tuition by driving. Again, it is best to keep this on a strict business basis, balancing salary against tuition charges.

Leaders in youth-serving agencies are a good source of drivers because of their training and experience.

Men who have recently retired often find driving to be a part-time job that helps them to adjust more gradually to retirement, and are frequently of a much higher caliber than one could otherwise expect for the modest remuneration involved. It is advisable, however, to set some age limit, and to require more frequent physical examinations.

It is important that a substitute who has learned the route in advance be prepared to take the place of each driver. Salary paid to these people for learning time is a worthwhile investment.

Driver Training

A separate meeting for drivers might well be included in the pre-camp training session. Topics to be discussed could include the following:

—Public relations, including such things as appearance, road courtesy, and parent-driver relations
—Discipline (The policies and attitudes of the camp should be outlined and discussed.)
—Health of camper and driver
—Safety measures
—Care and use of camp-owned cars
—Specific procedures such as attendance, messages, absences, etc.
—Procedures to follow in case of
  a. Mechanical breakdown
  b. Accidents (See Appendix.)

Liability

The liability of a camp that provides transportation is one that cannot be evaded. Whether charges for this service are separate or are included in an overall fee, the camp may be liable in case of accident.

When staff or parents use their own cars, the director should make certain that coverage is complete by communicating directly with the insurance company. Written confirmation of the coverage should be required and filed in the camp office before the opening date. When the "rider" co-insuring the camp is purchased from the insurance company directly, a contractual relationship exists, affording the camp greater protection. Since the legal aspects vary greatly from state to state, the counsel of an attorney is recommended.

Automobile insurance is covered in another chapter, but one point should be emphasized. Additional expense for the highest limits possible may some day prove to have been a most valuable investment.

Supervision en Route

Many children who would benefit by a day camp program are deprived of the experience because of fears related to their transportation. Any procedures that make the home/camp transition more comfortable are worthy of consideration. One camp told of a driver who, when checking his route, stopped at each home saying, "I am _____. I will be coming for Johnny on Monday, and so I thought I would stop a minute to get acquainted." What a wonderful feeling of confidence this gave the parents who were entrusting their children to this person, and to the children who left home on the first day with a friend rather than a stranger. If this is not practical, it is definitely advisable to arrange a camper-driver meeting prior to the opening date of camp.

Upon arrival at camp it should be clear that the driver is responsible for each child until he is assured that another adult has assumed the responsibility. There can be no "gaps" in the proper supervision of campers.

Some campers will need to be reassured frequently on the first day that they will get home safely. Campers (especially in uniform) will look surprisingly alike to counselors and drivers, so a system of identification for the first few days is helpful. Tags, buttons, or pins; different colors for each vehicle—the methods will be as unique as the camps which employ them.

Whatever the procedure for boarding the vehicles at the end of the day, it should be discussed and rehearsed during the pre-camp training session.

For the safety and security of all passengers, a few simple rules should be decided upon at the outset and consistently applied.

—Seats should be assigned
—A seat for every camper—and every camper in his seat—should be insisted upon
—Moving about, loud talking or shouting, and comments to passengers in other cars or to people on the street should be forbidden.

The details of transportation procedures, routes, and so on, are often organized by one individual, who may be called a traffic manager. The duties of this person would be as follows:

—Protecting the health, safety, and comfort of the campers, reporting at once to the director any unusual incidents or behavior problems
—Interviewing and employing drivers (including a road test)
—Training and carrying on a continuous in-service program for drivers with meetings, discussion, conferences, and so forth.
—Supervision of driving personnel
—Handling parents' calls that relate to transportation
—Planning routes, having them printed and posted, or placed in strategic spots. (It is a good idea to ride or drive over each route once. Problems that do not show up on a map will become obvious.)
—Making arrangements for insurance on "other owned" vehicles
—Keeping financial records with frequent analysis of costs

Where buses are used, adequate supervision is necessary. One or more counselors (exclusive of bus drivers who should be able to give their whole attention to the safe operation of the bus) should be employed.

The duties of the bus supervisor or captain could be as follows:

—To become thoroughly familiar with the route before camp opens
—Whenever possible, to see each camper before the first day of camp.

—To receive parents' calls relating to absences; to accept messages (if oral, make notes), and to deliver to the office nurse, or counselor as directed

—To keep attendance and turn in required reports at the camp office

—To report to the director any problems with campers, counselors, parents, drivers, or buses

—To keep order on the bus. To arrange seating with an eye to discipline, expediency in getting on and off the bus, and for those with known tendencies toward car sickness (check with camp nurse and seat them near a window or in the front of the bus.)

—To give notes, bulletins, newspapers, or notices from the camp to each camper just before he leaves the bus

—To check the bus when the last camper leaves to be sure clothing or other articles which may have been left on the bus are returned to the owner

Bus assistants or "jumpers" (as they are often appropriately named) should also have prescribed duties such as these:

—Assisting campers on and off buses when necessary

—Taking children across the street or to the door of the house if this is required

—Sitting at strategic spots on the bus assisting the supervisor with attendance, discipline, and program

Route Planning

In a large day camp the planning of routes is a time-consuming task. It is a waste of time to do it before the enrollment is almost complete, since the addition of one passenger can often involve several changes.

The latest maps available should be used in planning routes, but there is no real substitute for a personal check on the territory.

When large buses are used, campers are usually picked up at street corners, the local playgrounds, schoolyards, or other specified meeting places. Whenever door-to-door service is possible, it is preferable.

It is always wise, when planning routes, to have in mind the most expedient method for reaching the driver en route. Some bus companies now have commercial radios in each bus and this is the ideal method of contact.

Program

The time a camper spends going to and from camp is as important as any part of the daily program. The trip should be not only a means of getting to a desired end, but also a happy experience. Singing is a pleasant way to pass the time. There are many camp songs which have endless repetition or numerous verses which can be very monotonous for adults. Children enjoy these songs and they are peculiarly well suited to traveling, since the very monotony is soothing.

Accidents

Every person who accepts the responsibility for transporting children dread the time when a real accident may occur. The thought is so unpleasant that the subject is often avoided, but it is far better to discuss the possibilities at a drivers' meeting and try to plan for every contingency.

The driver's first responsibility is to the children. It will save time and trouble if two reports blanks are kept in the glove compartment, one of which has been filled out in advance and can be given to the driver of the other car. It would contain all the information he needs.

Rules for reporting accidents vary, even from one community to the next. It should be the responsibility of the camp director or the owner of the vehicle to find out where, how soon, by whom, and under what circumstances reporting of accidents is required. In some cases this is determined by the estimated cost of damages. Reporting of accidents should be done. If the driver is required to go to the police station to file a report, the owner or director should go with him.

An accident should be reported promptly to the insurance company, by telephone if the accident is serious, or, for lesser accidents, with a written report not later than twenty-four hours after the accident. Forms for these reports should be kept in the office files.

Vehicles

Recent studies show that for large day camps chartered buses and counselors using their own cars are the least expensive methods of transporting day campers. Chartered minibuses are far more expensive.

If the day camp also operates a nursery throughout the year and maintains minibuses in any case, this will affect the analysis. It is not economical to own buses or minibuses if they are to be used only eight or nine weeks a year.

Chartered buses are preferable for many reasons. There will be an experienced driver who picks up school children the year round; and, if he is absent, the bus company will provide an experienced substitute. Buses are large and heavy and tend to go slowly. If there is a collision with a small vehicle, it is most unlikely that any children will be injured. They are safer in a large bus. For all these reasons most day camps now use chartered buses to transport their campers.

It is interesting—even exciting—to see the children leave a well-organized day camp at the end of the camp day. At a sign from the person in charge of traffice the buses start lumbering out and the line looks like elephants parading in a circus. Then comes the minibuses and finally the private cars. In less than five minutes five hundred children have left the camp. This most-valuable cargo is on its way home.

A lot of preparation has gone into this quick and orderly exodus. The bus counselors and drivers of private cars took attendance in the morning. They have just received notes from the office listing every child who was delivered by a parent and must be added to their roll. The office also provided the name of any child who was picked up earlier by a parent or is to remain in camp. Also there are notes for children who are going to a friend's house on another bus or are just being dropped at a different location by the same bus. The second bus also has received a note. Everything must be in writing. The camp cannot afford to make mistakes.

No car or counselor leaves until every camper has been accounted for. This is most important for, should a bus counselor say, "I am missing Johnny Smith," the director will immediately check with Johnny's counselor. If the counselor says, "I escorted him to the buses" then we will make a quick search and probably find Johnny in his locker room looking for a baseball glove that he ran back to find. Or the counselor may state, "Johnny was just picked up by his mother" who, it is clear, failed to mention the matter to the office. If the counselor has already left, a link is missing in this most vital operation. The day camp director will experience many agonizing moments before the problem is resolved.

To reinforce the statements at the beginning of this chapter—transportation is the heaviest burden a camp director must bear; there can be no margin for error where the safety of children is involved. However, there are many other safety factors to consider while camp is in session; and these, with precautions for health, will be discussed next.

chapter 10

Health and Safety

"A camper is missing! Has he wandered into the woods? Did he decide to walk home? Could he be in the lake or pool?"

"Johnny has a fever!"

"Fire!"

"Johnny hit his head on a rock and is unconscious!"

"The axe slipped!"

"Winds of hurricane force are predicted!"

"The water is rising rapidly!"

"Mary is complaining of stomach pains!"

"Those thunder clouds look ominous!"

"A strange-looking man accosted us in the woods!"

"Susan's group stumbled into a hornet's nest!"

Certainly all of these dramatic incidents will not occur in any one camp or may never happen; but if they do, a camp director who has taken all possible measures *before* the incident occurs will be better prepared to meet the situation with equanimity. The emphasis is on practice as well as planning. No director can afford to take an "it can't happen here" attitude. When he accepts the responsibility for the care of other people's children he is obligated to provide staff with written plans, and train them with actual practice in all measures of health and safety. He is ultimately responsible for the health and safety of the campers.

There are three stages to the precautions he is obligated to take:

—First, he must have carefully designed plans covering all contingencies.

—Next, this plan must be in writing and given to each employee.

—Third, the plans must be practiced during precamp staff training sessions. There is no substitute for a "dry run" when behavior is not affected by stress.

Safety

Safety in the day camp is the responsibility of every member of the staff. There are dangers in every aspect of program, in every moment of the day, and adequate protection calls for constant vigilance. The following suggested plans require cooperation, concern, and conscientious observation.

Fire

It is well known that young children have more curiosity about fire than fear of its dangerous consequences. The day camp has an excellent opportunity to satisfy this curiosity and at the same time teach the child the basic rules for safety. Instead of sneaking behind the garage to play with matches, the campers learn in the campcraft program how to build a fire, what to build it with, when and where to build it, and how to make sure it is properly extinguished. Literature and audio-visuals that will help to dramatize the dangers of and destruction caused by careless firebuilding can be procured from state forestry services. The local fire department will usually be glad to send a fireman to talk to campers about fire hazards peculiar to the camp environment.

If it is not the practice of the local fire department to make an annual check of fire-fighting equipment in the day camp, such an inspection should be requested. They need to be alerted to the existence of the camp, and arrangements should be checked for quick notification in case of fire.

Fire drills should be held regularly with a log kept recording the date, time of day, and time taken to clear all buildings and account for all campers and staff. It should be made clear that children do not stop to gather belongings.

Each group should be assigned a meeting place and procedures for counting campers, checking against attendance, and reporting to the director shoud be planned and practiced. If the director stands with a watch, commending those who respond promptly, campers will take pride in competing with their own record.

Staff should be aware of the location and proper use of all fire-extinguishing equipment. If the day camp headquarters are in buildings with a fire alarm system, it is essential for more than one person to know the location of the shut-off, especially if it is connected to the local fire department. These systems sometimes go off unintentionally, and a quick call could save the expense and embarrassment of having equipment sent.

Program Hazards

There are some hazards connected with every activity offered in a day camp. Directors are usually cognizant of the dangers of activities such as archery, riflery, riding, swimming, and boating, but may overlook the less-obvious exposures to risk. Some of these that should be pointed out during precamp training are as follows:

General Camp Area

—Poison ivy (Many counselors will not even recognize it!)
—Carrying glass containers (Sometimes used on nature walks for specimens.)
—Toasting marshmallows (Hot sugar produces severe burns.)
—Keeping children dry on a rainy day
—Excessive activity in hot weather
—Location of poisonous plants, berries, and the like
—"Off limits" areas
—Awareness of allergies

Camp Fire Area:

—A counselor must always be in attendance at a camp fire.
—No running or horseplay in area.
—A bucket of sand and a bucket of water are to be kept within camp-fire area.
—A counselor must be sure the campfire is totally extinguished before leaving area.

Hikes

—Two counselors (one may be a junior counselor) should always accompany groups of campers under age eight. (If accident occurs, one can stay with campers while the other one goes for help.)
—Notify unit leader and office before going on a hike, giving planned itinerary.

Carpentry

—Establish strict rules for use of tools, supervision, and camper-counselor ratio. Print and post near area.

Environmental Hazards

American Camping Association Standards state that the director of a camp should have a written accident plan regarding risks to humans

from both natural and man-made site hazards. This plan would include:
1. Identification of the risks
2. Education of campers and staff
3. Establishment and enforcement of necessary rules and regulations.

These rules and regulations might include such things as:

—Identification and warning of the location of poisonous plants (poison ivy, oak, sumac, etc.)
—Location and identification of plants and berries that children might put in their mouths
—Safe storage of all power tools, and identification of persons who are permitted to use them
—Safe storage of gasoline, kerosene, explosives, and flammable materials with assurance that these materials will only be handled by persons trained in their safe use
—The same care must be applied to the storage of all narcotics and medicine that may be dispensed only under the specific directions of a licensed physician.

Permission Slips

Kidnapping is an ever-present threat in today's society. It is not only the child of the affluent parent who is at risk; divorced parents who have not been given custody may try to take the child from camp, and there have been numerous cases of children of bank employees being used as hostages in robbery cases. It is essential that permission slips be discussed and signed by parents. Where there is potential risk, photographs of authorized persons should be furnished. The following permission slips should be included in camp enrollment materials:

—————————————————————**PICK-UP AUTHORIZATION**

I hereby authorize 1. _____

| Name | Telephone No. | Relationship |

_____

| Name | Telephone No. | Relationship |

2. _____

| Name | Telephone No. | Relationship |

_____

| Name | Telephone No. | Relationship |

to pick up my child at the _____Day Camp. If there are any changes in these arrangements, I will give advance written notice. (NOTE: If there are any special instructions, or any persons who are never to be authorized to pick up your child, please list below.)

_____
Signature of Parent/Guardian

PHOTOGRAPHIC RELEASE

I hereby do _____
    do not _____ consent and authorize _____
Day Camp to use and reproduce photographs taken of my child and to circulate same for advertising and publicity purposes of every description.

_____
Signature of Parent/Guardian

FIELD TRIP PERMISSION

I hereby do _____
    do not _____ give permission for my child to be taken on field trips, either on foot or in an authorized vehicle, supervised by staff members of _____ Day Camp.

_____
Signature of Parent/Guardian

Director's Walk

A conscientious director will not rest easy because he has planned and practiced safety measures; he will want to make certain they are in effect. Periodically a director should walk about the buildings and grounds, figuratively looking through the eyes of:

—a parent
—another camp director
—a neighbor who wants to see what goes on in "that place"
—a licensing agent on a required inspection, or
—the fire department looking for hazards and methods for getting children out quickly, and finally
—his own eyes, which will reflect pride in his camp.

The points that follow may be considered as a safety checklist.

I. *People*

    1. Did you see children unattended? Children in forbidden areas? Children in dangerous play?

2. Inadequate adult/child ratio?
3. Children hurting other children?
4. Inadequately or improperly clothed children?
5. Adults and children engaging in rough play?

II. *Environment*

Indoors

1. Are floors slippery from sand, spills? dirty or splintery?
2. Are passageways clogged? Are there obstructions in front of doors?

Outdoors

1. Are there depressions that will hold rain and breed mosquitoes?
2. Are pools locked when unsupervised?
3. Is there poison ivy that needs treatment?
4. Is equipment broken or dangerously worn?
5. Are there exposed nails or screws, sharp edges or points?
6. Did you see evidence of hornets or wasps? Is there a nest that should be destroyed?
7. Are toilets clean, inside and out? Handbowls scrubbed? Adequate paper supplies?
8. Are animals and their immediate environment adequately cared for? Clean?
9. Are children protected from animals—and animals protected from children?
10. Are emergency procedures adequately posted?

Emergency Signal Systems

An emergency signal system should be set up and tested under all kinds of weather conditions. The signal should be clearly audible from the farthest corners of the camp. It can be a bell, siren, loudspeaker, metal wagon wheel with a striker, or trumpeter; and, in cases where the acreage is extensive, it may be a team of runners.

This same system could be employed for emergencies, which might include hurricanes, floods, tornados, smog alert, lost child, or a dangerous person.

Notifying Parents of Emergency

A prearranged plan should be in effect for notifying parents as quickly as possible in case of emergency. If news of an unusual occurrance reaches parents by radio or rumor before they have heard from the camp, telephone wires may be tied up with incoming calls from anxious parents.

A chain system of telephone calls works very well. For the sake of expediency, it might be advisable to have arranged in advance for the use of one or two neighboring telephones.

Health in the Day Camp

The responsibility for the health of the campers during the camp day rests primarily on the shoulders of the director. He may delegate this aspect of his obligation to a camp nurse or some other qualified person, but, ultimately, he is accountable. He cannot do it alone; counselors and parents must all be aware of campers' needs and be involved in meeting these needs.

The first step in setting up a health program is to check with state and local licensing authorities to determine their requirements.

Next, the director will prepare the forms and written materials that will insure that the requirements are being met.

Medical Forms

Health History—A record of past illnesses and medical treatment. Description of any physical conditions requiring special consideration.

Health Examination Form—Licensing will require a record of recent health examination by a licensed physician. The time of this examination may vary from as recent as two months to one year prior to enrollment in the camp. The form we recommend is one developed by ACA. This form must be in the camp office on the grounds at all times.

Parents' Statement—In addition to the report from a physician, it is wise to require a signed statement from parents on the first day of attendance at camp, giving the following assurances:

—The child is, and has been, in normal and good health
—The child has not recently been exposed to a contagious disease
—The parent or guardian gives permission for the child to be in camp with the understanding that the parent or guardian will be notified immediately should sickness or accident occur. This statement should include a provision that, should the camp be unable to locate the persons designated to be notified in case of emergency, the camp authorities may take such temporary measures as they deem appropriate, but only with medical advice.

All of the foregoing information is included on the Camper Health form printed by the ACA. It may also be found on p. 77 of *Basic Camp Management*.

SUGGESTED PARENT BULLETIN WITH HEALTH INFORMATION

Our concern for your child will not be limited to "learning" but will encompass the physical and emotional sides of his/her development. We ask for your complete cooperation in accepting the rules we have made for the health and safety of each child, and in turn we pledge to you our diligence in maintaining good practices. If at times you are inconvenienced, we ask you to remember that in protecting someone else's child you will also help maintain a safe environment for your own.

Sickness—Please keep your child at home if he/she seems listless, unusually irritable, complains of a stomachache, headache, or earache, or seems to be unusually pale or flushed. It is better to be overcautious than to risk exposing the rest of the children and staff to contagion.

A child should remain at home for forty-eight hours after a temperature goes down, and for twenty-four hours after a minor upset.

Please notify the camp immediately if your child *incurs* a contagious disease. If the other campers are to have preventive shots, there is usually a time limit.

Please notify the camp if your child is *exposed* to a contagious disease. The director or camp nurse will notify you if and when it is necessary to keep him home. This will be decided according to the rules of the local board of health.

Please see that your child keeps reasonable bedtime hours. His day and ours can be spoiled if he is tired and whiny.

Please notify the camp if you are going to be away for several days, since your absence may account for unusual behavior on the part of your child. Also, it is important for us to know who is responsible while you are away.

Throughout the season, if there is anything unusual going on in your home, please let the director know. Even though your child seems not to have been affected, it may show up in his behavior—his second language.

The information on the following questionnaire will aid the camp in helping your child to have a good experience.

—————————————————— PARENT QUESTIONNAIRE

Name of Child _____

Nickname (if commonly used) _____

Does your child have any special fears? (Animals, storms, loud noises, people, illnesses)

Does your child have any special tensional outlets? (Thumbsucking, nail biting, pulling out hair, withdrawal)

Have there been recent occurrences that might have affected your child emotionally, such as moving, illness, illness of a relative, death of a relative or pet, divorce, involved in or witness to an accident?

Does your child have any allergies? Have you notified the nurse of treatment?

Are there any restrictions on your child's participation in camp activities?

Is there anything else we should know about your child?

Have you given us more than one emergency number?
_____ Yes   _____ No

Is the person likely to be there if called?

Do they know we have been given their number for this purpose?

_____ Yes   _____ No

Staff Health Requirements

Staff are also required to have physical examinations. In some cases arrangements are made for a doctor to be available during precamp training, and the cost of the examination is paid by the camp. It is also necessary for all staff, including drivers and food handlers, to have tubercular tests. These reports must also be available on demand.

Two incidents demonstrate the importance of staff records.

In one case a counselor had a seizure. There was no record of epilepsy on file, no emergency numbers listed on his application.

In another camp a junior counselor slipped by without a physical examination and deliberately withheld the fact that she was diabetic. In the beginning stages of diabetic shock the individual appears to be surly—and it was not until the situation became more serious that staff nearby went for the camp nurse. Fortunately she recognized the symptoms and was able to take immediate action.

Health During the Day

Daily Inspection

Each day every camper should be checked by the camp nurse, director, unit leader, or some authorized person. The method to be used should be discussed and practiced during precamp training.

Look for red throat or white patches. Note if unusually pale or flushed; for red or runny eyes, bruises, lesions, rashes.

Any suspicious symptoms should be referred to camp nurse or person responsible for health program.

In some camps it may be necessary to look for head lice.

During the day staff should be tuned into any unusual patterns, such as frequent trips to the bathroom, restlessness, irritableness, complaints of stomachache, headache, or earache. Also watch for runny eyes, runny noses, coughing, or wheezing.

All camp staff should be told if a child has a severe allergy that could be potentially lethal.

On very warm days staff should watch campers carefully for signs of sun stroke. On wet days it is the responsibility of staff to see that campers are kept dry and clothing is changed promptly when necessary.

Daily Health Log *(See suggested form in Basic Camp Management, p. 76.)*

A daily health log should be kept in every day camp. The director should look this over at the end of the day. If a parent calls to complain about minor scratches or bruises he will be able to explain what happened and what was done about it. Ideally, parents will have been notified *before* the child reaches home, but this is not always possible. The entry should:

—Describe the injury
—Note the time it occurred and who observed the incident
—Describe the treatment and who administered it
—Note the time parents were notified.

Physical Hygiene

Children are not usually too concerned about personal cleanliness. They must be instructed to wash their hands each time they go to the toilet and before meals. In addition, counselors should find time to wipe dirty, sweaty faces and grubby hands just before the campers leave. Parents will appreciate this little extra bit of personal attention.

Dispensing Medications

No medication (even aspirin) may be dispensed without written authorization and instruction from parent and physician.

—————————————————————————**ORDERS FOR MEDICATION**

To be completed by physician:

If it is absolutely necessary for the camper named below to take medication during camp hours, please complete the information requested, sign, and return this form.

Child's Name _____ Address _____

Diagnosis _____ Medication Prescribed _____

Dosage _____ Time of Administration _____

Possible Side Effects _____ Special Instructions _____

_____ _____
(Physician's Signature)   *(Address)*

_____ _____
(Telephone)   *(date)*

—————————————————————————**MEDICATION REQUEST**

Name_____ Date _____

Medicine	**Dosage**	**Time Given**	**Caregiver's Initials**

Signature of Parent/Guardian

Caring for a Sick Child

A sick child should be made as comfortable as possible in a space set aside as an infirmary until someone arrives to take him home. He should *never* be left unattended.

Contagious Diseases

As soon as it has been determined that a child has a contagious disease a notice should be sent to parents of all campers who may have been exposed. This could include children in group, car or bus, or who have engaged in the same program activities.

_____ CAMP *Important Notice from Director*

We have had a new exposure to: _____ Mumps
_____ Chicken Pox
_____ Scarlet Fever
_____ Other _____

The incubation period for:

Mumps is 12 to 26 days. Please watch for signs of sickness, headache, fever, chills, swelling of one or both glands from _____ to _____. Child must remain out of camp for one week from onset of illness. If at the end of one week salivary glands are still swollen, child must remain home until swelling is completely gone.

Scarlet fever is 7 to 21 days. Please watch for signs of sore throat, temperature, fine, pin-point rash (usually starting around the abdomen) from _____ to _____. Child must remain out of camp for one week from start of medication, or 10 days from onset of illness.

Chicken pox is 13 to 21 days. Please watch for spots that look like mosquito bites on the back, abdomen, and face from _____ to _____. Child must remain out of camp for one week from onset of illness.

OTHER:

Sanitation

It goes without saying that toilets should be cleaned thoroughly several times each day. There is no substitute for frequent and generous applications of soap and water and a disinfectant. It is the director's responsibility to provide adequate cleaning supplies and equipment, and to assign the responsibility to specific individuals.

There is no possible way to prevent it but children should at least be cautioned about urinating in the swimming pools. It is a good practice to take the little ones for toileting just prior to their swim period.

Some day camps require each camper to go under the shower before they enter the pool; some have them step into a footbath of disinfectant. Chlorination is usually required by law.

Towels. Some camps provide one clean towel a day, others two, and the majority expect campers to bring them with their bathing suits. It is difficult, but extremely important, to impress counselors with the need to keep these towels separate, and make sure no two campers ever use the same towel.

The same precautions should apply to rest mats, blankets, or sleeping bags.

First-Aid Kits

The following suggested list is minimal. Each camp will modify according to needs.

100 bandages 3/4''
2 first aid cream 1.5 oz.
2 Red Cross bandages 2'' x 126''
12 Steri-pads 2'' x 2''
3 ammonia inhalants 4 c.c.
1 triangular bandage
6 John's eye pads

6 eye pads
1 tweezers
1 adhesive tape 1'' x 180''
3 gauze bandages 1'' x 126''
1 Red Cross bandage 8 ply 4-1/2 x 36'
12 Steri-pads 3'' x 3''
1 Red Cross Cotton 1 oz.
1 scissors
1 First Aid guide booklet

The above materials should have been in your original first-aid kit. Please replace the necessary items.

Accidents

If an accident occurs counselors should be instructed to send immediately for nurse, director, or first-aid person. Until assistance arrives they should follow the following basic first-aid procedures:

—In case of fall do not move victim when there is danger of head or spinal injury or broken bones
—In case of severe bleeding apply direct pressure to wound
—If breathing stops, clear airway and apply mouth-to-mouth resuscitation
—In case of burns apply ice or cold water.

When attention beyond environs of camp is required, the following emergency procedures are recommended:

Emergency Procedures

1. Before you take the child to the hospital, call the parents to inform them of the accident and where you are taking the child, or be sure someone is doing so while you are en route.
2. Take with you child's Health Form and Emergency Medical Permission slip.
3. If ambulance must be called the director or other responsible person should accompany the child and remain at the hospital until the parent arrives.
4. Someone should call the hospital to tell them you are coming.
5. Make a note that the child has left camp in case a driver or someone else comes to pick him up later.
6. Reassure other campers.
7. The counselor will immediately go to the office and fill out an accident report. The nurse will record incident in health log book. (See Accident Report Form in Basic Camp Management, pp. 48 & 49.)

The camp director should have important telephone numbers readily available for emergency use. The chart on the following page provides an excellent reference that should be kept near the camp's telephones.

EMERGENCY NUMBERS
(to be kept near phones)

For	Contact	Address	Tel. No.

1. Director
2. Police
3. Fire
4. Ambulance
5. Appliance Repair Service
6. Board of Health
7. Consulting Physician
8. Electric Company (town)
9. Electrician
10. Glass Company (broken windows)
11. Hospital
12. Locksmith
13. Plumber
14. Poison Prevention Center
15. Public Health Nurse
16. Water Dept. (town)
17. Wires Dept. (town)

* * * * * *

Waterfront

Most day camps use pools for swimming and ponds or lakes for boating. These safety points are written basically for this type of arrangement, but, of course, they apply to any swimming area.

—There must be a competent, certified person in charge of and responsible for all phases of the swimming program.
—No child should go into the water until counselors are in position to watch the area.
—When watching swimmers, counselors should stand a few feet back from the edge of the pool so that they can see those right *near* the edge as well as those farther away. They should constantly be scanning the area and not hypnotize themselves by looking at one spot.
—Counselors should stand apart from each other and not engage in conversation while on duty. Their eyes and attention should never leave the water.
—A waterfront at a camp should always have someone on duty even when no one is assigned to swimming, unless the pool can be securely locked. The four-foot fence requirement of most states is no barrier to the average camper.

—Small children should not be left alone in or near any water, even a wading pool.

—Never push a child into the water, duck him, splash him, or in any way intimidate him at the waterfront. Rough play by staff or campers should be forbidden.

—All equipment, unless it is being specifically used for a lessson, should be forebidden. This would apply to rafts, snorkels, fins, etc.

—Before children may swim in the deep-water area they should have shown an ability to swim at least three times the distance that could possibly become necessary and to feel at home in the water in different situations and locations.

—The diving area should be reserved for divers and divers should be taught to swim out of the area immediately after completing their dives.

—Counselors should be careful that children are not exposed to the sun too long, particularly at the beginning of the season. They should also be aware of any child getting cold or tired.

—If a child is floundering in the water it is very wise to put an arm under his legs, lifting them gently, rather than to make a dramatic save.

—Children should be taught to respond with absolute quiet to a whistle at the waterfront. It is also a good idea to teach them that three or more rapid whistles or some other signal means all out promptly.

—Counselors should never leave the area while children are swimming and should be certain that no child is left in the pool.

—When boating, all nonswimmers (those who have not passed ARC Beginners or equivalent) should wear life-preservers.

—Everyone should leave the water when thunder is heard and remain out of the water until fifteen minutes after the last sign of thunder or lightning.

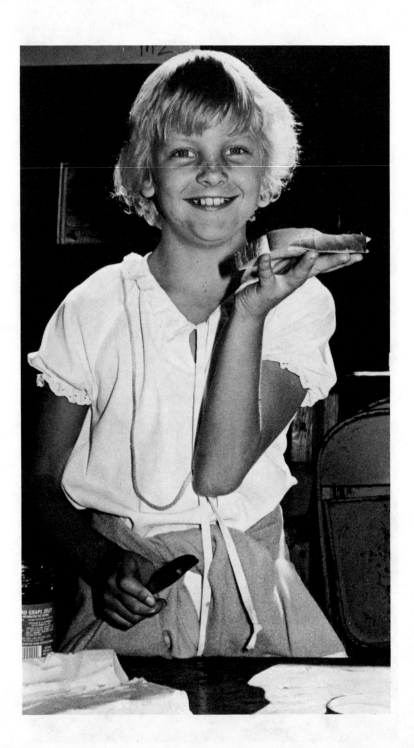

chapter 11

Food in the Day Camp

In the years since this book was first written there has been a growing body of knowledge about the effects of nutrition on a child's emotional state and intellectual prowess. A poorly fed machine cannot operate at full potential—and the human body is the most intricate machine ever invented.

It isn't necessary to be a vegetarian or a health-food enthusiast to recognize the importance of helping children develop better attitudes about food, and particularly snacks. Nearly all doctors and nutrition specialists agree that sugar and chocolate are harmful. Many cookbooks are being written now that offer healthy snack food ideas. The camp director should take the responsibility for setting the standards, since most adults grew up in a world where chocolate chip cookies and a sugary punch were standard fare.

People have also tended to associate sweets with a reward, a treat, or to celebrate a special occasion. Honey milk treats, consisting of non-fat milk, peanut butter, raisins, and a little honey, can be made and enjoyed by campers of all ages. Such books as *The Training of the Candy Monster* by Vicki Lansky and *Snackers* by Maureen and Jim Wallace offer many alternatives to sugar-laden treats.

Cold Lunches

These are usually brought from home by the camper, although in some camps box lunches may be purchased. In one case, sandwiches are made by counselors-in-training under adult supervision.

If milk is served, standards require that it must be pasteurized or certified according to state regulations, and that it must be obtained from an accredited source. If refrigeration is not available, milk must be kept in the shade and well iced. It is important to find out where the ice comes from because campers will eat it when they can. If milk is kept in a box in a stream, the box should be insulated and waterproof. In one camp, water from a source of pollution upstream was found coursing through the box in which milk was kept.

Lunch boxes must be stored in a cool place and out of the reach of animals. If a large storage box is not available, the individual lunch boxes may be hung on a line suspended between two trees.

Parents should be told of the facilities for refrigeration as a guide for lunch preparation, since bacterial growth in sandwiches subjected to moist heat for several hours can cause serious cases of food poisoning.

There are now available thermal boxes and bags that provide adequate protection.

Camper-Cooked Meals

In some situations, campers will prepare their own noon meals each day. This is not practical or possible in every day camp, but it is certainly desirable to give campers this experience as often as is feasible.

Inquiry would seem to indicate that this is one phase of day camping that has been explored more thoroughly and is practiced more regularly by agency or public day camps than by the private camp. In some cases facilities are the stumbling block, but more often it is lack of imagination and appreciation of what constitutes adventure for children.

Cooking in camp should be an experience quite different from home-style backyard barbecues. Hot dogs, hamburgers, and toasted marshmallows are not "camp fare" and offer little challenge in the way of planning or preparation. The techniques of stick cookery, foil cooking, and menus for one-pot meals are described in many excellent books. (See Bibliography.)

In many day camps the preparation of the noon meal is the major feature of the daily program. Each camper will bring what he needs for his own lunch, or the group may plan a day in advance to cook a one-pot stew, and each camper will bring one ingredient. Sometimes the camper can bring a sandwich or dessert to supplement the meal. In a day camp where meals are included in the fees the food for a cookout will usually be furnished by the camp, but campers may still have the fun of planning and occasionally can do some of the shopping.

Snacks

Working and playing out of doors produces healthy appetites that may need to be appeased more frequently than our customary three-meals-a-day routine allows. In many day camps a snack or light lunch is served in the morning, mid-afternoon, or just before the campers go home. This provides a welcome stopping point in the daily program; a chance to rest, visit with friends, and renew physical energy. In one camp it may be milk and crackers, in another lemonade and cookies. On a very hot day, fresh fruit or ice cream may be desirable; and, on a cold or rainy day, hot cocoa or soup may "hit the spot."

When Meals Are Served by the Camp

If meals are served in the day camp, then the same practices and procedures should be followed as in the resident camp. These are described very well in *Basic Camp Management* (see Bibliography). In most states it would be a requirement that the meals be approved by a qualified nutritionist. If it is not feasible to have a nutritionist on the staff, the cook or director can plan the menus in advance, and submit them to a nutritionist for approval.

Meals served vary from a simple soup and sandwich to a full-course dinner. It is important to plan menus with an eye to color, texture, and appeal, as well as to nutritional balance.

Some day camps have a caterer prepare the food and serve it from heated containers on a mobile unit, thus eliminating the trouble of purchasing food and employing a kitchen staff.

It is often more economical to use paper dishes and plastic cutlery, which can be destroyed after each meal, than to employ dishwashers and to comply with sanitation standards for dishwashing equipment. This is known as single service.

It is recommended that, in day camps in which meals are served, menus be sent to parents in advance. This not only helps parents to avoid repetition in the evening meal, but is also an indirect method of suggesting nutritionally balanced menus.

Supervision

The atmosphere in which people eat is of the utmost importance, not only for the formation of desirable habits, but also for digestion. Whether a cooked meal is served outdoors with the ground for a table, on picnic tables, or in a dining room, some methods and techniques for supervision should be established and discussed during precamp training. The following practices are suggested:

—The same counselor should sit with the campers each day during lunch periods and should be able to report on eating habits. When campers bring their lunches, the counselor should know whether the child is eating his lunch, giving it away, or swapping food. If a camper is consistently bringing a lunch that is inadequate or inappropriate, the counselor should report this to the director, who may be able to make some tactful, but positive, suggestions to the parents.

—Counselors remain seated while serving, and during the meal. If the campers are not old enough to pass plates around the table, one person should be chosen as waiter. This may be another counselor, a junior counselor, or an older camper.

—Conversation is encouraged, but shouting and horseplay at the table are not allowed. If two counselors are eating at the same table, they should not engage in conversation that excludes campers.

—The counselor will set a good example by saying, "Please," and "Thank you," but will not make a child conspicuous by insisting on such expressions. Manners are best taught by example.

—It is not reasonable to keep a whole table waiting for one or two slow eaters. It should be taken for granted that eating is a pleasurable activity and a necessary function. The counselor's attitude is "matter of fact." He will not threaten, urge, or coax the children to eat, *but* the director should be told of consistently poor eaters.

—If campers are expected to wait until all have been served, it is usually better for them to nibble on the raw vegetable or salad than to fill up on bread and butter.

—The server should start with very small portions. It is far better psychologically for a child to ask for more, than to be discouraged by a loaded plate. As the season progresses, the counselor who is serving will become familiar with the capacity of the individual child.

—A positive attitude is encouraged at all times. Campers are not allowed to announce or discuss their dislikes, nor should counselors comment adversely about the food.

—Consumption of food is never associated with discipline. Dessert is an important part of a balanced diet and should not be withheld as punishment or until a camper has "cleaned his plate."

—Counselors will avoid getting into an "issue" over food or eating. Problems should be discussed with the unit leader or director; but, until that is possible, it is better to be lenient than too arbitrary.

| chapter 12 | # The Day Camp Staff |

The spirit that is the heart of camping must grow out of the strengths and sensitivities of the individuals who make the heart beat. The camp that takes pride in a fine physical plant and excellent equipment but at the same time employs an indifferent, unimaginative staff, is like a robot that moves with precision but without feeling. Children will be influenced to a far greater extent by the people with whom they are associated in the course of a camp day than by program or places. Therefore, the careful selection of a staff is one of the most important considerations of day camp management.

Determinants for Selection of Staff

How does the camp director go about the business of finding and choosing staff? He keeps in mind certain standards, he must keep within the camp budget, and he is guided by the method of camper grouping in operation in his particular camp.

Qualifications of the American Camping Association

The Standards provide guidelines for such qualifications as age, education, and experience. The prescribed camper-counselor ratio will help the employer to determine the number of counselors needed in relation to the size of the camp.

Budget

The budget is usually a primary factor in staff selection. Payroll is the major cost item in any business and day camping, be it private-nonprofit or private-for-profit, must be operated on a businesslike basis. In a nonprofit camp, where the goal is to stretch the funding to accommodate the largest possible number of children, staffing may often be supplemented by volunteers.

This practice has some drawbacks. With all due respect to the good intentions of the volunteer the commitment is not always as secure as with the individual who signs a contract. The director should spend as much time interviewing a volunteer as a paid-staff person, stressing the need for regular attendance, training, participation in special camp functions, and a sincere acceptance of the philosophy and practices of the camp. Parents and visitors who observe inappropriate behavior will not know that they are looking at a volunteer.

The private day camp owner, presumably an astute business person, will know that the success of his business will be directly related to the quality of the service, and the people who work directly with the campers dictate that quality. There is a tendency for the public to look upon the private-for-profit operation with suspicion, fearing a "watering down of the milk" in the interests of profit. It is possible to do this in the selection of staff, meeting only the barest minimum requirements for age and maturity and experience, but the owner who makes this mistake will spend the difference in advertising and promotion. He will be beating the bushes for new staff each year, and will still be advertising for campers right up to the opening day.

Children are honest in stating their impressions and in describing what they see, hear, and experience. If they are unhappy and dissatisfied, bored or overstimulated; if they do not like the food or their counselor or the program, parents will hear about it. Some of those parents will investigate the complaints, knowing that children are also clever at exaggerating when it is in their favor, but many more will take the easier course of withdrawing the child or looking elsewhere another year. One of the best measures of the quality of a camp is the rate of return of staff.

When counselors elect to stay in the same camp all the way from camper status through C.I.T. programs; as junior counselors, and finally as leaders, it tells a story that cannot be disputed. They must be happy, enjoy their work, feel that they are treated fairly, and believe in the stated philosophy of that camp. When this happens a spirit is generated, a magical *esprit de corps* that practically guarantees an environment that will attract the same children for as long as they are eligible, and bring them back when they are employable. Children emulate the attitudes and behavior of admired adults, and when the staff is happy, the campers will be also.

There is no accepted formula for the percentage of the budget that should be spent on payroll but it is safe to say it will be the largest item of the budget. This is a sound investment because a well-qualified and well-trained staff will operate more efficiently. They are resourceful and less likely to depend on artificial materials and expensive equipment to insure good program.

Organization

A second factor in the selection of a staff is the type of organization or method of camper grouping, and this will be as different as every day camp, every day camp director, and every group of campers. Each individual camp director or each camp committee will need to develop a system adaptable to the program, facilities, and purposes of that particular camp.

Some day camps divide the campers into three or four camper groups, each constituting a unit. In this case one qualified person may be the unit leader with a general counselor in charge of each group, or the leader may also have the responsibility for one of the groups in the unit.

Frequently units are physically separated and operate with considerable independence within the overall framework of the camp. If there are certain activities that require the common use of a facility, such as a swimming pool or an archery field, then some sort of scheduling has to be done. Where the unit system is adopted, an attempt is usually made to make units as self-sufficient as possible from the program viewpoint. Leaders are recruited with the idea that they will provide the major leadership for program activities as well as for supervision.

Since it is not always possible to employ the "many-talented" individual, a camp may have one or more specialists in certain program fields, depending on need and interest. Such a specialist might be attached to a unit and assume some responsibility for group leadership and still go from one unit to another teaching a particular skill. In some camps a specialist will stay in one place, such as an arts and crafts shop, with camper groups coming there for instruction. The time of a specialist may be scheduled or left open, subject to requests from groups or units. A staff specialist might attend the precamp training session and give the staff members enough skills to get them started in his/her particular activity and then visit the camp once or twice a week. When a specialist works directly with the campers, the counselors should be expected to participate also, so that they can carry on with the activity between visits.

In another plan of organization campers are divided into groups by age, sex, or skills, with a senior counselor and a junior counselor, C.I.T., or camper aide attached to each group. In this case specialists employed to teach camping skills might also double as senior counselors and be responsible for a group. While the senior counselor is teaching a specialized skill, the junior counselor accompanies the group to scheduled activities. This system usually operates on a master plan, and a group would normally stay together throughout the day, moving from one activity to another.

Organization Chart

In most day camps there will be some overlapping of staff responsibilities. The director may also be the business manager; the nurse in a small day camp will frequently have other duties; staff members often transport campers, and the maintenance man may drive the camp bus.

A staff organization chart puts the whole picture into context, enabling the director to see where duties can be combined without curtailing efficiency or safety. A chart also helps each staff member see the lines of responsibility and his/her own place in the over-all staff structure. (See "Camp Administrative Forms and Suggested Procedures in the Area of Personnel," published by the American Camping Association.)

Staff for Multiple Camps

In multiple camp operations, such as those sponsored by public departments or youth-serving agencies, many of the administrative and supervisory duties for several camps may be covered by one person. Guidance counselors, program specialists, and maintenance supervisors may also work out of a central headquarters.

Near large cities where there are many private day camps in a localized area this same procedure may work to the advantage of all. By sharing the expense of program specialists for such activities as music, nature, or Indian lore, private camps can enrich their programs and offer a wider variety of activities. These specialists would usually act as resource people, giving inspiration, guidance, and assistance to regular staff members, rather than actually conducting program with cameprs. They may also assist in pre-in-camp and in-service demonstrations and workshops.

Sources for Staff

Recruitment of staff often begins with a tentative agreement with counselors at the close of a camp season and continues throughout the year, with the greatest concentration of effort in January, February, and March. The problems of securing a staff should decrease each year as satisfied employees return and recommend qualified friends.

One point of inquiry is among friends and acquaintances. However, because too intimate a relationship between employer and employee can lead to embarrassment, some directors establish a policy excluding employment of relatives or close friends.

Some American Camping Association sections have a counselor referral service, or serve as a clearinghouse through which camp directors can pass on to each other the names of counselors they are unable to employ.

College placement offices usually have a list of students who want camp positions, and are glad to post notices of vacancies on their bulletin boards.

In some communities, a state or federal employment service will have a list of prospective counselors. As a service to teachers seeking summer employment, school officials may be willing to issue bulletins describing camp positions available.

Positions may sometimes be listed in the news bulletins of teachers' associations, or the publications of professional educational organizations.

Churches are often glad to help their young people find desirable camp jobs. Sunday-school teachers and volunteer workers in youth-serving organizations often have had some training that is valuable for counseling.

Special-interest groups such as archery clubs, Audubon societies, rifle associations, or science clubs are other possible sources for camp counselors.

Leadership courses in agency programs or colleges should provide desirable candidates.

Senior citizens may be explored as possible camp staff. They can bring a level of maturity and responsibility that adds strength to the staff and can often bring skills that add new dimensions to program. Retirement at age sixty-five leaves many people bored and with a feeling of uselessness. Whether sharing a hobby, supervising woodworking, or teaching outdoor living skills—senior citizens are a valuable resource often overlooked.

Steps and Techniques for Developing a Staff

The first step in the employment process is the filling out of an application. (See Staff Application Form in *Basic Camp Management*, p. 19.)

Regardless of age or qualifications of an applicant, any person applying for work is entitled to the courtesy of an answer. In some cases a form letter is used which makes one of these statements:

1. An application blank is being sent
2. No vacancy exists
3. The application is being placed on file for later reference

References

Camp directors who use written references as a basis for selections may want to develop a "quick check," or a "yes-or-no" form. Such simplified forms are usually appreciated by busy executives. A stamped, self-addressed envelope should accompany every request for a reference. Some directors prefer to check references by telephone whenever possible, since many people will disclose in conversation information they could not or would not put in writing. When this is done, a written record of pertinent information gained through the call should be attached to the counselor's application. (See *Basic Camp Management*, p. 21.)

Job Descriptions

In preparation for an interview the director will have prepared written job descriptions for all positions. A job description should not be confused with a contract. It does not restrict the employer from altering the duties of an employee to suit the needs of a camp. It does give an employee the assurance of efficient administration and the security of knowing exactly what his duties and responsibilities are. Oral descriptions lead to misunderstandings, confusion, or overlapping of effort. Written descriptions give status to a position and build pride in the staff member toward his job. It is important that the language be simple and concise. Information should include these items:

—Title of the position
—List of the specific duties entailed
—The person to whom the staff member is responsible
—The extent and limitation of responsibility
—The relationship to other positions in camp and to total camp program

The following will give some idea of the detail that each camp director will want to make a part of the description for each job, fitting into the context of his overall plan.

Job Description: *Unit Leader*

The Unit Leader

1. takes attendance for the unit, inspects each camper for general physical condition, and gives absentee list to the junior counselor who takes it to the office;
2. reviews morning and afternoon plans with each counselor. Notes where they plan to be so that campers can be located in case of emergency;

3. offers suggestions to the counselors as necessary for activities, projects, and games to help them provide creative and varied program for the campers;
4. seeks out the "quiet" campers so that no child is overlooked;
5. helps counselors create opportunities for *all* campers to feel capable and successful, particularly children with special needs;
6. affords opportunities for the junior counselor to improve his/her skills through weekly program activities;
7. discusses his/her performance with each counselor and junior counselor *every* week using informal discussions to help counselors assess their daily program and relations with campers and other staff;
8. promotes positive attitudes toward the environment through personal example, camper activities, and general campground care;
9. has a daily concern for the health and safety of all campers and staff;
10. reviews fire drill and emergency procedures with counselors and campers at the beginning of each session;
11. conducts a weekly unit meeting to discuss camper relationships and program plans. (Note: Try to communicate announcements through memos, bulletin board, or speaking to individuals so that unit meetings can focus on sharing ideas and problem solving.)
12. selects and trains one counselor on how to take over unit leader responsibilities when unit leader is ill or away from unit site.
13. informs camp director of any problem or incident that might become a concern of parents, campers, or staff;
14. maintains contact with parents who have expressed specific concerns;
15. utilizes a system of shared coverage so that counselors who need a ten-minute "breather" can have one;
16. plans and supervises an "all-unit" special day once every two weeks;
17. coordinates the unit's contributions and participation in "all-camp" special days on alternate weeks;
18. arranges over-days or over-night program and field trips;
19. makes certain that all counselors in the unit are aware of campers with allergies, special diet, medication, etc.;
20. daily inspection of area covered by unit for such things as vandalism, new growth of poison ivy, faulty equipment, and general appearance;
21. accepts any other responsibilities that the director determines necessary for a safe and challenging camp program.

Interviews

When the necessary background information has been obtained through an application and references, an appointment can be made for an interview. If travel expense is involved, some camps share this with the applicant.

A hiring interview should be a two-way proposition, the objective being to place a competent counselor in a desirable working situation.

The employer frequently must decide on the basis of one interview whether this person has a working knowledge of camping skills and the ability to work well with children, and whether he will fit harmoniously into the total staff picture. The applicant must decide whether he feels he is qualified for the duties outlined, whether his personal beliefs and philosophy are "in tune" with the philosophy and program of the camp, and whether he will be happy in this particular camp. The prosaic, unimaginative counselor who may be heavily endowed with maturity and responsibility will be uncomfortable in a camp where a creative program is stressed, and the creative individual will be frustrated by a completely preplanned program. The individual who believes in camping in a literal sense will not be happy working in a camp where the major emphasis is on an athletic program, and the person who is accustomed to routine and regimentation will be miserable in a situation where freedom of choice by the campers is encouraged.

Group Interviews

To hire a competent, versatile, mature staff is no easy task; when it is necessary to schedule several consecutive interviews, it can be exhausting. Some employers find that the group interview offers many possibilities for evaluating applicants. Social poise, participation in discussion, and reactions to the group process are only a few of the characteristics of the individual that may be discerned through this method.

Recording Interview

A post-interview information sheet should be filled out by the employer immediately after the meeting and clipped to the application blank of the person interviewed. This would include impressions of the suitability of the applicant, notations of his special characteristics, and details of any commitments.

When a great many applicants are interviewed such details as physical characteristics and mannerisms will help to recall the individual. Example: Red hair, freckles, slight wiry build. Looked me in the eye when we talked. Gave answers in a straight-forward manner. Poised and articulate. Overweight, pudgy. Slouched in chair. Did not stand when Midge came into room. Very limp handshake.

Contracts (See Basic Camp Management, p. 29)

As soon as a decision is reached, a contract signed in duplicate should be offered by the employer. The employee should sign and return one copy to the employer if accepting the position; otherwise, he should return both copies unsigned. Some day camp directors prefer the word "agreement," rather than "contract," but in any case, the signing of a written document inspires a feeling of mutual confidence.

Personnel Policy

Although some of the details of employment may be included in the contract, it is best to describe the policies of the camp in a separate personnel policy. This would be used as a tool in the initial interview and should be included in the camp manual. Some directors give a copy to each employee and require them to sign a statement that they have read it and accept the terms. Generally it might include such items as:

—Dates and conditions of employment (state whether precamp training is included or will be paid for as an extra)
—Fringe benefits
—Sick leave
—Health insurance
—Workmen's compensation
—Authorized absences (time off)
—Leaving before termination of contract
—Conditions for dismissal
—Camp rules and regulations
—Opportunities for professional growth
—Opportunities for advancement

A sample personnel policy is furnished in *Basic Camp Management* on p. 28.

The following sample is a composite of several personnel policies used in day camps:

PERSONNEL POLICY — CAMP _____

* * *

FINANCIAL POLICIES

Each staff member will be paid for regular camp days, orientation day for campers and parents, and precamp training days. Failure to attend any one of these will be adjusted on pay check. Unit leaders are responsible for keeping accurate attendance and submitting reports of absences to the office.

Salaries are set for each employee according to agreement between the employee and director and subject to approval by the board of directors.

Salaries are based upon educational background, experience, and job responsibilities. Extra compensation may be given for unique talents, over-days, or over-nights.

The payroll schedule is biweekly starting with the week campers arrive.

All employees are covered by Social Security and Workmen's Compensation Insurance.

Medical insurance is available only to year-round employees.

All questions about the above should be discussed *only* with the director or the person to whom he may have designated this authority.

HEALTH REQUIREMENTS

All staff (including the director) are required to file in the camp office a completed health form and a report of a clear skin test *prior* to beginning employment. Physical examinations are required annually, TB tests every three years. Food staff must have TB tests *annually*.

Absences due to illness *may* be compensated at the discretion of the director. There is no policy for guaranteed sick leave.

All staff are expected to use good judgement in deciding when to call in sick, taking into consideration the health of the children as well as their own well-being. When in doubt it is best to let the director help make that decision. Sometimes it is possible to work at another job for the day where no one would be subject to contagion, thus avoiding the loss of a day's pay.

If you are too ill to come in, notify the office between seven and eight a.m. so coverage can be arranged. If you expect to be absent two or more days, please let the director know as soon as possible so a substitute can be found.

ARRIVAL AND DEPARTURE TIMES

All staff are expected to be at their assigned stations in the parking lot by 8:40 a.m. Campers arrive at this time and must be met and supervised.

Counselors will not leave until *all* children are in their proper vehicles and accounted for. Camp vehicles will leave the parking area *before* any counselor cars.

TIME OFF

It is intended that each staff member will have at least fifteen minutes of free time daily, but it is also assumed that no counselor would insist upon taking this time at the expense of the safety and health of the campers. Unit leaders will arrange this time (usually during lunch and rest) so each person has a "breather" while campers are still carefully supervised. Specialists may be called upon to fill in during these rest breaks.

USE OF TELEPHONE

Phone calls during the day will be limited to those related to camp business and can be made from the telephone in _____. If it is necessary to make personal calls during camp hours they should be made in the office. These should be limited to calls that *cannot* be made after camp hours.

TIPPING

We abide by the ruling of the American Camping Association that staff will not accept tips or other extra remuneration from parents. Parents are informed of this policy in a bulletin but if you receive a gift or tip, please ask the director how it can be tactfully returned. Failure to do so is cause for dismissal!

CAUSE FOR DISMISSAL

Immediate dismissal may be deemed necessary by the director for a violation of confidence, such as discussing a child's behavior with anyone other than the responsible staff; harsh and/or abrupt physical or verbal discipline; violation of the terms of this policy; failure to perform at a reasonable standard of excellence; insubordination; or consistent behavior destructive to morale. Wages will be paid through the period worked.

RESIGNATION OR RELEASE

Termination of employment may be at the request of the employee or the director. Employees will be asked to submit resignations in writing, giving two weeks' notice, and shall be compensated through the last day worked. A termination interview with the director is encouraged.

Smoking, Alcohol, and Drugs

Smoking is permitted only in the staff area during free time. A counselor may smoke at an over-night *after* the campers have gone to sleep. Extreme precautions must be observed because of the constant fire danger in our woods.

No drugs are permitted on the campgrounds at any time unless prescribed by a doctor and screened through the camp nurse or director. Anyone using illegal drugs will be dismissed and the local police will be called by the camp lawyer.

No *alcohol* is permitted on the grounds at any time, including overnights, over-days, and evening staff meetings.

Professional Behavior and Appearance

Staff are expected to serve as good models for children. Their appearance and manners as well as relationships with other staff will be the first thing noticed by parents and other visitors to the camp.

Dress should be casual and practical. Shirts or knit tops should cover fully from shoulder to waist (no bra tops or tank tops with low necklines, please!)

Shorts should be of medium length and not skimpy or tight.

Bathing suits should be one-piece or full two-piece—not bikinis. (Small children will grab anything when frightened.)

Footwear should be worn at all times, except at poolside, by both staff and children.

Staff are requested to wear a camp T-shirt (provided by camp) on special days for easy identification by parents and visitors.

* * *

Qualifications of Staff

The following paragraphs give some idea of the types of skills and the duties required of the various staff members and the qualifications for which to look.

Director

In most private day camps the owner will also be the director. In agency camps the choosing of a director may be the most important task of the camp committee, executive board, or recreation board. Considering the weight of responsibility carried by this one person, it is hard to conceive of anyone performing the task adequately who does not have at least the minimum qualifications outlined in the American Camping Association Standards. (See Appendix.)

Nurse

Day camp Standards require a doctor on call and a registered nurse or qualified first-aider on the staff. Medical students are not acceptable. unless they hold a current certificate in advanced first aid. When a nurse is not available, or has other duties, it is helpful to have several staff members who are qualified first-aiders. This could be one of the extra talents that would justify additional pay.

In some states there is a requirement for ALL care givers in a day care center to be trained in first aid. Even though it is not mandated, it is certainly a desirable goal for staff in a day camp. Training can often be given on the campsite. Consult local Red Cross for advice.

Office

The duties of office personnel, in addition to bookkeeping and secretarial work, may include supervision of camp supplies and equipment, purchasing, library work, and even supervision of campers. The office staff are certain to have many contacts with campers, so an interest in children is a definite asset.

Unit Leader

The unit leader stands in the same position to the unit as the camp director does to the entire camp. In the same way that the director is responsible to a board of trustees, a committee, or an owner, the unit leader is responsible to the director. Ability to supervise and guide group counselors is a necessary qualification, but the primary obligation of the unit leader is to the campers in the unit. The unit leader should have personal knowledge of the needs and progress of each child and be able to report on these at any time to the director or to the child's parents.

General Counselor

The true value of the camping experience for the camper rests with the counselor. Not only does he maintain a close, intimate relationship with the campers in his tent, cabin, or group, but he becomes the model from whom each child will copy personality traits, behavioral characteristics, and even physical mannerisms. A good educational background is an asset, but degrees and diplomas cannot supersede the less-tangible qualities of imagination, enthusiasm, creative ability, love of children, genuine warmth, and a love of the out-of-doors.

Junior Counselor

A junior counselor should not have direct responsibility for campers, but should receive some training that will prepare him to assist counselors or specialists. Some camps cannot pay these young people because they cannot be counted in a camper-counselor ratio, but the energy, spark, and enthusiasm they contribute to the camp program can be invaluable. The director must make certain that they are not pressed into service as substitutes in positions for which they are not qualified, or given responsibilities they are not ready to assume.

Counselors-in-Training

Some day camps have a counselor-in-training program for youngsters who think they are too old to be campers, but who are still too young to be junior counselors. These training programs offer the following advantages:

—A counselor-in-training program is an aid in preparing future leaders for camping. When a leader has come "up through the ranks" as a camper, counselor-in-training, and junior counselor, he is thoroughly indoctrinated in the philosophy and practices peculiar to that camp and so is more valuable.

—A well-planned counselor-in-training program will satisfy some of the adolescent drives that so often get youngsters of this age into difficulty. A chance to be independent—but not too independent; to take responsibility—but no more than he is capable of handling; to work—but still have some time to play, and most important of all, to "belong" to a society in which he has a legitimate place.

A counselor-in-training program should be planned and administered by an individual who is sensitive to the needs and whims of the adolescent and who really enjoys being with young people of this age.

Staff Relationships

We started this chapter with emphasis on the careful selection of staff, but the task does not end there. Building a group of individuals with varied backgrounds, talents, and personalities into one harmonious whole, all in a short eight weeks, is a real challenge. Creating an environment of openness in human relationships, a sensitivity to the needs and rights of others, and a method for expression of feelings is an ongoing challenge.

Staff Morale

Morale is the business of every employee in the day camp. Breakdown of morale can be so subtle, so insidious, that even the perpetrator may not be aware of what he is doing.

"I never gossip. If I have anything to say I will say it to a person's face," the counselor asserts self-righteously, and yet with a shrug of the shoulder, a facial grimace, or a sly wink he sets the wheels in motion that can lead to the destruction of an individual or a team.

It is possible to convey thoughts, ideas, emotions, anxieties, and even aggression without uttering a word!

Positive Grapevine

This can start with the director who states at a meeting, "There are so many great things happening I can never hope to see them all and you have even less opportunity to observe them. You may be modest and hesitate to talk about your most successful projects, but you can report on each other in a very positive way. For example, a staff member said to me, 'You should get out there and see what John Doe is doing with his group. I could hardly believe my eyes when I saw that Billy Jones was so involved he forgot to be a nuisance!'"

"I watched Judy handle a situation between two kids who were fighting. She gave each one a chance to talk—and they ended up friends."

Such reporting is contagious. A positive grapevine—as opposed to malicious gossip—will be reflected in the morale of the entire camp!

The members of a day camp staff can never "rest on their oars while floating downstream," but must keep the boat moving upstream with constant challenges and new interests. Some ideas for doing this will be found in the chapter entitled "A Bag of Tricks."

In public day camps where attendance is voluntary, the campers will not return if they are bored or dissatisfied. In private day camps where the child carries home a daily report of his activities, parents are quick to react if the child's enthusiasm is lagging. Good leaders accept these conditions as a daily challenge to improve their program and skills. To help them meet this challenge, the director should provide precamp and in-service training as described in the next chapter.

chapter	Staff Training and
13	Supervision

A visitor in a day camp once said to the director, "As I walked about this camp I sensed something very special, which I cannot seem to define. What is it?"

"I know what you mean," was the reply. "For want of a better name we call it 'spirit.'"

Spirit is an indefinable characteristic of a camp that sets the stage for the environment of fun and relaxation we are trying to create.

At Green Acres, as I talk about "spirit" at our precamp training session, I frequently note a look of skepticism on the faces of new counselors. Usually, however, by the end of the second week they admit they have caught it. It develops as we gradually change from a heterogeneous group into a harmonious working unit; it happens when each one is finding joy and satisfaction in his work, and when he/she has found his/her niche in the framework of human relationships that constitute a staff. We know that when our counselors are happy this will be reflected in the behavior and attitudes of the campers; though children are quick to detect a lack of harmony, they are equally responsive to adults who are comfortable and relaxed.

A director must not only use every tool at his command for careful staff selection, but, through staff training, must lead them into the cohesion that sets the tone for his camp, and all this in a very brief span of time. Where a school teacher might reasonably expect to take eight weeks to become well enough acquainted with people, policies, and procedures, to feel "settled in," a day camp counselor must achieve this state in a few days. It can be done when the director provides each member with orientation, direction, instruction, and supervision; for only as the individual knows what is expected of him, and how he is measuring up to those expectations, can he find the greatest satisfaction in his work, and contribute significantly to the total program.

Staff training begins with the signing of an agreement and continues throughout the season. The standards require twenty-four hours of pre-in-camp training, but before that, there are many methods by which a director can indoctrinate his staff.

Precamp Training

After the contract is signed the director will realize that, while preparation for camp is his first priority, the prospective employee is usually still deeply involved in his studies, teaching, or another job. Concrete suggestions and strategically timed reminders will be needed if staff members are to be motivated to make advance preparations for their work. The devices described in the following sections have been used with success.

News Bulletins

In addition to routine information and announcements, these bulletins may contain news about old staff members, thumbnail sketches about new employees, and news of improvements, changes, or additions to camp facilities.

Recommended and Required Reading

Very few day camp counselors have the time to do any extensive or intensive reading before or during the camp season, but they will usually read a pamphlet, a selected section in a book, or printed materials if the director can offer or suggest articles that are brief, concise, and easily accessible. What information will be most helpful to a camp counselor in his work?

First, background information on growth and development will help him to understand behavior. A counselor forewarned that "fours" are unbearably silly, and prone to use what they consider to be bad words; that "sixes" tire easily and have many fears and that eight-year-olds are inclined to be bold, brassy, and boastful will greet these traits with composure rather than annoyance.

Second, the counselor will profit by reading a few pamphlets on child guidance, methods of control, and understanding children's behavior. When the director provides the materials it can be assumed that they will express the philosophy of the camp.

Third, a counselor can brush up on the skills needed in his program. The resource books in the camp library will be used more readily during the camp season if staff members have had an opportunity to look them over before they have urgent need for specific information.

Books for suggested reading should be those most likely to be found in local or college libraries. It is unfair to *require* reading unless it is provided. Pamphlets are often inexpensive enough for a camp to purchase in quantity and can be mailed to staff members with precamp bulletins.

Correspondence Course Letters

A director who recognizes the value of this precamp preparation might work up a mini-correspondence course with periodic mailings, each designed to cover one aspect of the camp program. To be truly effective there would need to be some method for reactions and response. This could be in the form of a brief check list to be returned at the time of reading, or questions which could be followed up at the pre-in-camp training session.

Notices of Special Training Courses

Staff should be notified of professional meetings through the year, and encouraged to participate in those related to camping. Many camps pay all or part of the expense for attending conventions, lectures, or courses such as these:

—District, Sectional, and National meetings and workshops of the American Camping Association
—Nature courses, offered by the science museums, park commissions, or Audubon societies
—Special schools on skills such as archery, boating, riding, aquatics, and campcraft, which are usually held on a campsite in June and last from three to ten days

Staff Meetings (Prior to opening)

If it is possible to find a time when the majority of the staff will be available (perhaps during a spring vacation), a staff get-together for socializing, orientation, and program planning will afford the director an opportunity to "size up" staff members for later assignments.

Staff Manual

The manual is a publication of the camp that serves as a guide and source of information for members of the staff. Whenever staff members can participate in the composition of the manual, they will take more interest in reading it. For example, a list of rules and regulations they have helped to develop will be adhered to with more respect than a set of laws laid down arbitrarily by the administration. One leader will enjoy making a map of the grounds; to another there is real fascination in working out an organization chart. A committee may take on the task of writing a job description, or the artist on the staff may volunteer some clever illustrations. All these joint efforts will help to make the final product come alive.

The task of planning the contents of the staff manual is often most easily approached by putting oneself in the place of a new counselor, and by attempting to visualize things he needs to know, such as:

1. What has gone before?

   a. History and development
   b. Development of physical facilities
   c. Individuals who have played an important part

2. What are we trying to do for campers?

   a. Philosophy
   b. Aims and objectives

3. Where are we going to do it?

   a. Map or diagram of site and buildings
   b. Names and locations of special areas

4. Who does it?

   a. List of personnel (Who's Who)
   b. Organization chart

5. When?

   a. Daily schedule
   b. Rainy-day program

6. How?

   a. Brief description of each activity in the program, with emphasis on those considered most important
   b. Description of procedures for campers

      1) Arrival and before-camp supervision
      2) Opening circle
      3) Mealtime
      4) Rest hour
      5) Special services
      6) Closing circle
      7) Leaving camp (transportation procedures)
      8) Emergencies related to health or safety

7. Counselor-parent relations

    a. Open house
    b. When parents visit
    c. Telephone calls
    d. Special conferences

8. Rules and regulations for staff

9. Job descriptions, outlining the general responsibilities and specific duties for each position

10. Personnel policy

11. Records to be kept by staff, with samples

12. Outline of reports to be submitted by staff

A good manual will grow out of the needs of the people who use it. To be of value it must be kept up-to-date; therefore, a loose leaf binder is suggested. The manual should be available for easy referral during the camp season.

Pre-In-Camp Training

It is a requirement of the American Camping Association Standards that a minimum of twenty-four hours be devoted to the training of staff on the campsite prior to the opening of camp. Full attendance at *all* sessions should be required of *all* staff. It is hard to imagine how a director can expect to operate a camp without this minimal time to "organize the team," but common excuses are:

"I have school teachers; they are in school right up to the last minute." The answer then is to have training from 4:00 p.m. to 9:00 p.m. over several days.

"Our counselors come from different colleges—all getting out at different times. There is never a time when I can get them together." The director can, if he makes it a part of the contract at the time of employment." His insistence on the time for training is assurance that he has high standards and expectations for performance on the job. He is doing the counselor a favor by providing training that will make his task easier and more enjoyable. The director should not be apologetic or lenient about requiring attendance.

"I don't need to come," the former counselor may say. "I took the training last year." In answer to that, it is the responsibility of the planning committee to vary the procedures and content each year so that the program is stimulating and challenging for all present. Some repetition is necessary, and basic philosophy can be restated with new emphasis; but the brief time devoted to training is far too valuable to waste in "playing the same old record." The staff manual is a useful tool in eliminating such extravagance, but it may be advisable to require new staff members to attend an extra session when the contents of the manual will be reviewed and discussed.

Although it is expected that the major portion of this training program will be carried out on the campsite, it is not unusual for several neighboring camps to combine forces for a fraction of the allotted time, making it possible to engage outstanding speakers or specialists.

Tentative plans for the workshop should take concrete form by early spring. Program leaders, unit or group leaders, and other key people should be invited to share in the planning. If counselors are asked to evaluate the usefulness of the training session in their end-of-the season reports, their comments will be a valuable aid in planning for another year.

The purpose of pre-in-camp training is to:

1. Thoroughly acquaint all staff members with the philosophy and objectives of the camp;
2. Familiarize them with the site and facilities;
3. Add to their knowledge of the necessary skills;
4. Help them develop good working relationships with coworkers, campers, and parents.

Throughout the season, the director who has trained his staff well will enjoy a feeling of security and confidence which, in turn, is easily aborbed by employees. Counselors who have been thoroughly briefed on the "what," "where," and "how" of the camp approach the season with a greater degree of assurance, and discharge their duties with greater competence and enthusiasm.

The following principles and techniques (see Chapter 15, Program) will be important in planning for counselor training. These are as follows:

Balance

a. Alternating small and large group meetings
b. Observation mixed with participation
c. Lectures with small discussion groups
d. Discussion meetings and demonstrations balanced with music or active games

Variety

The director who insists on conducting all the meetings will find his listeners so attuned to the sound of his voice that they fail to comprehend what he says. Other staff members who are asked to speak or lead discussion groups should be chosen with care and given ample time for preparation.

Varying the locations of the meetings will also lend interest. Explanations and demonstrations of routine procedures such as eating, resting, or the closing circle will be most effective in the context in which they will take place. Skills such as archery, swimming, or campcraft should be explained or taught in the proper setting; small discussion groups can be held in comfortable outdoor areas, and unit meetings should be held in their respective unit areas.

Varied techniques, such as role playing, films, panels, symposiums, or demonstrations with puppets all lend variety and interest.

Tempo

The director who believes this to be an important factor in planning for children has an excellent opportunity to demonstrate it during the training session. It is possible to avoid a general feeling of breathlessness if the machinery is well oiled in advance.

The wise director will plan with extensive care to set the stage properly for the very first staff session. Teachers who have just finished winding up a school year need help in shedding the rigidity of school routines and to adopt the more relaxed attitudes necessary to good camping. Newcomers, who need to get acquainted, should be paired off with oldtimers for a friendly welcome and introductions.

Each day camp director will plan his training session to meet the needs of the camp, realizing that all of the important factors cannot be covered unless the program is well organized. A staff training session should include these features:

—General sessions
—Meetings of director with unit leaders
—Meetings of unit leaders with their staff
—Meetings of director or traffic manager with drivers and bus leaders

In-Service Training

The true value of precamp training will become evident after staff members have had an opportunity to test their knowledge with practical application. It is important to continue this training during the camping season, but finding a time when the entire staff can meet without neglecting the supervision of campers presents a difficult problem. Day camp directors have solved this problem in various ways.

Staff Meetings

1. Two meetings may be held during rest hour on a different day each week with one-half of the staff attending while the other half stays with the campers. This requires duplication of the content of the meeting, as well as doubling the time required of the leaders of these staff meetings.
2. A full meeting is held once a week during rest hour. On that day all campers rest in one area and are supervised by office staff or parents.
3. Emergency meetings of the whole staff are called only when circumstances make it necessary. One or two staff members lead the campers in singing or storytelling while the meeting is going on.
4. Three evening meetings are scheduled about two weeks apart. Staff are informed of the dates of these meetings at the time of employment.

Attendance at these meetings cannot be required unless the camp is prepared to pay overtime, so it behooves the director to make them interesting. If they include a meal and an opportunity to get to know coworkers socially, they will attract better attendance.

5. Some camps may never have full staff sessions, but arrange for small weekly meetings with a representative from each group to plan with the director. Whatever the plan may be, the following points bear consideration:

   —Every meeting should have a specific purpose
   —All meetings should begin and end promptly
   —The leader should adhere to a carefully planned agenda
   —Discussion of organizational details and announcements should be kept at a minimum. Such matters are usually best handled through unit leaders or mimeographed bulletins
   —Subjects discussed at full staff meetings should be of interest to everyone. The leader should be capable of tactfully putting aside matters of individual concern for a more appropriate time, without discouraging freedom of expression or wasting the time of the group as a whole

Topics to be covered at staff meetings might include discussion of the various aspects of behavior that show up in campers. By the end of the second week counselors will have encountered

   —the aggressive child
   —the shy child
   —the bossy camper
   —the camper who will not participate in any activities
   —the slow camper

On every day camp staff there are usually some persons who think they do not need help, and others who will not ask for it because they hesitate to admit their need. At full staff meetings these individuals are helped in two ways: first, they learn new methods and techniques, and hopefully gain a better understanding of children; secondly, they are reassured to find that others are faced with some of the problems they have encountered.

Midseason Slump

Some camp directors forestall a midseason slump by bringing in a specialist to give new ideas for some phase of program activity. Some of the successful projects being conducted by individuals on the staff can be shared with the rest. A joint meeting, where ideas may be shared with the staff of another camp, will often boost morale.

Evaluation

Evaluation is an ongoing process that is primarily the responsibility of the director, but active participation by all who have a vested interest in the camp is essential to effective growth.

There are some day camp directors who feel that end-of-season evaluation by staff is as important as precamp training, and require attendance at a meeting for that purpose after camp closes. This may be a full day, an evening, or less. If such a plan is contempated it should be made clear at the time of employment, before staff members make their vacation plans.

Midseason Evaluation

While end-of-the-season evaluation is helpful in planning for another summer, it is "after the fact" for the campers and parents whose expectations may not have been reached. When some midseason evaluation takes place it will help staff to grow in their jobs, and thus be a part of the staff training process.

A conscientious staff, trying to give their best to children, will appreciate opportunities for shared evaluation—a time to say: "How are we doing?"

"How many of the wonderful plans we started out with are materializing?"

"If they aren't, where did we err in planning?"

The following questionnaire has been used with good results:

MIDSEASON EVALUATION   UNIT STAFF

NAME _____

UNIT _____

DATE _____

1. Please comment on the *organization* and *cooperative* programs of your unit. Include at least two activities that were particularly enjoyable for your campers.
2. Please comment on the organization and activities of the specialists that your campers have used. Include suggestions for improvement.
3. What Special Unit or All-Camp activity has been the most fun for your campers? Why was it successful?
4. What has been the most frustrating aspect of your job so far? Is there anything the directors can do to make the summer more worthwhile for you and your campers?
5. Is there any program area in which you feel you need to develop your skills further in order to provide a well-rounded program for your campers?

Thank you,

John Doe
Director

End-of-Season Evaluation

Camp is over! The last camp bus has gone! The final goodbyes have been said, and the people who have lived so intensely for eight to ten weeks have gone on to vacations or back to their full-time jobs. As we stated in the chapter on Administration, this is the time for the wise director to take a long, hard look at the strengths and weaknesses of the season just concluded in order to plan better for another year.

The purpose of evaluation should be clearly stated when the following forms are distributed. Supervisors are not expected to downgrade their counselors, but to help them see their own strengths and weaknesses. There will be no "behind-the-back" reporting. Every staff member is entitled to see what has been written about him, and to attach comments if he does not agree with the appraisal. Specialists are in a good position to observe counselors, and counselors are the first to know which specialists have been the most effective. Their opinions should be respected.

A short form, shown here, for counselor evaluation is used by Deerkill Day Camp:

Evaluator _____

Counselor being evaluated_____

Date_____

Place a check mark at the appropriate point on each line.

1	2	3	4	5

Will work only under
constant supervision

Always helpful and looking
for something to do

1	2	3	4	5

Bored and listless

Always enthusiastic

1	2	3	4	5

Indifferent to welfare of
campers

Always concerned with welfare of campers

1	2	3	4	5

Shows no affection for
children

Shows real affection for
children

1	2	3	4	5

Campers are indifferent to
counselor

Campers have real affection
for counselor

What things do you *like* most about your assistant?

What things do you *dislike* most about your assistant?

1	2	3	4	5

I definitely would *not* like
the same assistant next
summer

I definitely do want the same
assistant next summer

CAMP NAME _____

End of Season Report   **Date**

Name   **Unit**

1. Please evaluate the swim program. Include specific suggestions for improvement. _____
2. Evaluation of specialty area. Answer the following questions for each area:

   a. What are the greatest strengths of these programs?
   b. How could this specialty be improved?

Arts & Crafts/Crafts Pavillion *(List each area of activity separately.)*

   a.
   b.

Nature

   a.
   b.

Music

   a.
   b.

3. Write about your experiences at camp this summer. Choose whatever aspects seem most significant to you.
4. Do you wish to be asked to return? (An affirmative answer is not considered a commitment by you or the camp.) _____

   Would you want the same job? _____

   If not, what position would you choose? _____

   The following materials must be turned in to the office and approved before you will receive your last paycheck.

   a. Camper reports
   b. Counselor report
   c. Personnel evaluations
   d. Library books

   *****   *****   *****

End of Season Evaluation of Counselors by Supervisors

Counselor_____ Year _____
Junior Counselor _____
Unit _____
Unit Leader _____
Supervisor _____

1. PROGRAM PLANNING This counselor:
☐ a. is consistently prepared with ideas and materials for creative program activities.
☐ b. is occasionally prepared with creative program activities.
☐ c. generally does not plan activities in advance.
☐ d. Other (specify):

2. SAFETY This counselor:

☐ a. is consistently aware and careful of potentially hazardous areas and situations.
☐ b. has difficulty anticipating and avoiding potentially hazardous situations.
☐ c. Other (specify):

3. CONTRIBUTION TO UNIT This counselor:

☐ a. is always ready to step in when he/she perceives a need and is an asset to the functioning of the unit.
☐ b. carries out unit responsibilities regularly.
☐ c. Other (Specify):

4. SWIM PARTICIPATION This counselor:

☐ a. participates constructively in swim instruction and free swim supervision.
☐ b. does not enthusiastically participate in the swim program.
☐ c. Other (specify):

5. EXTRA SPECIAL EFFORTS Please comment on the counselor's willingness to contribute to Closing Sing, Serendipity, Special Programs, Etc.

Place a (1) if it is one of the counselor's greatest strengths, (2) if it is a quality they generally demonstrate in their daily performance, (3) if it is a quality that needs further development.

☐ personal appearance
☐ maturity

☐ physical stamina
☐ emotional stability
☐ integrity
☐ judgement
☐ imagination
☐ creativity
☐ patience
☐ sense of humor
☐ rapport with children
☐ rapport with colleagues
☐ follow-through on suggestions

PART III: Please describe the counselor's performance, using examples if possible.

1. Supervisor's Commendations:

2. Supervisor's Recommendations:

Counselor's Comments

Evaluation has been read and discussed.

Supervisor's signature _____

Counselor's signature _____

*****   *****   *****

End of Season Report by Specialists

Name _____
Specialty Area _____
Date _____

1. Describe three or more *highlights* of your experience at camp this season.
2. What *changes* or *additions* could be made to your program to make it even more interesting, exciting, creative, and FUN? (You might want to include such things as: equipment, scheduling, personnel, organization, training, evaluation, administrative input, physical setup, etc.)

3. What *additions* or *changes* would you recommend in staff orientation and in-service training that would enable counselors to utilize your specialty more fully?
4. Do you wish to be asked to return? (An affirmative answer is not considered a commitment.) _____

Would you want the same position? _____

If not, what position would you like to be considered for?_____

It would be foolish to leave out the members of the camping community who have the most at stake—the campers and their parents. In most camps the responses will be positive, but constructive criticisms should be welcomed. If there is a truly disgruntled parent the director may want to follow up with a conference.

An End-of-Session Evaluation for Parents and campers

Your Name _____

Name of Camper _____

Unit _____

Counselor's Name _____

Dear Parent:

To continue our process of self-evaluation and growth, we are requesting that campers and their parents comment about our camp program. Section I is for parental responses and Section II is for camper responses. It would be most helpful to us if you would write in your child's answers to the questions using his actual wording.

Your assistance will be invaluable to us in planning and preparing for even more exciting and enjoyable camp experiences in subsequent sessions. Please fill in this form at the end of each session your child is enrolled. We appreciate your help.

Sincerely,

_____ Director

SECTION I: PARENTAL EVALUATION

1. What do you feel was the strongest feature of this camping experience for your child?
2. Did our camp program meet, exceed, or fall short of your expectations? Explain.
3. Is there any area of the camp's operation you wish to commend or make recommendations about?
4. Did you visit the camp during the session?   ☐ Yes   ☐ No

SECTION II: CAMPER'S EVALUATION

1. When were you having the most fun at camp?
2. Which activities did you enjoy? Why did you like them?
3. What do you remember most about camp? What will you miss?

When the responses of staff, campers, and parents are organized into a composite picture the director has a sound platform on which to build the program for another season.

| chapter 14 | **Discipline in the Day Camp** |

Day camp should be a time for *re*creation. The carefree days of Tom Sawyer and Huck Finn are a myth for most of our children who live in a tense, pressurized world where "Hurry" sets the tempo rather than "Stop! Look! Take time to listen!"

Parents in our highly competitive society have a compulsion to cram after-school hours with extra-curricular activities. Children no longer "just play"; they are taken for lessons in art, music, drama, dancing, skating, skiing, woodworking, gym, and even karate! These are all designed to satisfy the parent's need to grow "better and smarter kids." Competitive sports at an early age add to the pressures on children to measure up to parental expectations. Day camp should provide an oasis in the midst of this organized confusion.

It should not surprise us if children react to these pressures with behavior problems; behavior is a child's second language—a cry for help. Our goal then should be to create an orderly, calm, comfortable world in which our campers have no need to vent their negative feelings on others or to turn them in on themselves.

In this chapter we will try to focus on the reasons for behavior, to put help ahead of punishment, and thus to see ourselves as "counselors" in the truest sense of the word.

What are the first words that pop into your mind when you hear the word "discipline?" Obedience? Making kids mind? Punishment?

How often we hear people say, "That kid needs discipline." "That teacher has no discipline! Her kids walk all over her!" or "That kid is spoiled rotten! His parents never discipline him!"

The word discipline has a negative connotation, and even if we sweeten it up a bit by calling it "behavior management," the implication remains that someone (you, the counselor) will *do* something to someone, and because you are usually bigger and stronger than your campers your action will have a positive effect. We have only to look at our world situation to agree that "might does not always make right." When size is the controlling factor and the child responds through fear it is like sticking a bandage on an open wound without cleaning it. The bandage only holds in the infection temporarily. Eventually it will fester and erupt!

"I know all that," the frustrated counselor responds, "but what do I *do* when I am faced with a camper who is driving me up a wall—and knows it; with a child who has hurt another camper—or who kicks me in the shin. The child who destroys another's treasure, or whose pockets have to be examined every day before he goes home. The child who has just let loose a string of four-letter words—or who looks me in the eye and says, 'I won't—and you can't make me!'"

It is not easy to control your reactions while your shin is hurting, or while you are comforting the child who has just suffered an attack. The ability to pull yourself out of the "anger" track and cross over into one that says, "I wonder what can be going on in this kid's life that makes him have such a need to hurt!" is a special skill that comes with experience, but the first step is to make a firm commitment to "act your age." The counselor is not only bigger than the camper, he is older—and should be wiser.

Discipline begins with your attitude, which has been colored by your own experience. If you grew up in a harsh, punitive environment, you may see your role as a warden with your primary purpose to control and restrain lest the unruly child get out of hand. When you begin to see a child as "the enemy" you have already lost the battle; you are underestimating the skills and lasting power of your adversary.

But if discipline isn't a matter of control, what is it? James Hymes, author of "Teaching the Child Under Six," has given us a reasonable definition.

"Discipline is the slow, bit-by-bit, time-consuming task of helping a child to see the sense of acting in a certain way."

Discipline is teaching the art of living. It is helping children learn how to accept the rules necessary in a free society. Your task is to help each camper understand and accept the rules necessary in your camp. This part of your job will call upon all of your skills, imagination, and creativity.

It is important for you as a counselor to know something about age characteristics lest you punish or scold a child for "doing what comes naturally." For example, if you know that "fours" have a great need to expend energy, that "sixes" are inclined to be fearful, and "eights" are brassy and boastful, you can accept such behavior and say, "O.K., he's right on target!" Remember that the behavior you find annoying may be a necessary step of normal development. Children have to test their growing power against a force that offers some resistance in order to find their own limits.

One of your first tasks when you meet with the campers who will come under your supervision is to explain and discuss the camp rules—to let them know what is expected of them. Can you remember your first day in a new school—or camp—or job? Unless your "I AM, I CAN" was extremely strong you were probably uncomfortable—uncertain, until you knew the established limits. It is your responsibility to give your campers the security of edges. You have some very positive factors in your favor. Discipline stems from the word "disciple," and a disciple is one who is in strong agreement with the views of his leader. Your campers WANT to please you—to bask in the sunshine of your approval! They will identify with you—walk like you, talk like you, and even copy the way you dress.

John and Sidney were popular counselors. When they appeared in blue jeans cut off at the knee in jagged points, campers took the scissors to their own newly purchased jeans—to the horror of their parents.

It may be hard for you to believe that a child wants to please you when his behavior tells a different story, but if you try to resurrect that thought it may help to slow your angry response.

A second point that may offer some reassurance is that you are not expected to "make over" a child in four or eight short weeks. There are elements of his life that will remain unknown to you, circumstances over which you will have no control. This is both comforting and disturbing. You *can't* use it as a "cop-out," blaming everything on the parents or home environment. You *can* employ all of the patience and understanding you can muster. You can try to help the child cope with life *the way it is.*

It is easy to blame negative behavior on parents, but before you make assumptions it is wise to ask yourself whether you are trying to superimpose your values on theirs. Is your idea of teaching children that you should convert them to YOUR ways? How much are you being influenced by your own life experiences and attitudes? Are you trying to fit your campers into your mold?

A second point in your favor is that you are not alone. You are part of a team. Comparing it with a football team, your director is the coach: He makes the major decisions. In most day camps there will be someone else between him and you—a head counselor or unit leader. This person will be closer to the action—taking responsibility for calling the plays. When the staff functions smoothly as a team, each part supports the whole. The system works when each member of the team cares as much about the success of his teammates as he does about his own success. It is an exciting experience to work with others in a situation where you are almost mind-readers—where you become so "in tune" that you can communicate without words. When you find this harmonious combination you never feel lonely or overwhelmed because there is always support in time of need. Children are quick to sense this harmony and it makes them feel good—safe and secure.

When you can establish this kind of relationship with your coworkers they will stand by when they see a situation brewing, ready to intercept or support. Whenever possible we want to avoid a "locked horns" position, a situation where one party has to give in and lose face in the process. Another counselor can distract the child's attention, do something to draw the focus of the other children away from the scene, or take over and watch a group if it seems advisable for the counselor to remove the child from the scene.

These are some of the plays the team might plan and discuss in advance.

Hesitate

Try to buy a little time. Turn your back—walk away—or just stand there looking intently and directly at the child. This lack of immediate action is often a surprise that takes the child off guard. It may change his train of thought from "I'll get him!" to "What is he going to do?" and in that few seconds you may change yours from "He's doing it to me again!" to "What can be going on with this child that makes him feel so mean?"

"When I have tried this," one counselor said, "just staring into a child's face—at eye level—suddenly the corners of my lips have started quivering—my anger dissipated—and we both ended up having a good laugh."

This is not to suggest that you set aside your own feelings. Children need to know that adults do feel angry and sad; but you are trying to teach them how to control their own violent emotions. A child who misbehaves is already miserable and when you turn your anger against him it is like pouring fuel on a raging fire. The few seconds you give yourself to remember this while your anger cools down will enable you to deal with the problem as a mature adult, rather than as an opponent in a sparring match.

Think before you act. "If I do or say this what reactions can I expect? How can I avoid boxing myself in?"

Anticipate

You *can* train your mind to operate on two channels! One is paying attention to what is happening before you; the other is thinking ahead to what is coming next. This will help you when children are moving from one place or activity to another. If you turn them loose with, "O.K. kids, time for swim. Let's go!" pandemonium will result—and behavioral incidents are bred out of confusion. If you take time to explain what is going to happen next, and if you have established routines from the very beginning, your whole day will flow smoothly, seemingly without direction.

Investigate

When you find yourself dreading the day because a camper has suddenly become "the enemy," put on your Sherlock Holmes hat and start looking for clues.

What do you really know about this child? Who is his family? Does he have a father *and* mother or a father *or* mother? Has he brothers and sisters? What is his position in the family? The oldest? Youngest? A middle child?

Have there been any recent dramatic changes in his life? Moving? Divorce? Death? Is someone close to him away? Seriously ill?

Watch him closely throughout a day. Is he tired? Ask him what TV programs he watches. Could he be hungry? Nutrition affects behavior—could it be that he is having a steady diet of junk foods? Too much sugar?

What about *your* physical condition? Are you getting enough sleep?

Talk to the other adults who come in contact with him throughout the day—activity specialists, the person who picks him up at home and drives him to camp, and the camp nurse.

"Talk to me right off the top of your head about Sammy Green," a counselor said to a driver.

"That poor kid. His mother never comes out to say goodbye—she just shoves him out the door. Half the time she isn't there when we get home and when she is she just starts yakking at him before he can even get out of the car."

This person's observation may or may not be a clue. It would not be safe to make assumptions based on this one piece of information.

Has this camper been labeled in advance?

"You are getting Billy," one counselor commiserates with another. "Good luck! I had him all last summer! He ruined my summer!"

A parent announces on the first day, "I hope you can do something with him. He is beyond me! You have my permission to whack him if he's bad!"

Perhaps the problem may be a personality clash. Mixing ammonia and chlorine creates a dangerous gas. Sometimes two campers will have a similar effect on each other, or it may be two counselors who emit sparks whenever they get too close.

And don't forget to look at your program. A child who is bored—who never feels the fun of success—is also going to react.

Try keeping a diary for a few days. Is the behavior that troubles you the same act? Is it usually with the same people? What happened just before to trigger this act? What time of day is it most likely to happen? Sometimes if you keep notes a pattern emerges which provides some clues.

Mediate

Look for an opportunity to have a quiet talk with the offender when he is not in a crisis state. Deal with him honestly. Let him know that it is not bad to feel angry, but that he needs to learn to keep it under control. (I have heard adults under stress shout "Behave yourself!" or "Control yourself!" when it is obvious that if the child was capable of controlling himself, the action wouldn't be taking place.)

When you say to a child, "I know how you feel" you are offering him comfort. If you can take it a step beyond and say, "Sometimes when you do these things I feel so angry I want to yell at you, or even shake you—but I can't. One thing I have learned to do is to walk away and take some deep breaths, like this (demonstrate). After a few of these I can usually cool off enough to think clearly. Do you suppose that you might try that the next time you feel yourself getting mad?"

Another approach is "You see Janice, who is blind, and Davis, who has a brace on his leg. These are called handicaps—and your temper tantrums are also a handicap. The difference is that they can't do anything about theirs—they just have to learn to live with it. You *can* do something about your problem. There are ways to get rid of those bad feelings without hurting people or destroying property."

Offer acceptable methods for releasing feelings. "I can't let you hit me—or the other campers, but there are things you can hit. There is the tether ball, or this tackling dummy. We could take this bag and fill it with hay or crushed newspapers and hang it up where you can hit it."

"Pounding on clay—or hammering nails into a block of wood is like hitting, but it doesn't hurt anyone."

"I can't let you throw stones but you may throw these balls against that wall. I will throw the ball and you try to hit it with the baseball bat."

"Throw beanbags, or round balls of plasticene, or rubber-tipped darts against a target."

"When you are really mad, tearing something seems to help. I have a whole bag full of old shirts here. Tear them all to pieces if you like."

"Tear this newspaper into strips or crunch it into balls."

Sometimes the child will respond better to a soothing activity. Sand, water, and mud are relaxing media. Building a dam in a brook, or creating a stream and a miniature dam in the sandbox can be good activities. In summer camp things are possible that would be intolerable under ordinary circumstances. Set aside an area for digging, turn on the hose, and make a real mudhole. Let the campers put on their bathing suits and really get into it.

"I have a truly beautiful picture taken from a restaurant window in Gallup, New Mexico. Two boys, about six and nine, were playing in a mudhole. They were covered from head to toe—only they were fully dressed. I hope the fun they were having was worth the reception they must have had when they went home."

There should be places where children can be alone without feeling isolated. The most social beings have moments when they have too much "togetherness."

Many children can find solace in creative activities: painting, modeling, woodworking. If therapy is the goal, the activity should be undirected—simply a chance to explore and experiment with materials.

Writing or dictating is another form of therapy. Usually day campers cannot write fast enough to record their thoughts—the physical act of forming the words gets in the way of free flow of ideas.

"You are very angry. Come over here and tell me about it and I will write it down" said the counselor.

For ten minutes Jackie sputtered and steamed. When he finally stopped, the counselor read it back to him and then said, "What shall I do with this?"

"Keep it. I might need it again," Jackie replied as he ran off to join his friends.

The best way to manage behavior is to avoid mistakes. The following list of Dos and Don'ts used in the Green Acres staff manual for many years, seems to be as pertinent now as it was in the beginning.

DO expect the best from each child. They are not only intuitive, they are positively psychic. If you are afraid a child is not going to cooperate, he will sense your anxiety and test you. Anticipate appropriate behaviors and generally children will meet your expectations.

DON'T used negative labels and phrases. Fatso, Skinny, Slowpoke, Clumsy, etc., are damaging to the "I AM." The camper may pretend he doesn't mind, but the hurt is there.

DON'T make threats you can't carry out. Example: "If you don't hurry up we will go without you."

DO treat children with the same courtesy you would afford a guest in your home. If a guest spilled his drink on your table you probably wouldn't say, "There you go again! How many times have I told you to be careful?"

DON'T give choices when you don't mean it. Example: "Who would like to listen to a story?" when you expect everyone to sit down and listen!

DO be consistent. Be clear in your own mind what the rules and limits are. When a child tests you react always the same way.

DON'T be afraid to admit your mistakes. Children will respect you for it. It is good for them to know adults are not perfect.

DO avoid confrontations. Sometimes a nasty scene can be avoided if you seek help from someone who is not emotionally caught up in the situation. If you feel a "blow up" coming on call in the reserves: a unit leader or the director. That will de-fuse the situation, the problem can be resolved after everyone has a chance to cool down. *Never,* under any circumstances, *strike, slap, shake,* or *physically hurt a child!*

DON'T "horse around" with campers or "try to get down on their level." Do not allow them to hang all over you, jump on you. *Never* hold them by their arms (swing them around or skin the cat). A child's arm slips out of the socket very easily!

DO try to find at least one thing to love in every single child. If you have honestly tried—without success—talk it over with your director before the summer is spoiled for both of you.

When all else fails *act!* Do not rave and rant. Walk over to the child, take his hand in a firm grip, and start walking—somewhere out of sight and sound of the other children. Get down to his eye level, hold him firmly by the shoulders, and speak quietly and firmly, eyeball to eybeall. Know in advance what you can do—and what your limitations are. Do not try to handle a situation outside your experience or expertise. Ask for help! Above all keep your sense of humor and stay loose!

This book could have ended at this point. There are many excellent books available to help the day camp director plan his program, but books are expensive, and it takes years to acquire a good library. We know from our own experience that it is hard to select them from a list of publications, and many directors are not able to attend camping conventions and spend time browsing at the book table.

The Day Camp Program Book by Virginia Musselman was printed at the same time as *Fundamentals of Day Camping*—each one a companion piece for the other. It has recently been reprinted by Follett Publishing Company and is invaluable now as it was then. Just as *Basic Camp Management*, published by ACA, is a "must" for every day camp director, we would urge the purchase of this book as a first step in planning good program.

The simple ideas offered in the following chapters are intended as "springboards." They are offered with the hope that they will inspire counselors to plunge into the pool and discover many more ways to share summer fun with campers!

<table>
<tr><td>chapter
15</td><td>The Day Camp Program</td></tr>
</table>

Program includes everything a day camper does from the time he leaves home until he returns at night. It cannot be defined in terms of developing new friendships or of learning special skills, separated into time slots, or tied up in neat packages labled nature, arts and crafts, archery, or swimming. Program in a day camp can be rich and exciting or sterile and boring; it should strengthen the "I AM" and challenge the "I CAN" of each camper, recognizing that after ten months of marching to the tune cf a graded school system children are entitled to a change— a breather when they can develop their own special interests. Day camping is distinguished from other summer programs for children by the word "camp." It is based on the premise that camping is more than being *in* the out-of-doors; it is *living in* and relating all activities *to* outdoor natural surroundings. In most camps program will include some organized games and sports, but if this is the only emphasis it is not truly camping. Churches operate day camps, but moving a church school program outdoors does not make it a day camp. Day camping is an experience in group living that makes full use of the natural environment.

The program in a day camp will begin with a set of values and beliefs, which are then translated into goals and objectives. There is good reason for ACA Standards to require that these be stated in writing. It is a healthy exercise to seek answers to questions like the following:

Why do we want to start a day camp? Is it primarily a business venture or are we trying to meet a social need? Is it just an extension of a school program?

What do we want to have happen to the children who come to our camp? What will be the main thrust of our program?

What activities can we offer that will best accomplish our goals?

After all of the specifics have been outlined there is one goal that we hope will be common to all camps, however diversified they may be. It can be stated in one word—FUN! Fun for *every* child. A joyous experience that stores up memories for the camper to enjoy again and again!

Program Planning

The planning for program begins early in the spring when the camp committee or director and key staff sit down together and talk about what they hope Camp X is going to do for and with the campers.

Factors That Will Affect Program Planning

Nature of Sponsoring Organization. In the agency-sponsored, short-term day camp, a decision will have to be made as to whether it is best to offer a few activities stressing the quality of the experience, or to give campers a brief opportunity to sample a wide variety of new experiences. In a day camp where the average period is four or more weeks, there will be time to develop skills and carry out sustained projects.

In agency day camps, the program will be influenced by the year-round program and basic philosophy of the sponsoring organization.

The Organization Chart. The plan of organization of campers and staff will make a difference in the type of activities to be offered. Will the camp employ specialists? Will these specialists also be responsible for groups? Will they stay in one place or be roving resource people?

How much can be reasonably expected of counselors in planning and carrying out program? If the major effort rests on the shoulders of the general staff, who will supervise them? What plans can be made for evaluation and accountability?

The Campsite. Progam will necessarily be affected by the location, topography, and facilities of the site. It will be more difficult to create a camping situation in an in-town site, but with imagination much can be accomplished. The real tragedy is when the day camp leaders fail to take full advantage of every facility available. No activity should be carried on indoors that could possible be carried on outside, or that might better be replaced by a more "camp-like" activity.

Ages of Campers. Program planning must take into account the known facts about growth and development in planning activities appropriate for each age level. Preschoolers, six to tens, preteens, and teenagers all have different needs and abilities. Just as a director goes to a qualified nutritionist to have menus approved, he should also be willing to seek help from an educator in program planning.

Background of Campers. The social, economic, and educational background of the campers will have some bearing on the program. For the campers who live in crowded city areas where a tree is a novelty, the simplest outdoor experience may constitute high adventure. Counselors who work in city camps where facilities are limited are challenged to use their imaginations, as in the case where outdoor cooking, prohibited in a city area, was carried on in a steel wheelbarrow.

On the other hand, many children who live in suburban homes with landscaped lawns and gardens have a need for open spaces in which to run; for woods to explore. There are not many backyards today where the tree houses, huts, box-and-board-building play, and junkyard type of equipment would be acceptable, but this is the "stuff" that lends wings to imagination and turns the humdrum into adventure.

Staff Resources. Program will be geared to the special talents and abilities of the staff, and this will vary to some degree each season. In fact, changes may well develop after camp begins, for some of the best talents are not disclosed at the outset but are discovered as program unfolds.

Weather. Sudden or extreme weather changes will affect program; on a very hot day, quiet activities in a shady spot may be substituted for active sports, and longer or more frequent swim periods planned. Cool weather and cold water suggest that a carnival, circus, or field day replace swimming. Rainy days can be endured in a state of misery or filled with fun. (See Chapter 21.)

Elements of a Good Day Camp Program

Objectives. Putting these in concise, written form helps the staff to carry out the goals of the camp. The statement also serves as a basis for continuing evaluation.

Balance. A time for activity, and a time for rest; a time to be busy, and a time for leisure; a time to learn new skills, and a time to "just play"; this alternation is of utmost importance. Children with an over-abundance of energy cannot be trusted to recognize their physical limits. Periods of strenuous physical play should be alternated with quiet, "sit-down" activities. Campers should go home at the end of the day pleasantly tired, but not physically exhausted.

Tempo. Adequate time for transition of campers from one program area to another without pressure is the result of careful precamp planning. In their imaginations the director and staff responsible for setting up the program should think their way through an entire day, allowing ample time for such routine procedures as dressing and clean-up.

Small-Group Activities. The growing tendency toward decentralization in day camp program planning is in recognition of the advantages of the small group. When counselors are able to observe the needs and progress of each camper, the quiet, unobstrusive child is not lost in the crowd.

Large-Group Activities. Tradition and camp spirit find their beginnings when feelings and emotions are touched. The fun and friendship of camp programs, skits, or shows; the reverence and beauty inspired by a sanctuary program in a wooded setting; or the clear notes of the bugle as the flag is lowered at the end of the day: these are the moments a camper remembers.

Furthermore, "all-camp" functions often help to draw out the shy camper, who, in the anonymity of the large group, may lose himself in spontaneous participation.

Flexibility and Choices. The ability of a camper to choose his own program increases with age and experience. For the first week it is usually best to plan a program that exposes the camper to many activities. As the season progresses, more and more opportunity for choices may be offered. In some day camps the children have a planning period at the end of each day to discuss what they will do on the next day. In another, campers are given a choice of several activities with the leader keeping a checklist to insure some degree of variety in each camper's program. Program planning should allow for flexibility and for desirable changes.

The staff in a camp that had always adhered to the six-period-a-day master plan met to evaluate their program.

"There has to be a better way," sputtered Jane, the dramatics counselor. "Today I had a group of eight-to-ten-year-olds who were all hepped up about a play they had written. Just when they were really rolling the period ended and they had to leave to go to archery. They were angry and frustrated, and I'm sure the archery counselor found them less than enthusiastic. At the same time I was faced with another group, this time five-year-olds, and had to quickly shift gears and interest them on a different level."

"Most of our kids have to 'go by the bell' all year long," said Chuck. "It does seem as if they should have more chance to decide what they want to do here, not have some adult breathing down their necks all the time giving them orders."

"Furthermore," said Ruth, "learning to make wise choices is an important part of growing up, and day camp is an excellent place to practice."

"How can we do it and still be certain that we can account for every camper every minute of the day?" the director asked.

It was not easy to bring about the change—but it happened—and that camp has never gone back to the original plan with a master schedule. It was a gradual process, starting with a fairly well-organized structure and opening up slowly.

For the first week the counselors plan the entire program and assign children to activities. Starting the second week, each unit or group has a brief meeting or planning session in the morning, and each counselor describes an activity he has planned for that morning, limiting the number of children who could participate at one time. The size of the group is limited by the kind of activity and also to help the children learn about second choices. During these meetings you might hear the following:

> John: "I will take as many as six people to the pond. We will take nets and try to find . . ."

> Sarah: "I need six to eight people to prepare a play, which we will present on Friday."

> Ann: "I will be going into the woods to work on the hut we started yesterday. Today we will learn more about lashing. I can take five or six."

The children then decide which of these activities they would follow for the morning. If they want to make changes partway through the morning, the procedure has to be decided upon in advance.

There are other ways to develop a flexible program:

1. Program operates on a preplanned schedule in the morning. In the afternoon campers are given a variety of choices. In this way every camper is exposed to every aspect of program, but at the same time given an opportunity to pursue that which interests him most.
2. Each small group of campers meets at the end of the day to discuss what has taken place that day and to plan for the next day's activities.
3. Spontaneous Program. The following article, reprinted from *Camping Magazine,* is really an expression of a philosophy as well as a guide to another program method. At Green Acres it is given to parents each year so they will know what to expect, and to staff members as a goal to reach for. It *is* idealistic—someone has to "sell" the idea to the staff and train them in ways that make it work, but the results are worth the effort!

Spontaneous Program

It's the first day of camp. Ten eight-year-olds set out with their counselor to find a good spot in the woods to build a fort. An hour or so later, the fort well under way, the group starts back for its cabin, when one camper asks timidly, as he peers into the unfamiliar woods: "Are we lost?" Usually the counselor will reassuringly reply "Of course not" and the group will return and proceed to the next activity.

A counselor who's really on the ball might pause and say, "I know how to get back. Do you?" After three or four boys who are old-timers have boasted of their ability to find the cabin the counselor might extend the question even further. "Good—but will you be able to find the fort tomorrow?"

One boy suggests excitedly "We could make trail markers!" So the trip back to the cabin becomes a secondary program activity as campers invent their own system of trail markers and each one helps leave the trail. Just as the cabin comes to sight the counselor (or, if luck has it, a camper) begins to ponder out loud. "We wanted to keep our fort a secret. Now anyone can find it by following the trail. We need something that will let *us* find the fort, but no one else . . . What about a map?!"

Now the group is working on another activity, one which they chose themselves and one that developed directly out of their original, counselor-motivated activity. They go to the Arts & Crafts center for the materials to make their map, and then to the Campcraft counselor to get a compass and learn how to use it. While making the map they may decide they want to label the big tree that marks a left turn. Is it an oak or a maple? The counselor could answer that question himself— or he might suggest that someone go to the nature library and bring them a book on trees.

Of course, it might not go this way at all. The group might discover a blueberry patch so inviting that nothing less than an immediate berry-party will suffice. The blueberries get taken to the campcraft area to be made into muffins that are cooked on a hot rock and eaten with spoons which campers whittled while they were waiting for the muffins to cook.

Or maybe they don't find a blueberry patch, but a brush pile with chipmunks scurrying under it. They sit for a while quietly watching, and later they discuss what chipmunks eat, how they are like squirrels, how they are different from mice. Finally they decide they must go to the nature library to resolve all their questions.

By the end of their first day of camp this group will have participated in half a dozen activities and visited most of the camp's resource areas, all without a whistle blown or a bell rung to signal a change in activities.

This is spontaneous program. It is program that takes its roots in the natural energy, enthusiasm, and curiosity of children. Instead of channeling this excitement into a standardized program, it allows the program to develop out of the campers' interests. The transition between activities is so smooth it is invisible.

The campers will probably never realize that they were learning self-reliance in cooking and cleaning up for themselves when they made those muffins. It was just part of a perfect day to them. The campers go home ready for the next morning when they can make a flag for their fort, and they arrive at nine with their arms full of necessary old sheets for flags and with their heads brimming with ideas and enthusiasm.

Contrast this with an altogether too-familiar scene in some camps: the disappointment of a nine-year-old who needs "just ten minutes more" in woodworking when the activity ends. Everything stops with the ringing of a bell that signals the moment when Group A must switch from nature to athletics as Group B moves from athletics to leather-craft and so on down the line.

This traditional, six-period-a-day form of programming still predominates in many day camps throughout the country and there are still endless campers whose pleadings for ten more minutes are answered by a smile and a half-promise of "tomorrow." Too often, when tomorrow arrives the camper's enthusiasm has vanished, not only for his unfinished project, but for everything connected with that activity.

It is easier to administer the familiar structured six-period program and requires less skilled program leadership. A child's enthusiasm, however, is not as easily manipulated as time-blocks on a sheet of paper. Unlike a light switch, a child has no button readings *on* or *off* that we can use to engage and disengage his excitement when an arbitrary bell rings. Children are by nature enthusiastic, and camp should be a place where their enthusiasm for learning and living will have an opportunity to grow and take its own shape. A good camp both provides and encourages this opportunity. We succeed not by placing a child in a classroom-like atmosphere simply moved outdoors, but by allowing every child to contribute to the camp program. A camper's interest will not flag if he takes part in a program that evolves out of his own interests and that proceeds at the pace he sets for himself.

Today, with our heightened awareness of the concepts of open education and the unstructured classroom, many camp directors really want to free the day camp from its antiquated trappings but they are not quite sure how to begin. How can they bring about desired change?

Let's visualize a traditional day camp for a moment. It still hires as many specialists (an arts & crafts specialist, a nature specialist, a camp-craft specialist, etc.) as its budget will allow, and makes them responsible for instructing or entertaining the campers who come to them each day. A good specialist has traditionally been considered one who prepares his next day's program as conscientiously as a teacher prepares the next day's lesson plans.

In addition to the specialists, the camp employs general counselors to escort the campers from one specialist to another, while keeping a watchful eye on their health and welfare. As ambulatory babysitters they are not excited, and they serve as lackadaisical role models for their charges.

Now let's look at a less traditional camp. Specialists and general counselors are employed, but their responsibilities have been reallocated. Specialists are considered resource people, not instructors. They do not plan a day's program the night before and then expect every group to work on the same activities that day. Instead they are available to help campers solve any problems that arise in the course of the activities.

These specialists must be flexible enough to have three or four groups converge on them in a short span of time and still be able to help them all. Few specialists have assigned times; most are always accessible and their resources are easily mobilized. Although they answer questions, show technique and offer suggestions, their primary objective is not to "show and tell" but to help children discover—to ask the question which leads to the next creative response.

Counselors are not babysitters. A good counselor responds as sensitively to the needs and desires of children as a geiger counter does to uranium. When that counselor picks up the faint ticking of excitement from a camper who normally shuns all activities, he traces it to the mother-lode. He may find a child who loves nothing better than to draw.

That camper is then selected to draw the eagle on the fort flag, and he suddenly becomes important in the eyes of his fellow-campers, and his self-image is enhanced. Amazingly, that child will now attempt activities he had previously avoided. Success breeds success. The child who once tastes success can dare to risk an occasional failure, and so he can venture into new areas of program.

The general counselor's most valuable asset is the ability to pick up the signals children are always radiating. He must be able to see what sparks their interest and what bores them. He sees and hears not only the obvious signals, but in addition, reads the meaning behind a sidelong glance, a moment's hesitation, or tears in the eyes of his happiest camper.

Ability to comprehend a child's unspoken desires and help that child materialize them is an indefinable quality. There are some general principles that can be offered a counselor during his precamp training. A first concern should be to explain and to discuss the misunderstood words "unstructured" and "spontaneous."

A first reaction is to think this means a child may do anything he wants. Spontaneous does not mean chaotic. The counselor needs to be constantly aware that it is his job to provide a varied and balanced program for all of his campers.

There are some children who arrive at camp loving baseball. These campers would be satisfied to play baseball all day, and would never attempt anything new. Nothing would be easier than to let them go their own way. They would appear happy every day but they would be missing much of what a camp can offer.

With some counselor encouragement the baseball lover could play the leading role of Casey at the Bat in a skit presented to the rest of the camp. His counselor should always be striving to expose him to new experiences that will develop new skills and insight. A child who plays baseball well knows he plays well; he needs a chance to discover he can succeed in other fields.

Changing from the traditional structured program to a spontaneous one is not as difficult as we imagine. The major stumbling block is over-coming the restrictive structure we have imposed on our own lives.

It is too easy to impose on others the limits we have adopted for ourselves. In a camp where children bring their own lunches it should not matter much whether children eat at twelve or twelve-fifteen. Why must a group halt an activity that is near completion so that they may eat lunch at exactly noon?

How many rules and regulations are really necessary to safeguard campers, and how many are arbitrary? How many rules have never been questioned because they have been in practice so long they are traditions? We can begin to relax the structure of our camps by paring away limits that are not needed to insure safety of campers and staff. Rules should not exist to aid the administrative process; administrative practices should be designed to suit the needs of campers.

There is no precise formula that will ensure the success of spontan-eous program. If there was, it wouldn't be flexibile or spontaneous. When it is working well a spontaneous program is like life itself—never exactly the same for any two people.

Every activity reflects, in hundreds of ways, different interests of the campers participating in it. Each day becomes an adventure if at nine in the morning you can't read a posted schedule to learn where you'll be at two-thirty, or what you'll be doing. Such a camp teaches a child more than mere nature facts, archery, ceramics, and the other traditional camping skills. It helps him develop a sense of responsibility for living his own life in the best way possible.

By choosing one of the above approaches we are helping children with that most difficult process of maturation: moving from always following adult directions to making selections on their own. As adults they will have to make choices constantly and too often we expect them to be ready for this without having given them any experience along the way in making and living with the consequences of their own decisions.

When choices are introduced to children in the way suggested in the first plan, counselors are provided with a built-in self-evaluation tool. If no one ever chooses the activity a counselor offers, something must be wrong. The reason may become apparent if we ask the following questions:

What have you done to arouse and maintain interest? Do you always have materials ready so the activity will go smoothly?

Is the activity within the appropriate level of experience, allowing the individual child to know success?

Do you praise each child for giving you the best he can accomplish, rather than making him feel inadequate if he did not measure up to your predetermined standards?

Do you know how to "sell your wares?"

The Camper's Day

Many day camp directors dislike the use of the word "schedule," but it must be admitted that some planning for routine is essential. Campers arrive, eat, and go home at set times. That is the beginning of a schedule. If there is some facility that must be shared by more than one unit or group, such as a swimming pool, archery range, or woodworking shop, a plan is necessary. The following samples offer suggestions to the beginning camp director.

Plans of Organization

A master plan is drawn up by the director, head counselor, or program coordinator. It may be posted daily, weekly, or for an entire season. When there are more activities offered than there are periods in a day a system of rotation may be necessary. When a master plan is used campers go from one activity to the next as directed, keeping within the established time frame. A sample plan, as formerly used at Green Acres and typical of many day camps, would be as follows:

9:00- 9:30	Arrival. Opening Circle. Health Inspection.
9:30-10:10	Activities
10:10-10:50	Activities
10:50-11:30	Activities
11:30-12:00	Serendipity or Story Time
12:00- 1:30	Lunch and Rest Time
1:30- 2:10	Activities
2:10- 2:50	Activities
2:50- 3:30	Activities
3:30- 4:00	Closing all-camp assembly

In the unit system now used at Green Acres, the above framework is followed with one important exception. From 9:30 to 11:30 and again from 1:30 to 3:30 the units have activities with no restrictions of "periods." This means that a group deeply involved in a special project can stay with it as long as interest is sustained.

Daily Routines

Opening Circle. A certain amount of formality at the beginning of the day is a good introduction to the "business" of play. Procedures such as flag raising or the pledge of allegiance need to be explained, for a small child will often apply a ludicrous interpretation to words he does not understand. Daily announcements, reminders, and special words of commendation are all appropriate at this time.

Serendipity is the name we have given to a special time of day at Green Acres. From 11:30 to 12:00 the children gather in a quiet wooded area set apart for this program and not used for anything else. It is voluntary; small groups from all over the camp attend, but it must be the choice of the entire group, which in itself is another learning experience. A small, portable organ is used to help set the mood. Campers are expected to abide by the rule that respects the rights of others to listen and enjoy the program. The prettier songs are saved for this time; spirituals and rounds that teach simple harmony. The more raucous or humorous ditties are saved for the end-of-the-day assembly. Campers and counselors are encouraged to form choirs or to play musical instruments.

Each day one adult tells a story (never reads it) that does not necessarily have a moral but is not hilariously funny or silly. Such stories as "The Golden Windows," "King Midas," or "The Emperor's Robe" which have unstated morals are appropriate. The name "Serendipity" implies that one may expect to find something new and different—and that is the goal set for those who plan it on a daily basis. It is a good winding-down activity before lunch.

Time and again, when campers return as visitors, counselors, or parents of campers, they have described this as "the thing I remember most about camp."

Teaching Abstract Concepts (a note from Grace). "It is my personal opinion that we have gradually eroded the ability of children to relate to values and know the emotional satisfaction of patriotism, loyalty, and pride in our heritage. The pictures in the newspaper and the stories told on TV do little to encourage our children to believe in their native land. I think we have an opportunity—and a responsibilty—to help them know what it means to live in a free society. The spirit engendered in our bicentennial year revealed that people are hungering for reassurance that we are strong—and that our strength is based on the ideals stated in the Declaration of Independence. Respect and loyalty are values that can be taught and I believe we can bring about change in our demoralized society if we make them part of the day camp experience."

Lunch Time. (See Chapter 11, Food.)

Rest Hour. This may be called *siesta*, or quiet hour. The terminology is not as important as the acceptance of the idea that campers and counselors need a time to slow down in the middle of the day. The older campers may engage in quiet activities such as knotcraft, sketching, or reading. The success of the rest hour will hinge on two factors: (1) the counselor must believe it is necessary, and (2) the counselor must also rest with the campers. If he sits on a chair barking orders like a policeman, "Lie down," "Stop talking," "Who whistled?" he will supervise a wriggling, restless, resentful, and tense group of campers. If he stretches out on a blanket and says, "This really feels good. I'm tired after that long hike. Let's have a good rest, and then I will read some more of that story I started yesterday," his campers will follow his example.

Closing Assembly. This should be one of the highlights of the day: a time to enjoy camp songs, fun songs, and action songs; a time to experiment with rhythms. An element of surprise will sustain the interest of campers and help to get the stragglers there on time. (See Chapter 21, A Bag of Tricks.) The period is usually concluded with some procedure that becomes a part of camp tradition. Flag lowering is most impressive when accompanied by "Retreat," or "To the Colors" played on a trumpet or bugle, but a clarinet, trombone, recorder, or any other wind instrument may be used. Good recordings of all bugle calls are available and, while the personal element seems to add to the ceremony, a recording can be a satisfactory substitute. One popular ritual is for campers and counselors to join hands and sing a special camp song. A note of solemnity helps to tone down exuberance before the serious business of getting to cars and buses.

Traditions and Rituals. There is something comforting about the sameness of rituals. Doing things in a certain way, saying the same words, or singing a particular song gives one a sense of belonging. This is not limited to children: the many clubs, fraternities, societies, clans, and brotherhoods; each with its own secret signals, rituals, and regalia, is proof that man needs to maintain this sense of membership in a group. Certain procedures become "the way we do it at *our* camp" and oldtimers are heard carefully explaining it to newcomers. We can capitalize on this "togetherness"; it becomes part of the mystery and excitement of the camp program, but with one caution: Cliques or small "in groups" that put down or exclude their peers should be discouraged. In a happy day camp there are no outsiders!

Spiritual Emphasis in Program

Day camps operated by a particular religious organization may include some special instruction or services in their program, but the great majority of our camps will include children of all ethnic and religious backgrounds and therefore will refrain from introducing anything of a religious nature in the program.

Theme Camping

All of us like to step out of character occasionally and pretend we are someone different, and theme camping provides an opportunity for the camper to enjoy this kind of dramatic play. Announcing the theme to campers with such a statement as, "This summer we are all going to be Indians," or even asking "How would you like to be Indians?" will usually elicit a negative response. A more subtle approach would be to bring in some interesting artifacts and pictures, or to tell a story about some central character, incident, or time. Once the natural curiosity of the camper is aroused, it is up to the counselor to "fan the fire" with intriguing suggestions.

For the younger campers, going to day camp is usually theme enough. The older, more sophisticated campers, having accepted an idea, will make suggestions faster than the leader can keep up with them, and program will move from one exciting adventure to the next.

The following suggestions have been used:

Indians	Sailors
Pioneers	Cowboys
Frontiersmen	Various Nations
Mountaineers	Knights of King Arthur
Woodsmen	Robin Hood
Moon Dwellers	Space Men

Planning the Program from Day to Day

In a small day camp the director is immediately at hand and knows what is going on, but many of our day camps have from 100 to 800 children. In this case it seems advisable to have some organized plan for assuring the quality of the program. It would be all too easy for glorified babysitting to take the place of meaningful activities geared to children's interests and abilities. Presumably there will be supervisors or unit leaders, each responsible for a given number of campers and staff. The following plan sheet is used in our camp. At the end of rest period, each counselor hands his supervisor a plan for the following day. It can be subject to change, but it eliminates the possibility that a counselor will arrive without an idea in his head—or with a very good idea but no materials with which to carry it out.

DAILY ACTIVITY PLAN

Counselor.....................
Unit..........................
Date ....
Activity   Approx. Time ....
Special materials needed   Approx. Length................

Back-up Activity:

Special Comments:
....

chapter 16

Arts and Crafts

In a creative program arts and crafts will not be an isolated activity, but will serve as a useful supplement to other activities. Illustrating favorite camp songs, making and decorating rhythm instruments, or making puppets to dramatize folk songs are only a few of the ways in which music and art can be combined. Sketching with a piece of wood or charcoal from the campfire, making dyes from berries or bark, or making attractive jewelry from natural materials will integrate art with nature. Designs for articles made in the woodworking shop will come from the art department, and dramatics will go hand in hand with art in the making of scenery, costumes, and properties.

In planning for an arts and crafts program, these two points should be kept in mind:

1. Experimentation for the sake of finding new ways, new uses, and new inventions is a basic part of the creative act. A day camp program can provide the materials and the atmosphere that will encourage children to see and work in relation to their own needs, abilities, and interests.
2. Freedom is important—in physical arrangements, in allowing time for campers to create, and in lack of adult interference. But the point that freedom must be purposeful is often overlooked. There must be guidance, motivation, creation, evaluation, and quality according to the ability of the individual.

Materials for Arts and Crafts

A constant attempt should be made in the day camp to offer experiences different from those of school. Therefore, concentration on the use of natural materials should be stressed rather than on media available throughout the school year. In most day camps some of the

163

following could be found and used: straw, corn husks, cat-tail leaves, goldenrod, sumac, bamboo, cornstalks, wheat, rushes, seeds and grains, squash seeds, watermelon seeds, corn, rice, nuts, woods, and the bark of trees, driftwood, shells, sand, rocks and soil, pine cones, clay, berries, flowers, leaves, and moss.

Some of the very best arts and crafts programs involve the least expense. Their very value lies in the fact that campers are encouraged to make the best use of the materials around them.

The resourceful counselor or camp director may find businessmen who are glad to donate materials for the arts and crafts program.

A printer may give scrap paper or cardboard, and the narrow strips that fall into the waste basket from his edger are good for weaving chains and for false hair.

The upholsterer will have samples and scraps of leatherette or heavy plastic material.

Clothing manufacturers may donate remnants of cloth, and a manufacturer of waste once gave a camp a bale of good white cloth which was used for costumes, dyeing, and other projects.

A wall-paper store has sample books or odd rolls of paper which can be used on the blank side for murals, on the other side for weaving, or covering for books.

The rug man will save the cardboard tubes from the centers of his rugs, which may become the neck of a giraffe, the trunk of a tree, or the smokestack on a ship.

A department store may donate remnants of contact paper, oilcloth, or felt.

Campers love to bring things from home. A list of odds and ends needed that can be found in most homes, such as yarn, candle ends, foil containers, and fancy papers, might be sent with a precamp mailing.

Tools

An elaborate outlay of equipment will not be necessary, but the tools provided should be of good quality. Nothing is more frustrating to creative effort than trying to cut with dull scissors, pound with a hammer that is too light, or paint with poor brushes.

Also, these tools and materials need to be accessible. An arts and crafts room or shop is a fascinating place, and may make a more elaborate program possible. However, if using it limits the activity to a small number of campers for scheduled periods, it is far better to use portable kits, which can be moved with a group into a unit area, a shady spot under a tree, or to indoor facilities available on a rainy day.

Time

A final plea is for time. "I like it here," said a nine-year-old girl. "At the other camp I went to I never had time to finish anything I was making."

Activities Using Natural Materials

Build an Ant Farm

Partially fill a gallon jug or other similar large containers with soil. Find an ant hill. Shovel the surrounding dirt and debris into the jar. Cover the jar with dark paper to encourage the ants to make tunnels. Place some cotton on top of the dirt and pour a little water on it every few days. Feed the ants crumbs of bread and cookies, honey, or sugar water.

Make an Insect Cage

1. Roll an 8" x 18" piece of screening into a tube and secure with staples.
2. Place upright in disposable pie tin, fill with plaster, and let set.
3. Remove tin and use it for lid with string handles. (See illustration.)

Have you ever watched a spider spin a web?

Spider's Web

Here's how to collect a spider's web:
1. Find a suitable web on a quiet day.
2. Spread newspaper behind the web.
3. Spray lightly on both sides of web with white paint.
4. Place dark piece of construction paper behind web and gently lift.
5. Cut web guy lines at edge of paper.
6. Let dry.

Nature Plaques

Use old boards, shingles, plywood, etc., for base. Use natural materials such as dried foliage, dried branches, dried flowers, cattails, dried grasses, driftwood, fungi, lichen, moss seeds, or pods. Attach with glue or cement.

Nature Windows

Using clear contact paper (in desired shapes) place natural materials on sticky side and back with colored tissue; string with yarn to make necklaces, name tags, wall hangings, or mobiles.

Nature's Paintbrushes

Try painting with sticks, cattails, pine spills, twigs, or grasses.

Nature Mobiles

Use sticks or coat hangers for a base. Attach string to nuts, leaves, rocks, shells, or seeds with glue or cement. Attach strings to stick or hanger and balance. Use shells to make wind chimes.

Leaf Rubbing

Collect many varieties of leaves and bark and evergreen spills. Place between folded manila paper and rub with flat side of crayons.

Sand Painting

Children color sand with thin tempera paint and allow to dry; then make mosaics, designs, and pictures by sprinkling sand onto areas of paper coated with thin glue.

Rock Paperweights

Rocks of different sizes and shapes are used, along with ink, enamel, paints, or magic markers. Study the rocks and select one that has noticeable characteristics or a shape that resembles a figure or face. Wash and clean the rock and then color or decorate as desired. Varnish to protect design.

Indian Mat Loom

Weaving materials: grass, straw, rushes, cattails, etc. Materials are woven through strings attached to sticks .

Indian Puppets

Make Indian finger puppets by gluing acorns with caps into the top depression of toothpaste caps. (Little fingers will fit into the bottom of the caps.) Attach paper strip headbands and feathers.

Leaf Transparencies

Place leaves between waxed paper (keeping waxed sides together) and iron gently. These transparencies can be hung in a window.

Grass Weaving

Weave grasses, long day-lily leaves, ribbons, or strings into plastic vegetable baskets. Add ribbon handle. Make wall hanging by weaving grasses through strips cut in squares of cloth or paper.

Animals and People from Nature Objects

Create animals and people from natural objects, such as pine cones, acorns, pine spills, oak galls, grass, and pebbles.

Shingle Collage

Glue natural objects to swatches of wooden shingles and varnish over. Piece of bark (do not tear from trees) or dark cardboard can also be used.

Dyeing

Put sufficient water in an enameled pot to cover cloth to be dyed. Add concentrated dye to water and bring to a boil. Place dry cloth in dye bath to desired shade (will lighten somewhat when dry), remove, wring out, and dry. To make dye fast, treat cotton, linen, or rayon cloth before dyeing with one-quarter cup washing soda to gallon of water. Boil cloth at least one hour, rinse well and dry before dyeing.

Tie Dyeing

Tie dyeing is a technique of dyeing designs in cloth by tying off or knotting sections of the cloth before dipping the fabric into the dye. With practice, experimentation, and experience, unusual designs can be created turning ordinary white sheets and old dress shirts into attractive garments or fabric.

Natural Dyes

Use to dye cotton, woolen, rayon, or linen materials. Not as reliable color or colorfast as commercial dyes, but much more fun!

Natural Dyes

Materials	Color of Dye
onion skins	red or yellow
raspberries	dark red
beets	red violet
strawberries	red
mountain ash berries	orange
goldenrod (plant & flowers)	yellow
pear leaves	dull yellow
sumac leaves	yellow brown
elderberry leaves	green
rhubarb leaves	light green
blackberries	blue
dandelion roots	magenta
walnut hulls	rich dark brown
sumac bark	brown
bayberries	yellow

Gather barks in spring and early summer, leaves at full growth, flowers at peak bloom, berries and seeds when ripe. Experiment in making dyes by soaking materials in water overnight, and then boiling for an hour or more for desired intensity. Strain well to remove all plant materials.

Preparation of Various Dyes

Goldenrod. Chop flowers and plants into small pieces. Add water and bring to a boil. Simmer several hours and then cool and strain. After 24 hours reheat and add cloth to be dyed—simmer to desired color.

Pear Leaves. Pound the leaves to shreds and bring to a boil until maximum color is attained.

Berries and Stems. Boil in very small amount of water for two hours. Strain well, add one part wood alcohol to three parts dye to prevent spoiling.

Barks and Roots. Boil four to five hours in small amount of water. Strain and add one tablespoon of salt to each pint of dye.

Onion Skins. Boil in small amount of water for two and one-half hours. Add cloth to strained dye and boil one hour.

Natural dyes are fairly permanent and should be used while hot on dry materials.

Activities Using Easily Found Materials

Boats from Corks

Make boats by driving nails through corks. Add sails. Use also walnut shells, plastic dishes.

Boats with Magnets

Make a small paper boat with paper clips around edges. Use magnet to steer it.

Peanut Finger Puppets

Break peanut shells in half to form thimbles, making one for each finger. Put a face on each shell with ink. Place shell face on each fingertip and make conversation.

Finger Puppets

Wrap a facial tissue over a cotton ball on a stick, or over finger, with elastic around the neck. Draw on face.

What else could you use to make finger puppets?

Styrofoam Prints

Press-carve a design into the smooth bottom of a styrofoam meat tray. Paint over with water-soluble printer's ink. Lay paper on top and lift off prints.

Potato Sculptures

Combine potatoes with toothpicks, small nails, or pins to make sculptures using straws, screw eyes, buttons, beads, cloth and trims, wire bits, cone cups.

Potato Printing

Cut potato in half or thirds. Cut or scratch design into flat surface of potato, *brush* on paint and use as printer. (Dipping potato directly in paint tends to cause blotting.)

Crepe-Paper Dye

Children make dye by soaking crepe paper in water. Lay wet streamers on cloth so the colors "bleed" into a design. When the cloth is dry, the counselor can iron and finish edge. Use the cloth for special parties, a theatre curtain, doll's bedspread, or curtains.

Papier Mache

Tear toilet paper or newsprint into small pieces. Add flour and water mixture until soft and gooey. May be used instantly. Mold like clay, the more it is worked the softer and smoother it gets. Form into shapes, dry, and paint. Apply to framework of chicken wire to make huge animals or objects.

Wood Sculpture

Provide an assortment of small pieces of wood of all sizes and shapes, including dowels, spools, throat and popsicle sticks, and toothpicks. Use a strong adhesive (preferably glue). Children will create with same absorption they give to other media. May work individually or in groups.

Sawdust Sculpture

Recipe 1. Two cups sawdust mixed with one cup wheat paste and enough water to hold it together. Will get very hard.

Recipe 2. Mix one part flour or wheat paste and two parts water. Heat until clear and thick (stirring). When cool add sawdust until a thick modeling material is formed.

Recipe 3. Add sawdust to liquid glue to form a thick paste. Use for modeling or spread flat on waxed paper and cut into forms like cookies. This material can be sawed, filed, whittled, or sanded.

Cement Mixing

Mix equal parts of sand and cement. Add water a little at a time until it reaches a thick consistency. Let every child take a turn with the mixing. Very young children can fill a paper cup with the cement and when it hardens they have something they have created. Slightly older children can make a wooden frame and fill it with cement to make stepping stones. They can mark numerals on it while it is still wet. This is a good time to talk about Graumman's theatre in Hollywood where the stars make their prints.

Grandma's Salt Beads

Recipe. 1 cup salt, 1/2 cup cornstarch, 1/2 cup boiling water, 1 drop food coloring, 1 drop perfume.

Mix salt and cornstarch; add boiling water and coloring. Cook over moderate heat, stirring constantly. Add perfume and mix well. When cool enough to handle, form mixture into small balls. Run a stick pin through the center of each ball and place upright in the ridges of corrugated paper to dry. String on heavy thread.

Texture and Techniques—Onion Bags

You can do many different things with plastic onion bags. (a) Weave with pipe cleaners. (b) Weave with yarn using blunt needle, bobby pin, toothbrush needles. (c) Make crayon rubbings through paper laid on top. (d) Cut open and stretch over four nails in corners of a frame and use as weaving base.

Toothbrush Needles

Break the brush end off and file to blunted point. Use hole in handle as "eye" for threading.

Woodworking

Woodworking enables a child to work off strong emotions by pounding and sawing. It is an excellent way to strengthen math concepts and develop manual dexterity and eye/hand coordination. Some children will become creative at the woodworking bench even though they have resisted all other art media. Many feel great personal satisfaction as they become skilled in using tools and learn new techniques.

Woodworking can be dangerous. It requires close supervision with at least a one-to-four ratio. Young children can begin with such activity as driving nails into blocks of styrofoam. Provide them with pieces of styrofoam, large flat headed nails, hammers that are not too heavy. Just pounding the nail into the styrofoam is a beginning experience. For variation draw designs with magic marker and nail on the lines.

Children will be frustrated by saws that are not sharp enough to cut, hammers too light to drive a nail and screwdrivers too worn to turn a screw. (NOTE: left-handed children will have difficulty *tightening* screws, which are threaded against their natural wrist motion. *Removing* the screw will be easier for left-handed children.

Establishing a Woodworking Center

This is a noisy activity. It should be away from traffic and closed off securely when not in use.

The workbench must be the right height and solidly built. Tools should be hung on boards, each tool over a silhouette or outline marking its proper space. Rules for the care and use of each tool must be explained and rigidly enforced. The tools are not to be considered toys.

Nails are sorted into containers by size and weight. A heavy magnet attached to the bench by a rope serves to keep the floor clear of nails. Box nails, small and medium finish, 6 and 8 lb. common, and roofing nails work well. (Roofing nails are aluminum and will not adhere to the magnet.) Supply wood screws of assorted lengths and thicknesses.

Bench Accessories

1. two vises—fastened to bench
2. two coping saws
3. one box coping-saw blades
4. one brace—assorted bits
5. four claw hammers
6. two rip saws—16" or 18" blades
7. one smooth plane
8. two screwdrivers
9. one small tri-square

10. two compasses
11. two rulers
12. four pencils (large, soft, black)
13. two pkg. medium-grain sandpaper
14. screws—different sizes
15. one pkg. carpet tacks
16. blue nails
17. 1-1/4 '-2 " nails
18. water-based paint
19. white glue
20. dowels—different sizes, lengths
21. soft pine wood (different widths and lengths). Masonite plywood and any other hard wood will frustrate child to the extent that he may not try again, and thus will miss a good experience.

It's Easy to Make Musical Instruments

Interesting and useful instruments can be made from materials to be found around the home.

Drums

Wastebasket
Nail kegs
Coffee tins
Pottery flower pots
Wooden tubs
Chopping bowls

Suggested Materials.

Heads:
  Used drumheads
  Wet linen—shellacked
  Rubber tubing
  Muslin and airplane dope

Sticks:
  Rubber balls on sticks
  Large corks on sticks
  Soft cloth wound around a small ball

Rattles and Maracas

Small tin boxes with rice or pebbles
Plastic salt and pepper shakers with bright colored buttons

Toilet floats with rice or shot
Plastic Christmas bells and rice
Gourds

Maracas made from gourds are one of the simplest instruments children can make. The best gourds to use are those grown and dried in California. Only a small hole has to be cut and the gourd can be cleaned by shaking it and scraping it out with the end of a knitting needle. After the gourd is clean, one can put in dried beans, rice, small pebbles, bells, screws, and other such materials, and tape the hole up. Poster paints can be applied easily for decoration. After the paint is sufficiently dry, the gourds can be shellacked.

Tone Blocks

Darning eggs
Bones
Broom handles
Half a rolling pin (Saw about two inches across diameter.)

Bells

Sleigh
Christmas decoration bells
Elastic with bells attached to be worn on wrists or ankles
Wooden spoon handles with bells attached
Knitted cuff with bells attached

Chimes

By cutting rods and tubing into different lengths one can obtain varied pitch and tone quality.
Window rods
Copper pipe
Chrome tubes
Towel holders
Brass tubes

Tambourines

Tin pie plates with bottle caps
Paper plates with bells
Embroidery hoop with bottle caps or bells

Cymbals

Pie tins
Pot covers

Sand Blocks

Sand blocks make raspy sounds that fit into all sorts of rhythms and pantomime. They are a bit like woodblocks, except that they are solid, have a knob for holding, and their sound is made by rubbing them across each other instead of being tapped with a wooden stick. They are easy to make.

They are used in pairs. Each is a small block of wood 3" x 5" or 4" x 6" and about an inch thick. One flat side is covered with coarse sandpaper, securely fastened to the narrow sides with thumbtacks. The other flat side of each block should be nicely sanded, and can be painted or shellacked. A knob or bar of wood should be screwed into this flat side. A sand block is held in each hand by this knob.

Guiro

The guiro (Spanish for gourd, pronounced gweerah) is also made from a gourd. The guiro is shaped like a curved cucumber. Again, the gourd must dry out thoroughly. Then cut a piece from the narrow end and scrape out the inside, seeds and all. Leave the hole for a finger to fit into. The outside of the guiro should be sanded and smoothed. It should then be scored with a knife or file, the ridges running across the *width* of the gourd.

To use a guiro, fit it securely on a finger of the left hand. Hold a piece of wire, a long nail, a fork or other thin metal length in the right hand and stroke it against the ridges in the gourd.

To improvise when gourds are not available, use a block of wood. Thumbtack a piece of canvas or leather across one side, so that the left hand will fit through it, holding the board comfortably. Sand the other side until it is very smooth. Then using a steel-edged ruler as a guide, score lines across the board, making them deep enough and close enough together to make a fine rasping sound when a thin-edged tongue depressor is stroked over it.

Rhythm Sticks

Can be made of two pieces of doweling wood about one foot long and one-half inch in diameter that have a pleasing sound when struck together. Discarded chair rungs are satisfactory. They can be painted or shellacked.

Claves

Can be made of broom handles. Two pieces should be cut about seven inches long.

Coconut Clappers

Saw a coconut in two equal halves; file the edges of each half. Clap together to imitate sounds of hooved animals.

Gongs

Can be had by striking a (1) horseshoe, (2) round metal tray. Drill a hole and suspend with rawhide (3) heavy brass bowl.

Tuned Glasses (or bottles)

Tuned by pouring water into them—a small amount for a high note, a larger amount for a low note. Nail polish can be used to indicate level of water on glasses. Eight tuned vinegar bottles can be tied to a broom handle placed on the backs of two chairs. They should hang loosely and not too close together. Simple tunes, such as "Jingle Bells," "Row, Row, Row Your Boat" or "Three Blind Mice" can be played on tuned bottles or glasses.

Flower Pots

Can produce bell tones. Take four pots of different sizes. Invert them and insert knotted rope through the hole in each one. Suspend from a frame or broom handle.

<table>
<tr><td>chapter
17</td><td>Making the Most of Natural
Resources</td></tr>
</table>

At no other season in the year can we live as intimately with nature as in the summer. Every day camp can have a nature program, no matter how sterile or barren the facilities may be. If, under the worst possible circumstances, there is nothing better than an asphalt-covered playground, there is sure to be a blade of grass or a weed poking its way through a crack; if there is a building, there may be lichen growing on the bare surfaces (did you know that it takes twenty-five years for a piece of lichen to grow to the size of a quarter?); there will be insects on the ground and in the air to catch and observe. Campers can lie on the ground and look at the clouds in the sky above, and when rain falls from that sky it can open up a whole host of experiences. Appreciation of natural surroundings is a matter of attitude. We can take everything for granted and dull our senses to the excitement and beauty around us, or we can savor every small experience. It takes imagination, initiative, and a willingness to learn with the children. Usually, even in a day camp where there is not a nature specialist, there will be at least one person who is more knowledgeable than the rest, one who is tuned into the sensory experiences that can open new vistas for campers.

A nature counselor expressed his goals as follows:

"It is my intention to *present gifts* to the children. I hope that through active exposure to natural environments; through total *sensory* immersion, they will come to know the characters of these environments: not to know them in the sense of memorizing, but in the sense of understanding and appreciating. I want them to know that the white pine has five needles, but I also want them to remember the sticky feeling of touching—or even climbing—it; the soft feeling of lying on a bed of needles, the smell of the sawdust when they cut pine for firewood and the smell of the smoke when they burned it. I want them to remember the sense of adventure when they made tea from its needles, and the taste of that tea.''

Nature Resource Center

The nature program cannot be the sole responsibility of one person—a specialist who imparts knowledge in forty-minute time slots scheduled into the campers' day. Nature is there—all of the time—and some of her most exciting surprises are spontaneous, such as a beautiful rainbow or coming across a praying mantis. There should, however, be a place—a resource center where campers can deposit their findings, seek information about their discoveries, and find equipment that will inspire further exploration.

What might you find in this resource center?
—Nets to catch butterflies or fish for samples of pond life. These can be made by the older campers.
—Vials for bringing back dirt, mulch, mud, or water to study with magnifying glasses.
—Insect cages
—Magnifying glasses and microsopes
—Sturdy cages to house such animals as gerbils or rabbits
—A roll of clear contact paper for mounting and preserving

Of primary importance is the nature library. The children's books have two purposes. Some will inspire a desire to discover, others will help children identify the discoveries they have made.

For the counselors there should be books on a more adult level. These should not be books full of Latin names, but some of the fine books written by top naturalists. After reading a beautifully illustrated, well-written book about trees, you see trees through new eyes. There is an excitement that comes with knowledge and it is that sense of excitement that is somehow transmitted to the children.

But how can the counselor, who has had no special training or experience, conduct a meaningful nature program?

These are some of the ways:

—Together with the campers he/she can emphasize sensory experiences.

With *eyes* to *see* he/she can . . .

—Look through a magnifying glass at the activity in an ant hill.

—Lie on the ground and look at the clouds: white clouds in a blue sky; threatening black and gray clouds. Talk about the color and the shape. What makes them move?

—Look for the home of a spider, a bird, an insect, a fish, or other animals.

With *ears* to *hear*, he/she can . . .

—Sit very still and listen for nature sounds. (It will take a while before the inner-city child can tune out the sounds of trucks, planes, and sirens and hear the hum of insects, the chirp of a cricket, or the song of a bird.)

—Listen to the wind in the trees and detect the difference between a broadleaf maple tree and a pine tree.

—Listen to the different sounds of water—lapping at the edge of a lake, dripping after a rain, gurgling and murmuring in a brook, or swirling down a drain.

—Listen to the different sounds of the insects—high and low pitch, whirring, humming, buzzing.

—Put his/her ear to the ground and listen for the sounds of life underground.

With a *nose* to *smell*, he/she can:

—Identify the plants or weeds that have distinctive smells . . . sweet fern—pepper grass—wild onions—crushed leaves of yarrow—new mown hay—the root of a Queen Anne's Lace plant.

—Smell the swamp; compare the smell of dry sand and wet sand.

Taste is a sensory experience that must be undertaken with caution, stressing the dangers of putting unknown plants in the mouth. Many familiar berries and decorative plants are poisonous such as: the berries of bittersweet and the leaves of the rhubarb plant.

—But it is fun to make dandelion curls and taste them—to make staghorn-sumac punch—crush juniper berries and taste them—or pick blueberries and make muffins.

You and your campers can *feel*:

—A smooth beech leaf—the hairy elm leaf—a funny, felt-like mullein leaf rubbed against your face

—Prickly thistles—burdocks—chestnut burrs

—A fish—a worm—caterpillar—snake—frog—a bunny's face—the paws of a racoon—the underside of a mushroom

You can make a list of surfaces with different textures such as leaves, moss, trees, grass, mud, sand, concrete, asphalt, bricks, stone . . .
Make a list of descriptive words as children tell you how it feels to them—why they like or dislike it . . .
—Make rubbings. (See Art.)
—Blindfold child and ask him to identify . . .

What else can you do?
Nature is everywhere, and a nature program is less dependent on location than on the ability of a counselor to make the most of available resources.

What to Do in a Brook or Creek

—Fill a jar with brook water after a heavy rain and again on a clear, still day. Study with a magnifying glass.
—Use nets to dip from various parts of a brook or pond and put contents in a pail for further study.
—Turn over rocks and see what is under them. Remember to put them back.
—Walk with bare feet in sand or mud.
—Make a map of a brook showing the source and the end.
—Make stick boats with leaf sails and have a boat race.
—Build a dam and make a pool. Talk about beavers.

Things to Do in a Swamp or Marsh

—Look for the nest of the red-winged blackbird.
—Look on the underside of milkweed for the cocoon of the monarch butterfly.
—Look for and observe wild ducks, muskrats, turtles, frogs, birds.

At the Seashore

—Study the area between high and low tides. What can grow that is underwater half of the time and exposed to hot sun the rest?
—Put out markers and move them every fifteen minutes as the tide goes out. Measure the distance.
—Look for evidence of high water line—extra high.
—Collect shells to use in art projects.

Things to Do in the Woods

—Make and mark nature trails.
—See how many living things can be found in an old log.
—Collect seeds, rocks, berries, mosses, mushrooms.
—Hold treasure hunts and scavenger hunts.
—Go on hikes.
—Look for animal tracks.

What Can You Learn about Insects?

—Have you ever seen a praying mantis?
—Have you ever watched a cockroach clean its antennae?
—Have you ever chased grasshoppers in a field?
—Have you ever listened to crickets and katydids?
—Which insect makes its sound by rubbing its legs together?
—Catch a firefly in the evening at home and bring it to camp in a plastic container. (Let it go after you have observed it.)
—Have you ever seen mosquito wrigglers in the water?
—Have you ever watched a frog catch a fly?
—Have you ever watched a caterpillar eat a plant?
—Have you ever listened for the sound of a dragon fly?
—Have you ever made an insect cage? (See Arts and Crafts, Chapter 17.)
—Have you ever watched a spider spin a web?
—Have you ever collected a spider's web? (See Arts and Crafts, Chapter 17.)
—Have you ever watched ants come and go in an ant hill?
—How do they dig the hole?
—Have you ever watched them carry food, overcome obstacles and follow odor trails?

Feeding Live Insects

Grasshopper. Fresh grasses and weeds. Clumps of sod in the cage, watered occasionally, will last several days. Put soil in cage for them.

Beetles. Grubs, caterpillars, meal worms, a piece of rotten wood with soft insects in it will keep a beetle happy. Give him a tin of water, too.

Crickets. Wet bread chunks, lettuce, peanut butter. Give them soil to dig in.

Caterpillars, Tree Hoppers. Leaves from the plant on which they are found. Lettuce leaves. When they start spinning a cocoon they won't need anything.

Praying Mantis. Small, live insects, gathered by shaking a bush over newspaper, bits of raw, chopped meat.

What Can You Learn about Rock, Sand, and Soil?

Things to do in a grassy area:

—How many different plants can you find in a marked-off section? Compare this with an equal area of poorer soil.
—Look at a patch of grass through a hand lens. How many different colors are there?
—Blindfold a child and hand him something from the ground. How does it feel? Does he like it? Why?
—Show how grass helps save soil. Dig up a piece of sod and turn the hose on it to show how rain washes it away. Leave it with a fine steady spray and look at it from time to time. What happens?
—Watch water soak into the ground. Dig down and see how far it goes. Try a slow, steady spray and a forceful one. Which is better? A soaking rain or a heavy shower?
—Water goes down into some soils faster than others. Water carries soil from one place to another. This is called erosion.
—Stir different soils into a glass of water and watch the settling process.
—Plant seeds in different soils and chart growth process.
—Wet soil contains decaying vegetation called humus.
—Create a compost of leaves, small sticks, ground-up food waste, shells, etc. Plant beans, pumpkin, squash, or other fast-growing plants in mulch and some in regular soil; check the differences in growth rates.
—Dig up mulch from woods to show the differences in soil.
—Dig for worms in well-established mulch and in regular soil. Count. Where did you find the most life? What other things are in the two soils?
—Dig sand and gravel and count living creatures.

Trees

—How many different kinds of evergreens can you find?
—Can you tell an apple tree from a maple or an oak?
—Are you aware of the different branch patterns?
—Can you recognize a tree from a silhouette or a leaf?
—How many shades of green can you find?
—How do leaves grow on a branch? Opposite? Alternate?
—What textures can you find in leaves? Can you identify them by touch?
—How many different forms of animal life can you discover in and around a tree?
—How do different trees react to the force of the wind?
—Is there any tree you can recognize by the smell?

—What trees provide food? Have you tasted maple syrup? Spruce gum?

—Do trees smell different when they are rain soaked?

—Can you find any nut trees?

—What grows on trees that you can use for art projects? (Pine cones, pine needles, acorns, horse chestnuts, leaves)

—Can you find the stump of a tree that was chopped down?

—Have you looked at the roots of a tree?

—Do you know why one tree will blow down in a hurricane while another stands fast?

—Have you planted a tree? Watered a tree? Fed a tree?

—Look at furniture. Feel it. Can you tell what kind of tree it came from?

—How does rough wood compare with planed wood?

—Have you ever felt pine pitch on your hands?

—Have you ever counted the rings on a tree stump?

—Look for leaf skeletons. Why are they that way?

—Adopt a tree. Learn about your tree. Know the bark, the leaves, shape. How can you take good care of your tree? Measure the height and circumference. Write down; put in a safe place and measure again when you come back next year.

—Measure distance of shadow from trunk. How many people can sit within shadow?

—Can you find pieces of bark from wild cherry, sassafras, or black birch? Peel down bark and make lollipops.

—Stake off a small section of woods and clear away underbrush. Mark a section of the same size beside it and leave uncleared. Compare difference in growth of the trees the next year.

What Can You Learn About Growing Things?

—Plant and tend a garden.

—Plant sunflower seeds. They grow quickly to remarkable heights and attract birds.

—Plant scarlet-runner beans along a fence.

—Cut three saplings and lash them together at the top. Plant beans and let them grow up the poles, making a teepee.

—Show how house plants turn towards the light. Plants outside reach for the sun.

—Visit a market garden and ask about irrigation. Use plastic to create moisture.

—Visit an orchard and pick fruit.

—Conduct a controlled conditions experiment: in one cup put soil, seed, and water. In the second one just put the seed in water. In a third one, plant seed in soil but do not water it. Cover one cup with a dish to eliminate light. Cover one tightly to eliminate air. Resist the temptation to tell children what will happen. Let them discover . . .

Seeds

—Cut seeds open and examine parts.
—Look for seeds in plants and flowers. How many different kinds can you find?
—When there were no stores how did people get seeds? How could they make sure they would have a crop next year?
—Do potatoes and onions grow from seeds?
—Demonstrate power of seeds to grow. Plant in a baby food jar in water mixed with Plaster of Paris. Set in an aluminum pie plate. As seeds swell they will crack the plaster and break the jar.

What Can You Learn about Rocks and Stones? Sand and Soil?

—Talk about the differences between grains of sand, pebbles, stones, boulders, cliffs, ledges.
—Weathering rocks form sand and clay. Some rocks can crumble in your hand.
—Sand is fun to play with. Dry sand flows more smoothly than wet. Silver sand runs more freely than coarse. Very coarse sand is called gravel.
—Older children can make a bird bath.
—Put different grades of sand on a scale and see differences in weight.
—Put a limestone chip in one dish and another kind of stone in another dish. Pour a little vinegar on each stone. The limestone will fizz and bubble.
—Visit a quarry to see how granite and other stones are processed and cut into useful forms. Take a walk and look for stonework. Curbstones are often made of granite. Take a field trip to see cobblestones or show pictures of and tell how they are used.
—Encourage children to pick up stones at lake or beach on weekends and bring them in to display on table by size, color, and shape. (See many ideas for using Arts & Crafts, Chapter 16.)
—Study with magnifying glass.
—Look for a stone wall. Talk about origin—reason. (Older campers can read Robert Frost's "Mending Walls.")
—What lives in stone walls? (Snakes, chipmunks)

So we have given you more than one hundred suggestions—and we have only scratched the surface. We haven't even mentioned shadows, frogs, fog, wind . . . the world is yours—use it!

Ecology

The term ecology is one that is widely—and loosely—used today. For some it means "Don't be a litterbug." Others think of it in terms of conservation: "Don't use paper plates!" Pollution is very much a matter of public interest at the time this book is being written, and erosion is something that can be seen in almost any day camp. The subject is timely—and voluminous. The degree to which campers may become involved will depend on the knowledge and concern of their counselors.

Many of the activities listed above will serve the purpose of ecology as they help make children aware and appreciative of the natural world around them, as they begin to understand the interrelationships of all living things, and as they become conscious of the damage man does to his environment when he disturbs the balance of that relationship.

The activities described here are all so simple, so basic that *anyone* can engage in them. They are starting points—the beginning of a path which may branch off in many directions, but the counselor should bear in mind that the goal is to help develop a sense of awareness. It is not necessary to milk every experience for additional learning. It is better to stay loose, listen for cues from the questions the children ask. When it ceases to be fun and becomes a chore, back off and reassess your own goals.

chapter 18 | Adventures in Camping

What is adventure? My dictionary says it is "an unusual experience or course of events marked by excitement and suspense. An undertaking of a hazardous nature involving some risk." All of us have some deep-seated need for the experience that lifts us out of the ordinary, and children often live in a world of fantasy where they can be bigger, stronger, and braver than the person they see in the mirror. Unfortunately, in our society their needs are satisfied vicariously in front of the television set and their heroes are not cowboys and Indians but gangsters and killers. In our day camps we can provide experiences for our campers that open new areas of interest and excitement. They need not be elaborate or complex; they do not require counselors who have had extensive training—but they do rest on the ability of the adult to let his imagination take wing. An adventure can be as simple as cooking an egg on a hot rock in the sun, or baking a cake in a reflector oven. It can be as mysterious and as suspenseful as stumbling across clues to buried treasure—and eventually finding it. It can be building a hut—in the city from boards and boxes—in the country from saplings lashed together; it can be staying at camp until dark, sitting around a campfire listening to stories and singing camp songs.

Campcraft

Campcraft is an adventure to the growing child; learning how to build a fire and cook a meal over it; creating a bench, shelf, or table from wood which the camper chops or saws and lashes together with twine; washing with water out of a can suspended from the branch of a tree.

"That's all well and good if you have the facilities," one might say, "but how can you have a campcraft program on a city playground?"

187

The ideas offered in this chapter can be adapted to any environment if responsible counselors believe in the spirit of adventure and combine their energies to make it all come alive!

Campcraft Activities

The art of living out-of-doors without sacrificing comfort or safety is a totally new experience to most day campers—an introduction to a brand-new way of life. The wonder and amazement exhibited by the most sophisticated child when he sees a fire, food, or a useful gadget made with his own hands, guided by his own thought processes, is matched by noticeable changes in his total growth and development as he meets with success.

Though it is desirable to teach camping skills in a natural setting, it is possible to conduct a program in a very limited in-town environment. Fires can be built in metal containers (after the necessary permits have been obtained). Cooking can be more than roasting a hot dog or cooking a hamburger, and lashing and knot tying can be learned without the benefit of wooded areas. In planning a campcraft program, the director might keep the following points in mind:

—Allow plenty of time during the counselors' training session for demonstrations of, and active participation in, campcraft procedures. If possible, cook some of the meals, demonstrating various kinds of cooking.
—Provide a good resource book for every person who will be actively engaged in campcraft. The pocket edition *The Campcraft Book* by Catherine Hammett (American Camping Association, 1980) is inexpensive, basic in content, and easy to carry.
—Give campers sufficient time for happy learning experiences. This is not an activity that can be limited to a forty-minute schedule period.
—Keep camper groups small to insure participation and careful supervision.

The following suggestions could be made to the counselor who is responsible for the campcraft program:

—Become familiar with the grounds and all other areas to be used *before* camp opens.
—Get as much advance information as possible about the ages, experience, and abilities of campers who will participate in the program.
—Make a tentative plan for the season. Remember that *progression* is important. Each step must be within the camper's ability, and a completely satisfactory experience.

—Make a very specific plan for the first week. *Practice* everything you intend to try. You may learn with the campers, but in the beginning it is better to have them feel that you know and enjoy what you are doing.

Firebuilding

Whenever we ask children to do something normally forbidden, we have the beginning of excitement. Fingerpainting or playing in mud are activities which legitimize getting messy and dirty and children who have had cleanliness drummed into them find it hard to get involved.

Playing with fire is, of necessity, a "no no" and when we offer it as program it lends a bit of spine-tingling excitement, tinged with fear. The conversation that goes with learning how to build a fire is crucial. I use the word "conversation" because that means questions and answers, conjecture and discussion—not a lecture. What is good about fire? When is it bad? How did people make a fire before we had matches? This is a good time to make a design or sign by burning it into a piece of wood with a magnifying glass and explain how this same process can start a forest fire. (See Arts and Crafts, Wood Burning.)

Firebuilding for a Cookout

Children have a natural interest in fire and particularly in its creation. It is important to include fire prevention and the care of fire into program. Children need to learn what people do around a fire, and the rules regarding safety. Successful and consistent firebuilding takes much patience and practice. Children five and older should have the opportunity to help build and light a fire at some point during the summer.

Fire should be built *only* on sand, rock, or dirt, with no roots or other combustible material nearby. Cookout grills can also be used. Building a fire requires three types of materials:

—*Tinder* (finger wood) is used first because it catches fire very quickly and burns rapidly. Tinder includes small, dry twigs no larger in diameter than a small child's finger. It does not include newspaper, leaves, grass, or other materials like lighter fluid.

—*Kindling* includes wood that is dry and ranges in diameter from finger to thumb. It is usually six to twelve inches long. Kindling should snap when broken.

—*Fuel* includes pieces of wood and charcoal. The lower dead branches of trees are a good source. Green and rotten wood are poor additions to fire. Soft woods burn very quickly, hard woods burn slowly.

IT IS NECESSARY TO HAVE BUCKETS OF WATER AND SAND KEPT NEARBY TO EXTINGUISH A FIRE!

Hunter Trapper Fires

Three Stone Fire

Indian Fire

Fire Hole for Stewing

Building a Fire

1. Have a fireplace ready.
2. Collect tinder, kindling, and fuel and sort into piles by size.
3. Have safety pails ready with water and sand.
4. Keep the wind at your back.
5. Take two sticks of kindling to form an angle in the fireplace.
6. Pile tinder in the angle created by the sticks *lightly* so that there is air.
7. Light the wood at the *base* of the pile because fire burns upward.
8. As fire catches add tinder until the fire is brisk.
9. Add pieces of kindling one by one where the flames are strongest.
10. Gradually increase the size of the wood.
11. Gradually build fire in shape of teepee.
12. Slowly add fuel.
13. When fuel is burning well, cooking can begin.

Always make sure your fire is out completely before leaving the campsite or fireplace.

Additional Activities Related to Firebuilding

Experiment to see that fire needs air; put logs or sticks crosswise, and all in the same direction to see which burns better.

Build a fire with wet wood or on a rainy day. Know where to find driest wood, split logs, birch bark, fuzz sticks, and patience!

Know how to build trench, hunter's teepee, Indian, three stone, and altar-type fires and purposes of each one.

Outdoor Cooking

"Each camper will have a cookout once a week!" the brochure promises. What does it mean? All too often a visitor will find campers standing around watching the counselor as he tends hamburgers and hot dogs on a charcoal grill! That can hardly be described as an adventure! Cooking is exciting when you make your own stove and tools. In the city where fire building, as described here, might only occur in a metal wheelbarrow the following suggestions can still work:

—*Buddy Burners.* Take the lid off a tuna-fish can and make sure there are no sharp edges. Fold strips of newspapers the width of the side of the can. Dip in paraffin and coil around inside can until it is full. Use as you would Sterno.

—*Tin-Can Cooking.* Remove one end of a #32 can. Cut out a piece on one side (see sketch) and punch a few holes near the bottom on the opposite side. Make a small fire inside the can. Cook pancakes on top.

—*Box Oven.* Use a heavy carton with a central divider. Line *all* surfaces with heavy foil. Line flaps to serve as oven doors. Stand on end so divider forms a shelf. Place a pan of coals below and cook above.

—*Milk-Carton Cooking.* You can cook in a milk carton by cutting off the top, filling the carton with water, and setting it right in the coals to boil foods. (The water becomes heated first and carries heat away from carton.)

—*Paper-Bag Cooking.* Put two slices of bacon in the bottom of a paper bag. Break an egg on top of them. Fold the bag with a drugstore fold (several creases), put a stick through the bag, and hold over fire not touching coals. Food *will* cook, bag will *not* catch fire.

Clean Up

Know how to dispose of garbage, papers, and liquids properly. Know how to construct a grease pit or water drain and help make one for your unit site (either, both, or combination). Organize a good system for washing dishes either by constructing a dish stand or by taking charge of one part of cleanup after a cookout.

Making Your Own Tools

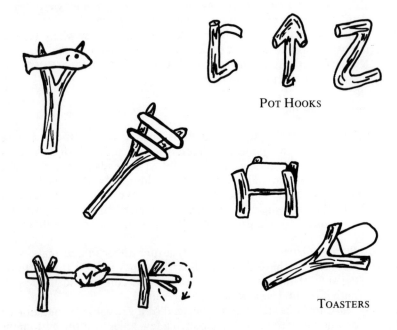

Pot Hooks

Toasters

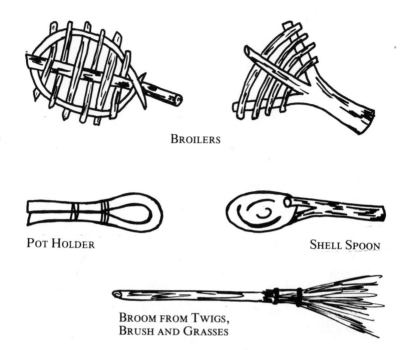

BROILERS

POT HOLDER

SHELL SPOON

BROOM FROM TWIGS,
BRUSH AND GRASSES

Man-made Tools

Every boy wants to use a jackknife. In camp where campcraft is stressed children will be taught how to use a saw, hatchet, and jackknife, but the potential hazards often scare off the day camp director from offering this experience. Certainly it is not to be taken lightly! It calls for adequate supervision, small groups (almost a one-to-one ratio), and mature counselors. When it does happen it is the ultimate adventure!

Lashing and Knot Tying

Instructions for these activities can be found in the Boy Scout Handbook. In the camp these represent an advanced stage of campcraft, probably beginning with eight-year-olds. Lashing could be used to make the tables and benches mentioned earlier in this chapter.

Other Activities Utilizing Natural Resources

The following activities might be considered introductions to campcraft since they lead to a familiarity with the woods:

Fishing. If campers can make their own poles from saplings they have cut down and if they can clean, cook, and eat the fish they catch, they will have had a memorable experience.

Trail Blazing. Divide into two groups. One lays the trail; the other follows. This is more exciting if the first group hides at the end of the trail to ambush those who follow. The final signal is a danger signal, so followers are warned.

Signs:

—On the trail—two stones—one on another, with one to right or left, give the direction.
—Go right or left. Three stones one on another is a warning.
—Stick pointing direction stuck in ground.
—Stick pointing direction placed on forked stick stuck in ground.
—Tuft of grass tied and bent in direction to be followed.
—Sticks or stones placed in V indicating direction.
—Danger. Three sticks in a row. Three stones one on top of other.
  Campers will enjoy making up their own set of signals.

Camouflaging. A variation of Hide and Seek in which players must hide in plain sight. This can lead into interesting discussions of the use of camouflage during wartime, and of how nature helps animals protect themselves by providing them with coloring to match their surroundings.

Hiking. There is nothing more exhilarating than swinging along a country road with congenial companions, sometimes with an objective, sometimes just for the fun of being out on the open road and in the out-of-doors. Hiking may well be a new experience for day campers, many of whom are accustomed to being transported wherever they go, and some real enthusiasm on the part of the counselor is often necessary to arouse their interest.

As in every activity, preplanning is important. If the hike will take campers off the grounds, it becomes doubly necessary to check all details. The steps to be considered might be as follows:

1. Discuss the trip with the camper group; where to go, what to wear, what to take.
2. Get permission from the director, if necessary, for the hike, and for use of any equipment or property.
3. Gather equipment:
   a. First aid belt—know how to use contents
   b. Compass
   c. Food, cooking equipment, canteen if needed
   d. Camp song book

4. Last-minute details:
   a. Drink of water or milk
   b. Everyone to the bathroom
   c. Distribute equipment to be taken
   d. Check each camper for proper attire; a sweater (which can be tied around the waist), comfortable shoes (sneakers are not suitable for hiking), and socks
   e. Tie lunches around the waist or over the shoulder or use pack basket. Walking is more comfortable if hands are free.

5. Sign out, listing these facts:
   a. Names of counselors and campers
   b. Time of departure and probable time of return
   c. Destination and planned route

6. Check arrangement for these services:
   a. Milk or equipment to be taken to destination
   b. Transportation for the return trip, if necessary

7. Rules of the road:
   a. A minimum of two counselors, one at the head of the group, the other bringing up the rear.
   b. Walk on the left side of the road facing traffic.
   c. No fires without permission.
   d. Do not pick wild flowers. Leave them for others to enjoy.
   e. Watch for poisonous plants and avoid contact.
   f. Remember, speed is not a consideration on a hike. Rest by trying "Scout's pace"—alternately walking twenty steps and running twenty steps. This lessens fatigue, and gives variety and novelty. Rest by lying flat on the ground with feet propped against a tree, thus letting the blood run out of the feet and resting them and the back at the same time. Rest at least one-half hour after lunch.
   g. Check for possible heel blisters. It is best to apply an adhesive bandage on a reddened area as a precaution.

Taking special kinds of hikes adds to the interest. On a *spot hike*, campers sit down a few feet apart every fifteen minutes and look for something interesting to describe to the others.

A *color hike* means finding as many yellow, green, or red things as possible.

A *tree hike* is a search for different kinds of trees.

A *touch hike* is to get the feel of different textures and surfaces— rough bark, furry leaves, soft moss, or prickly thistles.

Overnights

All campcraft procedures lead up to and involve practical application when the campers stay on an over night. This is usually the high spot of the season and a privilege younger campers look forward to eagerly. It has generally been found that seven-year-olds are capable of staying, but sixes have enough emotional and motivational adjustments to make without the added strain of sleeping away from home for the first time. Staying on an overnight can be compared with learning to swim; it often marks a definite upsurge of development in other areas. The camper gains a feeling of accomplishment and inner power which enables him to reach a little higher for success in other fields.

The advance notice sent to parents should be explicit and reassuring. It could include the following:

NOTICE TO PARENTS

—Aims of the over night
—Schedule of activities
—Menus for supper and breakfast
—Precautions for health and safety
—Clothing and equipment needs (to be marked)
—Extra charges (if any)
—Parents should be prepared to come for the child if it develops that he was not ready for the experience.
—Camp reserves the right to decide whether a camper is ready.
—Parents are asked to tell the counselors of any unusual eating, sleeping, or toilet habits.

SUGGESTED SCHEDULE

As soon as the other campers have gone, counselors gather over-nighters together and discuss plans, explain procedures, decide on necessary rules, and assign chores. A sample schedule might be this:

4:00-5:00 p.m.	Make up bed rolls on location where campers will sleep.
5:00-6:00 p.m.	Swim
6:00-7:00 p.m.	Supper. Clean up.
7:00-7:30 p.m.	Games. Flag lowering.
7:30-8:00 p.m.	Walk in woods.
8:00-8:30 p.m.	Campfire
8:45 p.m.	Bed
6:45 a.m.	Arise
7:30 a.m.	Breakfast
8:00 a.m.	Roll up bedding. Clean up camping location.

A Word to the Wise: Keep groups small. A camper/counselor ratio of five to one is desirable.

If campers sleep on the ground, a canvas square will keep heavy dew from soaking blankets.

If a walk in the woods after dark is to be included:

1. Take the campers over the route first in the daylight pointing out objects that might become frightening shadows at night.
2. Stop every fifteen minutes to listen for night sounds.
3. The walk will be exciting enough for most children without adult embellishments of ghostly noises or frightening stunts.

Homesickness often strikes right after the evening meal. Symptoms may be a headache or a stomachache. Try very hard to reassure the camper and encourage him to stick it out. Suggest that he try until bedtime with the assurance that if he wants to leave then, you will call his parents. Assure him that if he does stay you will sleep near him. Never insist that a camper stay if he really wants to go home. The time will come when he is ready for the experience, and forcing the issue too soon may only prolong that time.

Avoid ghost stories or other frightening stunts at the campfire or bedtime. It is usually the adult who thinks they are funny, not the camper, and the counselor will pay the price in lost sleep if nightmares result.

"Over-days"

Six-year-old campers, slightly envious of the tales told by over-nighters, but not quite ready to undertake the adventure themselves, can be satisfied with an over-day. This is good preparation for the overnight which will come later, just as the overnight in the day camp is a good introduction to resident camping.

The program will be similar to that of the overnight except that parents call for their children at eight o'clock.

Tents

Learn the meaning of terms—guy line, grommet, and the like. Help pitch and strike a pup tent.

Fire Building Contest

For as many groups as will participate, strings are set up as in diagram, tied between two stakes about ten inches off the ground. Two persons are chosen for each team; they will gather the wood, build, and light the fire. The first one to burn through the string is the winner. This can be very exciting with each group cheering on its team.

| chapter | Athletics and Camp Life |
| 19 | |

Our attitudes toward athletics and competition often mirror our social philosophies. If we believe that the world is a jungle where only the fit can prosper, athletics become a training ground for survival. Children have a natural drive toward competence, and an athletic program gives them an opportunity to master their environment. They learn on the playing field that hard work and attention to improve proper techniques are necessary elements leading to success. A child who learns to take pride in his "workmanship" will gain the discipline and self-confidence that will enable him to approach and master increasingly difficult tasks.

The success of an athletic program begins at the top—with administration. Attitudes, goals, and practices should be well thought out and articulated during precamp training. Possibly the most sensitive area would deal with competition. On the one hand there will be those who believe that competition is injurious, physically and emotionally, and should be eliminated in programs for young children. On the opposite side are those who argue that we are living in a highly competitive society; children cannot be protected forever, and sooner or later they must learn to function in a world which is competitive. Is there a golden mean between these opposing points of view? Possibly the answer lies in the age levels, with eight to ten at a time when competition can be introduced on a gradual basis.

Prior to that time it might be best to avoid games where the contestants "choose up sides." There will always be one or two who never are chosen and are constantly suffering humiliation. Athletics should be recognized for what they are—games. The reward should be for achievement, not for being best. When competition is treated at an adult level, children are inclined to "put down" the weaker members of their team, thus reducing the self-confidence and self-esteem of those campers who are less mature physically, less well coordinated, or simply less aggressive than their peers. It is the counselor who sets the tone for attitudes. He can encourage his campers to respect honest achievement and give credit where it is due and to help each other achieve. If he permits them to make insidious comparisons, "You are the worst hitter in the group!" he is teaching them that the way to success in later life is to climb over the backs of the weaker members of society. On the other hand, if he gives honest praise at every opportunity, "That was a good hit, you are really improving. Your hard work is paying off," he is providing a model which will be worthy of emulating. Counselors would be constantly aware that children will imitate their walk, the way they speak, their practices, and their attitudes. This is a great responsibility!

Athletics and Group Life

Pride in group accomplishment is just as important as pride in individual success. In a society where the population is constantly on the move, children have less opportunity to establish ties. Families go in diverse directions. Often they commute long distances and have little need to cooperate with or even establish a friendship with their neighbors. The ties people have to their communities are steadily declining. Volunteer associations that depend on the unpaid labor of women have felt the pinch as more and more women have joined the work force; churches have declined as a place where people come together and work for shared goals; and families, once dependent upon each other for production of the necessities of life, now go their separate ways.

Thus today, group athletics have become increasingly important as a means of developing a community spirit. It is on the athletic field that children learn that the members of a team must support and depend upon each other; that every cog in the wheel is important, and that the goal is not always winning but to put forth the best possible team effort.

Emphasis on playing well has another function. The more effectively a group of people work together, the greater their identification with the group, leading to a commitment to group norms and goals.

Growing up involves more than increasing autonomy from one's own identification. Societies in which citizens fail to extend their loyalties beyond their family circle have great difficulty in achieving national goals. The absence of wider loyalties discourages democracy and leads to economic inequality. When campers can learn to extend their loyalties beyond themselves and their immediate family, they are more likely to make moral and political contributions in their adult life.

Sex Differences and Athletics

Sexual equality is another sensitive area which might be brought out into the open and discussed at staff training sessions. We applaud the increasing recognition that:

—Members of the female sex are capable of achievement in the athletic arena.

—Women are entitled to the joys that come with common struggle toward victory on the playing field.

—Our own observation tells us that there are clear differences between male and female children which are relevant to the discussion of an athletic program.

—In strength and speed, pre-adolescent girls are the equal of boys.

—In stamina, most girls spend a disproportionate amount of time in physical activity and as a result, their stamina is not as great as their male counterparts.

—In skill and aggressiveness, we find enormous differences (author's opinion) between boys and girls. In a volleyball game, for example, when the ball goes over the net, eight-year-old boys are alert and ready to go after it, while even older girls, ages twelve or thirteen, will fail to shift position with the oncoming ball.

—Because of their greater skill, boys rarely sprain or fracture fingers while engaging in athletic games, but such injuries are common among girls.

—As attitudes toward the female sex have changed, we have noticed that girls are more seriously interested in athletic programs.

—The old views that boys and girls cannot and should not engage in sports programs together is as untenable as the new view that competitive sports should always be integrated. This ignores the fact that there are differences in skill, agressiveness, and interest. We believe that a responsibility policy requires respect for all differences.

Not every boy is wildly enthusiastic about athletics. It is wise to encourage all children to engage in some aspect of an athletic program which enables them to test their growing ability to make full use of their bodily skills. If at the same time we respect the diversity of interests among our campers we can teach them to be happy and tolerant in a society with ever more ambiguous role models. Thus freedom of choice is probably the best policy.

In conclusion, athletics are fun and should be a part of camp life. They are important for both the individual and group development, and today they present day camps with new challenges.

Swimming

This is usually the highlight of a day camp program, and thanks to the American Red Cross, most contemporary camps have good facilities and well-trained staffs.

A successful waterfront program must have the full cooperation of the entire camp community. No matter how good a waterfront staff may be, they will be ineffective without the enthusiastic support of the entire staff, the campers, and their parents. The commitment and involvement begins with the administrators, who set the rules and policies and communicate them to the parents when they enroll their children and to staff at precamp training. There are some aspects of the day camp program in which flexibility and creativity can be encouraged. Swimming involves an element of hazard, and so it becomes a black and white proposition with no gray areas. Reasonable rules are established and no exceptions allowed.

Parents are concerned about the swim program. Some will be anxious about health and safety and others about attention to skills and progress. These concerns should be anticipated and dealt with openly before the season begins. Policies should be in writing, but when parents visit before camp opens they can be given additional reassurance when the swimming program is explained to them ore explicitly.

During the season the camp newsletter, bulletins, or parent visiting days should continue to tell the story. When there is a problem, as with a child who constantly finds excuses not to go into the water, it is the responsibility of the camp director, or the waterfront director to call the parent and try to find the reason for the child's reluctance. It is much more than a recreational device; learning to swim may save a life in later years!

Rules will vary with each camp depending on such factors as the number of campers, the facility (pools or lake), the ages of the children, and the maturity of the staff. The basic rules that follow can serve as a starter.

Health

Licensing regulations may require showers or foot baths before entering a pool.

Whether the children will swim on a cold day or in the rain will be decided either by a camp nurse or the administration. In any event, it should be optional.

Counselors should watch children carefully in all weather. Some will be cold and shiver even on a warm, sunny day. They should be rubbed with a towel and allowed to lie in the sun.

Young children must be reminded to go to the toilet before a swim period and be warned not to urinate while in the water. Talking will not prevent it from happening, but presumably the chlorination process will compensate.

Safety

Even in the smallest pool, counselors must be stationed along the sides with their sole responsibility to keep an eye on every child. The swimming instructor *must* have this kind of support; he/she cannot teach and maintain constant surveillance at the same time.

Children should be taken out of the water during a thunderstorm. In a large pool or lake, lifesaving equipment must be immediately available and its use practiced on a regular basis.

Instruction

Parents should be assured that if a child is fearful, the staff will never force him, scold him, or make fun of him but they will use every means to encourage every child to participate.

Unless a child brings a note from home saying that he is to stay out of the water, every child will be required to put on a bathing suit and go to the pool.

Most day camps provide swimming instruction every day. Time is short and constant practice provides the physical conditioning that facilitates learning. This means that the waterfront staff must have the assistance and cooperation of every group counselor.

These people should receive some instructions during precamp on the basic methods to be employed.

Motivation

Children have an innate desire to achieve, to gain control over their environment, a natural drive toward competency. To a large extent, swimming offers its own reward. Children who make real progress on the waterfront are excited and proud, and happily expend remarkable energy. Some require more tangible motivation. The Red Cross has established a program of rewards (cards) for basic skills, but with very young children it often takes a whole summer to earn one card. Thus, Deerkill has established a whole series of symbolic rewards for swimming achievement.

We have a large bulletin board with the names of all campers, arranged alphabetically rather than by groups. A color code is used to indicate that a camper is working on beginner's skills, and a green number written beside his/her name as each test is passed. When all skills are passed, the numbers are covered with white surgical tape and a second row started with blue numbers. After a camper has passed the six easiest Red Cross Beginner skills he/she receives a Deerkill Beginner One card, which looks very much like a Red Cross card but clearly indicates what skills have been learned and identifies them with the phrase, ". . . has passed the following Red Cross skills." Most younger campers receive this card within two or three weeks of camps. They then begin work on the Deerkill Beginner Two card, which covers the next six skills. These cards provide intermediate goals which the children find exciting. Similar rewards are used for the Advanced Beginner and Intermediate levels, but only at the halfway point through their skills series, in contrast to the two cards given out at the beginner level.

Recognition for achievement may also be provided through the weekly camp newspaper which lists the names of all children who have received cards.

Some campers who are ten or twelve will require new challenges to maintain their interest in swimming. A competitive swimming program (ten-mile swim), water ballet, and lifesaving techniques offer inducement.

An excellent facility and a qualified staff will not insure a good swimming program. When it is fun for the campers, encouraged by the parents and supported by the administration and the counseling staff, it will be, as it should, the highlight of the whole camping program, and the greatest selling point a camp has to offer.

<table>
<tr><td>chapter
20</td><td>Musical Experience in
in the Day Camp</td></tr>
</table>

Music in the day camp is like a shiny gold thread woven through the tapestry of program; not a solid stripe of planned activity known as "the music period" but a sparkle of fun and joy woven through the entire day.

Everyone can participate in music in some way, even the person who says, "I can't carry a tune!"—"I sing like a frog!" Music and rhythm are like Siamese twins—they cannot be separated. If you can shrug your shoulders, clap your hands, snap your fingers, or stamp your feet you can have a musical experience with your campers!

Music helps to build camp spirit. When staff come together for training before the season opens, the singing of familiar songs and the remembering of old favorites sets the tone for an easy, relaxed atmosphere. It is the core of the indefinable something known as "Camp Spirit." But singing, probably more than any other aspect of camping, requires enthusiastic leadership. The camp director who is fortunate enough to employ a versatile leader is blessed, but more often than not this is a skill that is discovered rather than disclosed. Some people have not recognized it as an asset—others are shy about using it until they are comfortable in their surroundings. It was the archery counselor in one camp who developed a campers' choir and trained them to a level of achievement that gave them personal satisfaction and won the respect of their peers. In another case, the man hired to conduct a campcraft program turned out to be an excellent song leader. With an extensive repertoire of old and new songs he carried the entire camp through the season on a joyous musical "trip."

From him—and others along the way—we have learned a few pointers worth sharing.

Song Leading

Never try to teach a song by rote—"lining it out"—as they did in the olden days. Introduce it briefly and then say, "Now I will sing it and you help me just as soon as you know it." In the beginning select songs with a phrase or word everyone can join in on immediately, e.g., "Froggie Would A 'Courting Go." Everyone can sing the "A-hum." Do *not* exhort children to sing "nice and loud." Loud is not better. There is no need for sacrificing quality in a song session, and when shouting takes the place of singing, quality flies out the window!

Avoid negative exhortations such as: "Come on, I need you to help me! I can't stand up here and sing all by myself! *Sing* everybody!"

If your children are not responding, look at your agenda. Have you started with familiar songs? Have you planned variety—alternating funny songs with pretty songs? Are you having a good time?

Pitch

A good song is ruined if the leader starts it too high—or too low. Most people can sing comfortably between A and G. If the leader is not musical enough to be able to find this level, it is best to use a pitch-pipe or instrument bells to help. When the pitch is off it is far better to acknowledge the error and start over. A guitar or autoharp will alleviate this problem.

Tempo

Many song leaders have a tendency to D-R-A-G out songs. Try to keep them at an appropriate tempo; for instance, "She'll Be Comin' 'Round the Mountain" would be sung with more vigor than "You Are My Sunshine."

Resources

It is essential for the leader to know the words to a song before attempting to lead a group in singing it. It is also important to have a variety of songs ready to offer. It is so easy to get stuck in the "crack of the record" and sing the same songs day after day. A tool that will help counselors to introduce a wide variety, to sing at the right pitch and tempo, and to learn words is the tape recorder. One or two of the camp's most versatile song leaders can be asked to record a number of songs, and these tapes can be used by small groups or individual counselors.

There are many good song books available, some of which are mentioned at the end of this chapter, but sometimes it is only the reminder that is needed. The lists that follow serve that purpose. There are songs for every occasion: songs to help counselors through the day without constant nagging and issuing orders, songs to use when extreme weather interrupts program, and songs to fill in the moments when waiting is necessary. These lists will be supplemented by staff when the mood is set. "We sang this one when I went to camp!" "Did you ever hear this one?" "We had a song with our camp name in it—perhaps we could substitute this camp name!"

Singing Just for Fun

Everyone who ever went to camp remembers the silly, fun songs that barely fit into the category of music. These songs lend a note of humor and sheer rollicking joy to the song session. Spaced between the rounds and more harmonious songs, they allow the audience to move, and when participation is lagging, a song like "Michael Finnegan" will get everyone involved again.

The favorites listed here are only intended as reminders. Counselors will usually recall others they enjoyed when they were campers.

Supercalafragilisticexpialodocious
Clap, Clap, Clap Your Hands
Under the Spreading Chestnut Tree
Michael Finnegan
I Am a Fine Musician
She'll Be Comin' 'round the Mountain
John Brown's Body
My Hat She Has Three Corners
Did You Feed My Cow?
Fox Went Out on a Chilly Night
Animal Fair
There Was an Old Lady
John Jacob Jingle Heimersmith
Did You Ever See a Lassie?
Oh, the Noble Duke of York
Five Little Speckled Frogs
Little Rooster by the Barnyard Gate
I'm Going to Sing When the Spirit Says Sing
I've Been Working on the Railroad

Familiar Folk Tunes

When choosing songs to sing with young children we turn first to the familiar folk tunes passed on from one generation to another. They belong to everyone; they are easy to learn, within easy voice ranges, and have a simple basic rhythm. They have lasted because they came from the heart; they grew out of real-life experiences.

Sea chanties were sung by sailors who led a very monotonous life. Confined to ships for months at a time, far away from home and loved ones, they were overworked, often badly treated, and underfed. As they swabbed the decks, climbed the ropes, and polished the brass they sang to keep up their spirits. The rhythms of the chanties were a vital force in many of the shipboard tasks.

The cowboy riding the expanse of the great western ranges sang to himself, to his horse, and to his herds to dispel the loneliness and to calm the restless animals. As we sing his songs we feel the rhythm of his horse, loping along.

The men who built railroads across this vast continent and the blacks who picked cotton under southern skies spoke to us of the physical hardships they endured through the songs they have handed on to us. These folk tunes depict the very fibre of a developing nation and are a priceless contribution to our national heritage. As they are introduced to our children with brief explanations of their origins and uses, the child begins to have an awareness of his/her country's history.

One way to spark camp spirit is to make up camp songs, or individual group songs. There are many simple familiar tunes that lend themselves easily to improvising words.

The following songs are good for this purpose because the tunes are familiar, simple, and rhythmic:

Frere Jacques
Twinkle, Twinkle Little Star
The Bear Went Over the Mountain
What Shall We Do When We All Go Out?
Goodnight, Ladies
You Are My Sunshine
Jingle Bells
Little Brown Jug
Where, Oh Where, Has My Little Dog Gone?

Songs that Can Be Used for Skits and Dramatizations

Hole in the Bucket
Soldier, Soldier, Will You Marry Me?
Thorn Rosa
Minerva
Three Sailors Came to London Town

Songs for Beauty and Harmony

Contrast sharpens the edges of perception. We enrich the "feeling" side of our campers when we alternate fun songs with those pleasing to the ear. Introduce simple harmony as in rounds, inculcate values as in

"America, the Beautiful," or stir the sentiments as when we clasp hands at the end of a singing session and sing "Happy Trails."

Some favorites are:

Whole World in His Hands
Rock-A-My Soul
Kum Ba Yah
Down in the Valley
Hush Little Baby
All Night, All Day
Michael, Row Your Boat Ashore
Jacob's Ladder
When the Saints Go Marching In
Rise and Shine
Swing Low, Sweet Chariot
Home on the Range
This Land Is Your Land

Rounds

Rounds are the child's first introduction to harmony. The blending of tones comes as a surprise to young children and even seems to have a touch of magic. The following favorites can be found in most camp song books.

Row Row Row Your Boat
Three Blind Mice
Kookaburra
Little Tommy Tinker
White Coral Bells
Make New Friends But Keep the Old
Why Couldn't My Goose?

Another way to introduce harmony is to sing two songs simultaneously. For example, one-half of a group sings "Let Me Call You Sweetheart" while the other half sings "My Wild Irish Rose."

"Daisy, Daisy" and "Bicycle Built for Two"

"Frere Jacques" and "London Bridge"

Songs for Getting Acquainted

It's the first day of camp. Counselors and campers are meeting many for the first time. The immediate task at hand is to make the campers feel comfortable in this new situation, and to do this we start with the one familiar thing they brought with them—their names. When you address a person by name—pronouncing it correctly—you pay him an honor. You establish his "place in the sun" and you reassure him if he is anxious: "Someone knows me! I will not get lost in the crowd!"

One this first day it is important for each counselor to spend enough time alone with his group to help them get acquainted and establish the necessary ground rules for daily living in his camp family. Ideally he will have received a list of his campers in advance and will have memorized their names. Putting names and faces together can best be done with a few simple songs.

Planning and Conducting Large Group Assemblies

Singing is the alternating current that keeps an all-camp assembly alive. Such assemblies should not be all singing; they provide an arena for the presentation of skits, stunts, dramatic productions, announcements, and special commendations. Interspersed with these, the songs will be the spark that maintains the interest of the group.

The leader might find the following suggestions useful:

1. Have a planned agenda—a list of songs that will alternate sitting still with moving; listening with participating. Children cannot sit still for very long at a time—they need to "get into the act," and there are many fun songs that give them that privilege.
2. Keep it moving! This is another reason for the song list. There can be no delays while you try to think of another song—or ask the audience to suggest one. A song session should be fast, sprightly, and carry the audience along a note of fun and unity.
3. Insist that counselors sit with children, placing themselves strategically so they can reach out and touch a child who is acting up. They are expected to give the leader full support by singing, controlling behavior, and showing enthusiasm. Unless you make this clear from the outset, counselors will cluster together across the back of the group—and the hapless leader will be doing the job alone!
4. Each session should have a clearly defined beginning and end. Establish procedures in advance for ending session and moving away. Usually it is better to dismiss one group at a time.

Singing on the Bus

Day camp does not begin when the campers arrive at camp—it starts with the moment the parent hands the responsibility for the child over to a representative of the camp. In many cases this is the driver or bus leader. The ride each way may take as much as one hour and we cannot turn off the natural behavior of children for those two hours each day. If we expect them to become automatons we are in for a rude awakening. There are some games that can be played on the bus, but singing is the best method for keeping behavior under control. The rules for leading large group assemblies can be relaxed for the simple reason that you have a captive audience—anchored in one place. This is a good time to let campers test their leadership abilities—to teach the words to a new song, or to try a new round.

Singing name songs as children board the bus gives the day a nice start, and by the same token singing them off the bus is a happy ending to a good day.

Will you sing the same songs going home that were appropriate in the morning? Maybe, but these are not the same children. In the morning they were bright-eyed and bushy-tailed. Going home they are pleasantly weary and some of the littlest ones may drop off for a nap. This is a good time to sing the long drawn-out many-versed repetitive songs: the songs which bore adults to frustration but which children enjoy. They do help to wind down the day because they go on—and on—and on . . .

Samples are:

Around the Corner and Under the Tree
Hole in the Bucket
Patsy-atsy Oree-ay
Honey You Can't Love One
Ki-yi-Ki-yi-Kus
Old MacDonald
Coming Round the Mountain
Wheels on the Bus
Nick nack, paddy whack

Other Musical Experiences

Dancing

In some day camps this may be a specialized activity with instruction but Play Party Games for younger campers and square dancing for the teens are fun for all.

Older campers like to make up their own dances. Divide into groups of four to six. Give each group a song (example: A-Tisket, A-Tasket) and allow them ten minutes to create a dance, which they will then perform for the entire group. (See The Day Camp Program Book for further suggestions.)

Rhythm Band

Although this is often presented to kindergarten children, the real desire and ability to participate in such an organized activity is more appropriate for children six to eight. At this age the effect of motion and sound in unison gives a sense of satisfaction and they are able to listen and follow directions. At first it might be best to start with some of the records mentioned at the end of this chapter, but as children become more adept they will enjoy experimenting with combinations of sounds and rhythmic patterns on their own. It would be well to purchase a few instruments—cymbals, triangles, a Chinese wood block, and a good hand drum—but the real fun will be in creating sound effects with instruments made in conjunction with the arts and crafts department. (See Chapter 16, Arts and Crafts.)

Jug Band

This is an experience that can be as simple or sophisticated as the inclinations of the group who perform. It begins with the discovery that when you blow across the mouth of a small-necked jug it creates a musical tone. With experimentation specific notes or tunes can emerge.

Add to this a washtub drum, which produces a real bass note when the string is twanged. Fill out your band with various utensils gathered from the kitchen. A set of measuring spoons will make one type of shaker and a large salt shaker filled with pebbles, beans, or rice will produce a different effect. When the lids of aluminum, steel, copper, and tin pots are suspended from a string tied around the knob and struck with any metal tool they produce a variety of musical tones. The possibilities to be found in the kitchen are endless.

Musical "Instruments"

Fill eight drinking glasses with water at different levels and try to tune them to the notes of the scale.

Bring in a goblet of fine crystal, wet the edges and run your finger around the brim. It will make music and the children will be fascinated!

Make wind chimes with pieces of metal tubing, shells, bells, etc.

Experiment with a piece of hose. Blow through it. Blow across the end. Make holes in it and blow through it. Put your finger over one hole at a time and try again. Try it with a funnel on one end. Purse the lips and play it as you would a wind instrument.

Put funnels on both ends of a fifteen-foot length of plastic tubing. Talk through it. Hum a song through one end and let the person on the other end guess the tune.

Put a piece of tissue paper over a comb and hum through it.

Create sound effects to enhance dramatic production, shaking a sheet of aluminum to make thunder.

Coconut halves clapped together for the sound of horses' hooves. Strike a cymbal for a gong.

Use dowels of different sizes for clocks, i.e., broomsticks for steeple clocks, half-inch dowels for mantel clocks, and pencils for wristwatches.

Pinch the end of a drinking straw and make a diagonal cut to bring to a point. Blow through the straw to make sounds. Make several of varied lengths. Each will have a different tone.

Experiment with vibrations with the following demonstrations:

—Put elastic bands around a box and pluck them. Try different widths.
—Pluck a guitar and/or autoharp.
—Tap a drum.
—Place a hand on larynx and hum.
—Tie a string on each side of a cake rack. Hold the strings in your ears while someone runs a fork across the rack.

The ideas suggested here can be developed and extended with the help of the following books:

The Day Camp Program Book
  Virginia Musselman, Follett 1980
ACA Song Book
Children Discover Music and Dance
  Emma Sheehy, Teacher's College Press
Creative Music for the Developing Child
  Claire Cherry, Fearon
Fireside Book of Children's Songs
  Winn and Miller, Simon and Schuster
Making Music Your Own
  Silver Burdett

chapter
21

A Bag of Tricks

So now you are a camp counselor! Perhaps this is the first time you have been responsible for program—and you are feeling a bit anxious. The best thing you can do by way of preparation is to fill your "bag of tricks!" Start with your own childhood memories. What games did you like to play? Remember those silly riddles like "Knock! Knock!"

What simple magic tricks challenged your powers of observation and tested your wits?

What books did you like best?

If you can dredge up memories that elicit a warm glow, then you can be assured that these same things will appeal to your campers. As you think about them, jot down reminders—key words—punch lines. You may think you will remember them but when you are faced with a group of campers be prepared to have your mind go blank—it happens to the best of us!

Methods for Gaining the Attention of a Group

Before you can make use of the following suggestions you must first be able to get your campers to sit still long enough to hear about your ideas.

Probably the most important tricks in your bag are methods for gaining the attention of your campers. These are the years when voices are loud and everyone wants to be heard at the same time. The bewildered counselor stands in front of a group, "O.K. now, listen everybody!"

"Listen," he says, his voice rising. Snapping his fingers for attention and clapping his hands, he shouts in desperation "How can I tell you what we are going to do if you don't listen?" and finally he bellows "Q-U-I-E-T," the ultimate irony.

Some counselors rely on whistles to control their campers. They shrill their way through the day, blowing the whistle to signify "Go," "Stop," "Get in the pool," "Get out of the pool," "Someone is misbehaving." The whistle-blower feels powerful, the campers move like robots, and the environment is polluted with unnecessary noise.

No one expects lively campers to tiptoe around camp, whispering, but there are some simple, common-sense ways to oil the wheels of camp life so their squeaking doesn't frazzle the nerves. These should be discussed and practiced during precamp training.

The first, and most basic rule is never shout across the room, field, or playground at a camper or fellow counselor. It takes only another few seconds to walk over to him and speak in an ordinary tone of voice. If this one rule alone were to be practiced the difference in the overall tone quality would be startling!

A second rule is to plan ahead. This is especially true in moving from one place or activity to another. Instead of, "Let's see—now we go to archery. O.K. kids, let's go!" the counselor says, "We are going to archery now. You may go ahead of me but please stop and wait when you get to the flagpole."

Some ground rules should be established at the outset for group meetings. "One person will talk at a time—and everyone will have a chance to speak."

Body language can be an effective way of reducing unnecessary chatter. "Let's make a set of secret signals that give messages. For example, if I hold my hand up high with the palm up like this it means 'stand up' and if I hold it down here with the palm down it means 'sit down.' Now what other signals can you think of?"

(This would be a good time to introduce the game "Indian Chief" described later in this chapter.)

The time-tested method used by Scouts—the upraised hand—is a form of body language that works with large groups. The leader raises his hand high in the air. As others notice they follow suit, and stop talking. When all hands are in the air it is quiet and the leader can proceed.

Any one method gets boring if it is used too often, so we have used the following ditty which serves the same purpose:

Oh, you push the damper in   *(pushing motion with right hand)*
sol sol do do   do do do

And you pull the damper out   *(pull hand back)*
sol sol do do   do do do

And the smoke goes up the chimney just the same   *(Circling upward)*

Oh, you push the damper in   *(pushing motion with right hand)*
sol sol   do do do do do

And you pull the damper out   *(pull hand back)*
sol sol do the do do out

And the smoke goes up the chimney just the same   *(Circling upward*
sol sol do do do re me me re do re   *motion with index*
                                                   finger)

Just the same, just the same   *(open hands)*
me fa sol me re do

Oh the smoke goes up the chimney just the same
sol sol do do do re me me re re do

Repeat with motions only. This will reduce a group of fifty or more to complete silence and at its conclusion the leader can address them in an ordinary tone of voice.

Another way to quiet a large group without shouting is to start clapping, motioning to those closest to you to follow suit. The leader then manipulates the group by adjusting the rhythm (faster and slower) and the tone (loud and soft), by raising and lowering his hands, gradually winding it down until only the tips of the fingers are touching—very slowly.

Start singing a familiar song ("Jingle Bells") and when all have joined it tone it down—softer and slower until it is just a whisper.

Stand in front of a few children and start a motion (i.e., tapping top of your head). As more children join in, change the motion. When all are participating, slow down and bring to a stop.

Have drum signals with different meanings. Call it "drum talk" with signals meaning wash your hands, snack time, let's go outside, etc.

Get out a balloon or paper bag and start to blow it up. Children will stop to see what you are going to do.

One feature that distinguishes day camp from school is that camp counselors are expected to have as much fun as the kids. Traditionally, teachers stand in front of a group and instruct, but counselors participate in the action. This should be discussed at precamp training, stressing that when counselors have a ball the success of the program is assured. This is particularly true in the skits and stunts that add spice and an atmosphere of FUN to the campers' day.

Skits and Stunts

The word "skit" frightens some people who think of a prepared script and rehearsed presentations. Some planning certainly is necessary and costuming adds a new dimension, but preparations and rehearsals need not take so much time that they interfere with the counselor's first responsibility—his campers. Skits can be brief and very silly, bordering on the ridiculous—but never at the expense of another human being. They should never be crude or vulgar, or poke fun at ethnic groups or customs.

Nursery Rhymes

Counselors act out nursery rhymes, campers identify.

Dramatizing Familiar Songs

1. Four Green Speckled Frogs (counselors faces are made up with green paint.)
2. Soldier, Soldier Will You Marry Me?
3. Old Woman, Old Woman!

The Viper. Over a period of a week, month, or the entire season signs appear in unexpected places—"THE VIPER IS COMING." Occasionally someone will dash madly through the area shouting, "THE VIPER IS COMING!" Only one or two people are "in" on the secret so suspense builds among staff as well as campers. Finally the word is leaked out that "This is the day! The viper is coming!"

"Who is it?" What is it?" The excitement grows. During end-of-day assembly a disreputable figure, clothed in coveralls and carrying a pail and mop, ambles out in front of the group. "Get out of the way!" the leader shouts, "the viper is coming." "I am the viper," he answers slowly, "The Vindow Viper!"

Putting on a Face!

Blindfold two counselors, provide them with lipstick, rouge, eye makeup, and face powder and have them make up each other's faces.

Clown Act

Two counselors dressed as hobos or cleaning women chase each other around. One picks up what appears to be a pail of water, runs to the front and throws it at the audience. (Confetti has been substituted for the water.)

Small Car

Choose the smallest car available and hide as many counselors as possible in it, all dressed as clowns. They drive out in front of the audience and climb out—one at a time. (For the few moments the skit takes they can be stacked on the floor, crouched down in front, and even in the trunk.)

Barbershop

Customer enters barbershop and asks for a hair cut. Barber says, "I think you need a shampoo." The patter is important, "Oh my, your hair is in terrible condition, I'd better give it my special treatment" as he breaks an egg on the victim's head and rubs it in. "Have you noticed that your hair is falling out? If it keeps up this way you will be bald. I have something here that will feed it," as he pours ketchup on and smears it around. "Now we add some of this super distilled powder—make a paste and let it set for a few minutes. Close your eyes and relax. Shall I give you a transogenic rinse? It will make your hair shine and give it body!" At this point an accomplice sneaks up and dumps a pail of water over the long-suffering victim.

Towel Snatch

Two teams are chosen, six on each team. Each one sticks a towel in the back waistband of his shorts. Object is to snatch opponent's towel without losing his own.

Balloon Stamp

Same as above, only tie balloons to ankles. Try to stamp on and break.

Suitcase Relay

Two lines—one male and the other female. Males are given a suitcase with girl's clothing.

Girls are given a suitcase with shirt, pants, jacket, shoes, and hat.

First person puts on garments, runs to a given point, returns, takes off garments, puts them back in suitcase, and tags next in line.

Carnivals

Preparing for a carnival can be as much fun for campers as the actual event. The very word suggests color, music, and gaiety. A supply of flags, bunting, crepe paper streamers, pennants, and other decorations may be stored ready for use. Roofing buttons (tin discs, which can be purchased by the pound from building supply houses) may be used for money or awards, which can later be redeemed for more tangible prizes. Dried kidney beans serve the same purpose.

Games of Chance for Children

—Pitching tennis balls into a #10 can set on the floor, or fastened to a pole.

—Ping-pong balls rolled into a muffin tin set on a slant. (Holes are numbered.)
—Clothespins dropped into a milk bottle.
—Pennies or roofing buttons tossed onto numbered saucers floating in a tub of water.
—Wet sponges thrown at the face of a camper or counselor who puts his head through a hole in a sheet.
—A nail pounded into a block of wood with three blows.
—Jar rubbers thrown onto a board with numbered cup hooks.
—A candle flame put out with water pistol.
—Matches blown from a straw into a tub of water.

Olympics

—Shot put with balloons or blown-up paper bags
—High jump from standing position with broomstick
—Broad jump from standing position
—Javelin throw with drinking straws
—Discus throw with paper plates
—Standing broad grin—measure width of grins
—Running high whistle—time length of sustained whistle
—Feather blow relay—blow a feather, run and retrieve it, and touch off next player
—Foot race—measure combined length of both feet
—Jumping over a broomstick held in both hands.

Games

One of the most valuable resources a counselor can have is a variety of games suited to every occasion: quiet games for small spaces, active games for cool days when swimming is out of the question, sit-down games for hot days when active children are content to sit under a tree, games used to fill in waiting periods, games that develop the senses and increase awareness, and games just for fun.

There are many excellent books of games available but when the game is needed it should be in the counselor's head, not on the library shelf. Enthusiasm will be lost if the counselor has to hunt for an idea.

During the training period a game session will help to stimulate more ideas. In playing games with children, the following simple suggestions may be kept in mind:

1. Know the play interests or abilities of your group. When deciding which game to introduce, consider temperature, space, size of group, age and skill of players, time of day, mood of group.
2. Get group into game formation. Start with few directions. Then start playing. Learn by doing.

3. Know the game and the rules, and the song if it is a singing game. Know an easy way to play as well as ways to make a game progressively harder, depending on ages.
4. Watch for signs of fatigue and restlessness. Rest the group by alternating active and quiet games.
5. Play game only as long as it holds interest of the group.
6. Introduce a variety of games to group so each child may succeed.
7. Be absolutely fair.
8. Stress cooperation, not competition. Competition limits happiness and success to a few.
9. Avoid elimination games. Slow children are always eliminated first and they are the ones who need to play and develop skills.
10. Do not spoil the fun of playing games by granting special privileges, making unfair decisions, or using one person as the butt of a joke.

Games to Play with a Ball

Wiffle Ball: Needed—bat, wiffle ball, three bases, and someone to pitch. Adapt a small area by using one base. Everyone gets to hit and must wait on base to be hit home.

Soccer: Larger ball, two goals, two goalies, and a referee. Adapt to small area by using one goal and have several goalies as one team, and one player trying to kick it into the goal.

Kick Ball: One ball, three bases, and a pitcher—to be played like wiffle ball, except one kicks the ball instead of hitting it. Again, adapt to the area. One base may be used.

Toss Ball: All stand around in a circle. The ball is tossed up in the air, and a name is called. That person must run to catch the ball before it touches the ground. This person is now the tosser and will call another name.

Straddle Goal: This time the person in the center of the circle tries to roll the ball to the outside of the circle. The children may try to stop the ball with their hands. They may not close their legs or change the straddle position.

Air Ball: The ball, on a signal, is tossed up in the air, and all share in keeping it from hitting the ground. There is a "counter" who keeps track of how many times it leaves one child's hands and makes it to another before dropping.

Volleyball: The net can be any string tied at an appropriate height for little children, and the ball should be light and large. This can be a team effort or played by as few as two. Young children will catch ball instead of tapping it.

Balloon Volleyball: This is great for indoors. Add some paddles made by stretching a nylon stocking over a wire coathanger and you have a variation of badminton.

Very Active Games:

Duck, Duck, Goose: The children sit in a circle while one child walks around the outside touching heads, saying "Duck." When he says "Goose" the child he touches chases him around the circle. If he can make it back to the empty spot the "Goose" is "it."

Drop the Flag: Variation of Duck, Duck, Goose. The child does not say anything as he walks behind, and all wait for him to drop the flag (scarf or whatever). When it is dropped, that person is then the chaser.

Midnight: One child is the fox. A line is drawn for the other children to stay behind safe from the fox. The children start out slowly toward the fox asking, "What time is it, Mr. Fox?" Mr. Fox replies by saying any time he wants but when he says "Midnight" he starts chasing them. All who are caught then become foxes and join in on the chase until all are captured. Vary by providing several safe spaces.

Giants and Dragons: Two lines are drawn with a group of children behind each one. The giants tiptoe toward the dragons and can do so safely until the signal "The dragons are coming" is given. Then the giants try to get home without being tagged by a dragon. If tagged, they then become dragons and are still in the game. Game ends when all are dragons.

Rabbit: Children form groups of three: two holding hands to form a "home" and the third standing inside. In addition one child becomes the rabbit seeking a safe home and another the hunter. The rabbit who is being chased may go into any occupied home, displacing the child in that home who then becomes the pursued. If the hunter catches the rabbit that person then becomes the hunter.

Cat and Mouse: Good for older children. Form circle, holding hands tightly. The cat on the outside is trying to get at the mouse inside. Players help the mouse by letting him in and out of the circle. They can hinder the cat by keeping him from entering or leaving the circle. Can be rough.

Bean Bag Snatch: Make two lines facing each other. Give numbers to players on each side. When number is called, the two players run to the center and snatch the bean bag. Keep score—one point for each snatch.

The child who snatches the bean bag must try to get back safely over his own line without being tagged by the other.

Fun Activities for Large Group Assemblies

Whoa Dobbin (Indoor Activity): Leader: Listen! I think I hear a pony coming down the road." (Taps lightly on the floor with one finger nail.) "He's coming closer." (Taps with two fingers) "Closer!" (Taps with one hand, increasing speed) "Here he comes!" (Both hands, very rapidly) (Jumps to feet and shouts) "Whoa Dobbin! He's going away again!" (Reverse motions two hand, one hand, two fingers, one finger) "He's gone!"

Three Blue Pigeons:

Together— me re do   sol fa me
         Three blue pigeons   Three blue pigeons
           do sol do la sol   fa me re   do
         Three blue pi-i-igeons   Sitting on a fence
Leader, dramatically "Oh, look! One flew away!"
Audience groans—cries.
       One blue pigeon
       No blue pigeons

Audience gets more vocally grief stricken with each verse. Leader pauses—(walking around, head down, hands behind back and suddenly points and shouts) "Look! Look! One came back!" Audience claps and cheers. Repeat dramatically until all three pigeons are back on the fence.

Note: This is in the same category as fingerpainting and fire building. It gives children a chance to do that which is usually unacceptable. A great way to let off steam, really shout, and make a lot of noise.

The Bear Hunt: In this game the children sit in front of the leader who sits cross-legged. Audience repeats every word after leader. They follow his lead on action. The key is to overdramatize. Use your voice to build the excitement. "Let's go bear hunting! Take down the gun." (Reaches for the gun) "Look it all over. O.K. let's go. (Slaps hands on knees for walking) "Oh oh—a big hill" (Slaps slowly, grunting, as if straining up hill) "Ahhhh! We made it—run down the other side" (Slaps rapidly) (Walk some more) "Oh oh, tall grass" (Make breast stroke motions saying 'swish—swish') "Phew! (Wiping brow) "That was tough! Well, here we go again" (Slapping motion) "OHHHH! (groaning) a river. What shall we do? How can we get across?" (Looks around shading eyes with hand) "I see a boat!" (excitedly) "Come on. Get in the boat. Row across the river!" (Rowing motions, grunting with effort) (Walking again) "Now what?" (disgustedly) "A swamp!" (Pull one hand at a time as if pulling feet out of mud saying 'Uck! Uck!) "Now we are almost there. Better go slowly—walk softly." (slaps on knees softly) "There's a cave!" (whispering) "Let's look in! I see an eye! I see two eyes! It's a bear! Let's get out of here!" (shouting) (Reverse all previous actions—rapidly. Running, swamp, rowing, tall grass, running up hill, down hill, walking) "Home again!"

Train Station: A ball of string is the track the train must follow. The string is unwound, and every few feet there is a chair. The chair is the station, and each child has his own station. The signal is given, and directions are announced as to how they will get to the next station—hop, walk backwards, crawl, etc.

Going on a Walk: Dramatization of the oral commands of the leader. Decide what kind of walk it will be: a space walk, walk through the jungle, underwater walk, etc. Respond with the whole body full of exaggerations.

Sometimes I'm Tall: One child is blindfolded. The others stand and respond to the verse:

Sometimes I'm tall, Sometimes I'm small.
Sometimes I'm very, very tall;
Sometimes I'm very, very small.
Guess what I am now?

The leader decides which level the children remain at, and the blind-folded child's clue is during the last line when he tries to guess by the voice level.

Games of Skill

Drop Clothespin into Milk Container: Do this from standing position. Involves good eye/hand coordination.

Drop Ball Into: Coffee can, cupcake tins, egg carton, shoe boxes, gelatin mold pan, tire. Each of these containers might suggest a different kind of ball—ping pong ball, tennis ball, large beach ball. You could vary by suggesting balls be thrown, bounced, or dropped. You could challenge by drawing a line for starting, and use objects as targets. Possibilities unlimited . . .

Toss-Across Bean Bag Games: Targets for bean bags can be made very easily from cardboard boxes. Any of the above can be used as well.

Bean-Bag Tic-Tac-Toe: Can be made by taping form to floor and placing token where bean bag lands until three in a row is accomplished by one child.

Bowling Games: Use a variety of objects for pins: bottles, cans, paper towel tubes, blocks, boxes. Vary the kind of ball with the pins. Let the children come up with their own suggestions for balls and pins.

Table Hockey: Use popsicle sticks as hockey sticks and tiny balls of paper as puck. Set goals, and provide edges, using blocks, or set inside a clothes box with sides about two inches high.

Ping Pong Puff: One must blow the ping pong ball over the center line. The opposing players are defending their line and advancing toward yours. If the ball gets to the other side, hits someone, or rolls off, the opposition gets a point.

Fish: This is always a favorite, and great for the very young. Make your fish and attach a paper clip. Tie a magnet to the end of the line. Everyone is a winner.

Relays for Both Staff and Children

Potato-Sack Race: Traditional
Three-Legged Race: Two tied together
Wheelbarrow Race: Partners
Paper Plate on Head: Walk to goal without holding onto plate
Egg on Spoon: Does not have to be hard boiled
Roll Potato with Nose: Or one could use a popsicle stick
Pass Lifesaver Over Straw: Takes a lot of skill
Snow Shoe Race: Using paper as shoe, one cannot step until paper has been placed down under other foot. Two papers; that's all.

Quiet Games

Poor Kitty: Children are seated in a circle. One child in the center of the circle is on all fours and is the kitty. Kitty creeps to a child who must pat the kitty and say "Poor kitty" three times without smiling. Kitty tries to get the other to smile. When he succeeds they then change places.

Doggie, Doggie, Where's Your Bone? : The doggie is a blindfolded child seated in front of the group with his back turned. Another child sneaks up and takes the bone (block) and goes back to his place. The children chant "Doggie, doggie, where's your bone? Somebody took it from your home." The doggie now turns around and tries to find out who took his bone.

Who's that Knocking at My Door?: Child (blindfolded) with back to group tries to guess who knocked. The only clue is the vocal response "I did" which can be disguised. Child tries to identify.

What's that Knocking at My Door?: A variation of the above. The clue is the sound of the object, or it can be placed in the blindfolded person's hands and touched.

Indian Chief: All sit in a circle. "It" is asked to leave the area while the chief is chosen. The chief starts a motion, which all copy. When the other child returns, the chief changes the motion when he thinks that "It" is not looking his way. "It" has to identify the chief.

Spider Web: The first child touches something in the room, or if outdoors, something near him that everyone can see. The second child touches the first object and another across the room. Each child touches all previous objects, *in order*, and adds a new one. When a child misses one of the objects, he is "out."

The Minister's Cat: This is an alphabet game. Each child gives an adjective to describe the cat, in alphabetical order, after naming all previous adjectives; the seventh child might say, "The minister's cat is an active, brave, curious, dumb, eager, furry, gigantic cat."

I Went to New York: Form a circle. In the first round each player names something he took to New York—a bathing suit, a toothbrush, an apple, a pair of pajamas, etc. In the second round the first person gives a logical sentence about his object, and the others repeat the same sentence, substituting their objects. You could then have—"I went to New York and wore my bathing suit in the swimming pool at the hotel." (wore my toothbrush, apple, pajamas, etc., in the swimming pool at the hotel.) The results can be hilarious. *Note:* Best with no more than ten players. Counselor may need to help choose objects with varied uses.

Special Days:

Many of the themes suggested earlier can be used for one special day instead of a whole week. In addition, you might have:

Backwards Day
Swap Day
Color Day: Everyone tries to wear something of the color announced
    in advance. Program ideas center around the color.

Who Am I? Day:

Each camper decides who he is going to be; may or may not dress the part. Each one starts out with a small sack of roofing circles, tile chips, beans. Campers ask questions which must be answered "Yes" or "No." When another camper guesses his identity he gives him some of his "booty." The one who ends the day with the greatest number wins some recognition. (It would be wise to have each camper register with his counselor at the beginning of the day so he will not change his identity.)

Flags, Signs, and Badges

It is a good feeling to belong to a group. Left by themselves campers are likely to develop their own cliques—inevitably leaving some out. This can be avoided when there is a deliberate attempt to build group identity and spirit. After a name has been chosen, an arts and crafts activity could be the designing and creating of pins and badges. In similar fashion, a flag could be designed and proudly erected over the group area.

One interesting way to make a sign is by tacking or gluing rope onto a board.

Burning the name on a board with a magnifying glass held in the sun is an even more exciting experience. It should be carefully supervised and tied in with a discussion of fires, mentioned in Chapter 18, Adventures in Camping.

Riddles:

'I will place three counselors in a row, take off my shoes and jump over them.''

(Answer: Jump over shoes.)

* * *

"I will sing Yankee Doodle backwards in the same length of time it takes you to sing it."

(Stand with back turned and sing.)

* * *

"What questions can you ask that can never be truthfully answered 'no'?"

(Answer: How do you pronounce Y-E-S?)

* * *

"What question can you ask that can never truthfully be answered 'Yes'?"

(Answer: Are you asleep?)

Magic

Can you lift a small coke bottle with a straw? (If you bend the straw it will hook under the lip of the bottle and you can lift it.)

Stand over a cardboard box and drop playing cards into it. (Trick is to drop them flat side down. If on edge air catches side and they will not land in box.)

Put six glasses in a row. Fill numbers one, two, and three half full of water. Task is to move just one glass so every other one will be empty. (Solution: Pick up number two glass and empty it into number five.)

Games for Learning Names and Getting Acquainted

Roll A Name: Children sit on ground or floor in a circle. Leader rolls ball to a child saying, "Tell us your name."

Identification: Leader describes a child. First one to call out the right name describes another child, etc. Another version is: "I am thinking of someone who's name rhymes with track . . ." Make up verses rhymng names, such as:

Grace, Grace ran a race.
Jenny found a shiny penny.

Zim, Zam, Zum: Children form a circle. Start by having them learn the names of the children on their right and their left. "It" points to a child, says, "Zim" and counts. Child must name the camper on his right before the count of ten. *Zam* means the camper on the left; *Zum* means give your own name. If a child fails to give the right answer, he changes places with "It."

There will be no time when a full bag of tricks will be more appreciated than on a rainy day, usually faced with dread. These days can be the best!

chapter 22 Rainy Days Can Be the Best

A rainy day program cannot be "played by ear," but will hinge on two prime factors—*attitude* and *preparation*.

Counselor Tom Brown may not be overjoyed at the sight of rain, but he has the satisfaction of knowing he is ready for it. First, he makes sure he is going to stay warm and dry, knowing that his disposition will be related to his comfort. Next, he checks his schedule to see just what changes he can expect, what his duties will be, and for how many children he may be responsible. He can face the day with equanimity because he has made his plans and has the materials rounded up that he will need to carry them out.

Counselor Harry Jones opens one eye at 7:00 a.m., glimpses the gray skies and pouring rain, and groans, "Oh, no, a rainy day!" He arrives in camp inadequately dressed, prepared to be miserable, and starts spreading the contagion of his gloom with such greetings as "Nice weather for ducks!" Not having made any special preparation, he succeeds in making everyone who comes near him share his misery before the day is over.

Planning Ahead

The first stages leading to this all-important preparation are undertaken by the director long before camp opens.

Space

First, he will consider space. How many warm, dry areas will be available? If tents are used, will they let in enough light? How long can they be used if there is a cold, driving rain with high wind? If rain lasts more than one day? How much moving around in the rain will be

231

necessary? How many times will the campers have to put on and take off raincoats, hats, and rubbers?

It will take time and concerted effort to visualize a whole day's program with every camper accounted for all of the time, but it is easier to do it in advance than to struggle with last-minute arrangements or to squeeze too many children into inadequate facilities. A realistic approach anticipating the worst possible conditions may send the wise camp director in search of a clubhouse, church, recreation hall, or some other large indoor space that is available for emergency use. One day camp made use of a neighborhood clubhouse (seldom used in the summer); another had permission to use the town hall. In some cases it may even be necessary to cancel camp entirely on rainy days. In this event some plan will have to be devised for notifying parents. Radio or TV announcements on local stations may be used, or a telephone chain. The director calls ten key staff people who each call ten, and so on, until the last camper has been notified. If this system is used, the last person on each chain should call the director back to be sure no link was broken. The system should be explained to parents in a precamp bulletin. At the same time a thorough description of required rainy-day apparel could be included with a plea for marking every item.

Clothing

The day camp director who has been faced with innumerable yellow slickers and hats and as many pairs of unmarked rubbers will provide marking pencils or pens with instructions for counselors to inspect each article as it is taken off, marking where necessary. A snap clothespin for every camper, also with a name on it, will help to keep rubbers together. Decorating these clothespins could be an early crafts project and help the campers to recognize their own. If the group moves from one building to another, the clothespin should go along in the raincoat pocket.

Counselors, too, need to be reminded of the necessity of keeping warm and dry *all* day. An extra pair of socks or dungarees may be as necessary for them as for campers.

Program

When careful planning for physical space and comfort is complete, the director can then begin to think of program. What activities can continue as usual? If there is an arts and crafts shop, will it need to accommodate more campers on a rainy day? If so, the counselor in charge should be alerted.

What activities will it be necessary to eliminate? If there are specialists for swimming, archery, or sports, what other responsibilities will they assume?

In an early bulletin to counselors some suggestions can be made for program ideas, but in addition it should be stressed that every individual will be expected to come to camp with concrete contributions for rainy-day activities.

In our camp every counselor was expected to bring in a box or bag labeled "Rainy Days," which held the materials required for a particular activity. For example, he would have straws and beans ready for a relay race. Enough attention was drawn to these often gaily decorated containers to invite questions from the campers. Told that "We can't open them until we have a real rainy day," their curiosity was fired. Campers have been known to yearn for a rainy day, which sets a good tone when it happens.

During precamp training it might be good to devote at least one full session to a discussion of rainy days, with emphasis on attitudes, a check on schedules, and a demonstration of program ideas. Several programs could be planned, and the equipment for them secured, stored, and marked, ready for use.

The following list of suggestions will serve as a jumping-off place for the ingenious counselor who will be constantly surprised to find that the simplest devices are often the most fun. Perhaps it may be necessary to resort to movies if the rains come down for days on end, but these too can be related to camping.

Outdoor Activities

There are many fun things for campers to do in the rain if they are appropriately dressed. Unless the counselor can approach the undertaking with enthusiasm, it will be a dismal failure; therefore, the suggestion would stem from him, not from the director.

—*Drippy Walks.* One has only to observe the line of cars drawn up outside a school in suburbia on a rainy day to realize that walking with rain in your face is a rare experience for many of today's children. "What looks different in the rain?" ". . . smells different?" "What can you hear in the quiet of the woods?" Giving the excursion some purpose will make it more meaningful.

* * *

Have you ever walked in the rain?
I have . . .
The raindrops beating on my hat,
My boots sloshing through a puddle
And the wet, wet feeling on my face.
Have you ever walked in the rain?
I have . . .

Have you ever walked in the fog?
I have . . .
It closes in softly about you
And makes you open your eyes wide
To peer into nothing
Have you ever walked in the fog?
I have . . .

Have you ever run in the wind?
I have . . .
The rush of noise about your ears,
Hair whipping your head,
The feeling of fresh air warming your skin
Have you ever run in the wind?
I have . . .

(HAVE YOU EVER WALKED IN THE RAIN? by Helen Campbell)

—*Scavenger Hunt.* The list could include such items as a worm, a dry leaf, a bird feather, or an acorn.

—*Fishing.* Whether it is true or not that fish bite better in a rain will make little difference to the small boy who has never known the pleasure of fishing under these conditions.

—*Swimming.* Some of the older campers may elect to swim in the rain. This is usually permissible if caution is taken to be sure they are rubbed dry and do not get chilled. Never swim in thunder showers.

—*Campcraft.* Discuss techniques for keeping comfortable in the rain. Practice fire building. Plan and carry out a cookout in the woods on a rainy day.

Indoor Activities for Small Groups

Originality and imagination are welcome faculties in counselors when it comes to thinking up indoor activities for small groups on rainy days.

—*Collections.* This is a time when campers and counselors can share their special interests. A collection of bells, dolls, model planes, miniature animals, stamps, or other items can be carried from one small group to another, or six or eight displays might be set up in one large room. Articles that can be handled will be more satisfactory to children than those that can only be viewed, but both have their place.

—*Traveling Shows:* Short skits, plays, puppet shows, marionette shows, shadow box shows, or flannel board stories can travel from one group to another, providing entertainment for the performers as well as the audience. The preparation for these might have started at the beginning of the summer as a major project, or they may be planned and rehearsed in the morning for an afternoon performance. A counselor who plays a musical instrument might go about as a wandering minstrel, playing a few numbers at each stop. These travel shows give the campers a delightful feeling of suspense, since they never know what treat is in store.

—*Dress Up*. In one camp it is traditional for counselors to visit the costume room on a rainy day and deck themselves out in some outlandish outfit; Mr. John in a derby hat and a pair of shorts, Miss Sue in red flannel ski pajamas, or the director in a Peter Pan hat with a rakish feather sets the stage for a day of fun. Children, too, can spend happy hours with a few costume accessories. In one camp, second-quality crepe paper is purchased in quantity from a local manufacturer for the making of paper costumes on rainy days.

—*Cooking*. All ages can enjoy cooking on a rainy day. The very youngest campers (nursery) can make uncooked puddings in paper cups decorated with chocolate shots. Popping corn with an old-fashioned hand popper is fun, and if a roofed-over area is available, popping can be done over a charcoal fire.

Boys and girls will enjoy making cookies or cakes; indoors if a kitchen is available, or utilizing an indoor or outdoor fireplace with a reflector oven. The memory of the aroma of gingerbread baking in a fireplace will outlast the cake itself, and, if that gingerbread is baked in the shell of a scooped-out orange, baking becomes an adventure!

—*Ice Cream*. Making ice cream with an old-fashioned hand freezer and rock salt is another new experience for most day campers.

—*Parties*. Planning in the morning for a special party to take place in the afternoon can provide enough ideas for a full day's program. Children are intrigued by a Halloween or Valentine party out of season; invitations (it is fun to invite someone even if it is only the office secretary), decorations, favors, refreshments, and entertainment all help to make the day a busy and interesting one. An "Un-birthday" party inspired by Alice in Wonderland is a traditional rainy-day event in one day camp.

—*Picture Contest*. Each camper will lie down on a large sheet of paper and the counselor or another camper draws around this outline. He can place himself in an active position, running, jumping, dancing, etc. During the day he will fill in detail of clothing with crayons and paints. At the end of the day the pictures are hung on a wall and campers from another group try to identify them. (A variation is to draw a picture on a 12″ x 18″ paper and dress it with scraps of cloth, yarn, etc.)

—*Playmaking.* A counselor with some knowledge of the art of makeup makes up children as different characters. They then write a play and include each character.

—*Charades.* This is really a very basic beginning of dramatization. Write the names of objects, sports, occupations, or nursery rhymes on chards, which the counselor could whisper in the ear of a nonreader. Pictures could be used as well.

—*Puppets.* Making simple puppets and preparing a show can take up a large part of a rainy day.

All these possibilities can be discussed at the training session. Lists should be made of the materials and equipment necessary and where to get them. When the rainy day comes, each counselor should know where to sign up for any facility that has to be shared.

Indoor Programs for Large Groups

In many cases the rainy-day facilities available to a day camp will make it necessary to use one large room for several hours. If this building is away from the camp each counselor should know in advance what equipment he is to take. This should be set aside in a box or carton marked "For rainy days only." The director, program leader, or whoever is to be in charge of the overall program, and several key persons should arrive before the campers to set the stage. When the children do arrive, someone should be standing near the entrance with explicit directions for the care of outside clothing and storage of lunch boxes. If as much as fifteen minutes is going to elapse between the arrival of the first and last bus loads, a plan should be ready to occupy the early arrivals. Table games, listening to records, books, or inactive games may be best. If active games are employed, they should be well-planned and supervised. It will be a great temptation to campers to run or slide on a large floor space or to want to explore an unaccustomed building, but after fifteen minutes of such activity it will take a much longer period to get the group back under control.

When all have arrived and their belongings are settled, a brief assembly will serve to pull the group together. Rules should be established for the day, the location of toilets explained, and the day's plans outlined. If the campers are six-years-old or younger, they will need reassurance. A strange place will bring to the surface some old fears—"Will I get home safely?" "Will my car and driver know where to find me?" If the procedures are outlined in detail and the children are given a chance to ask questions, they can relax and enjoy themselves.

If the building is large enough, the group might then break up into smaller groups and go to different corners to plan a skit, stunt, or charade. A stage and a piano will be definite assets. Depending on the campers' ages and the facilities, the planning and preparation might take up the morning and the production the afternoon, or it might be all done in half a day. In this case a second plan would be necessary for the hours remaining after lunch and rest.

Another plan would be a variety show. Each counselor should be expected to be ready with a contribution. Campers should be given alternate opportunities to watch and to get into the act. Noisy, let-off-steam games or contests are alternated with quiet stories or music.

A prearranged signal is explained, demonstrated, and practiced (a whistle, gong, bell, piano chord, or upraised hand), which will be used throughout the day when it is necessary to get the attention of the group.

In conclusion, the counselor should remind himself that weather has little effect on the enthusiasm and exuberance of children. Every camp director dreads a prolonged spell of rainy weather, but in one camp when this did occur, the staff was amazed to discover at the end of the season that campers' enthusiasm and parents' reports indicated that it had been the "best summer ever."

chapter	Day Camping is for
23	Everyone

As a rule, when we speak of day camping the image that comes to mind is of children from ages five to twelve, but in recent years changes in our society have brought about new patterns for living, and some of these are reflected in the services offered by day camps. A brief description of day camps that extend outside the parameters of the usual may serve to arouse the interest of the reader and point the direction for further investigation.

The first, and most logical, step is to extend the age limits downward. As more and more mothers enter the work force and the need for child care increases, the gap between day camping and day care has narrowed—and the services have overlapped. It is natural for parents to want all of their children to be in the same place and this has led many day camp operators to add programs for younger children.

The Nursery Camp

These are sensitive years when good experiences can give children a real head start; but on the other side of the coin, their developing personalities are vulnerable. The day camp director who sets up a nursery camp is incurring heavy responsibility. The following suggestions stress the importance of the people, the place, and the program.

People. As a minimal requirement the supervisor of the nursery camp should have a degree in early childhood development. Her assistants may be students from a teacher training institute, mothers who have obvious intelligence and nurturant qualities, or teachers. Frequently, but not always, teachers of elementary or secondary schools find it hard to adjust their training and experience to this younger age.

The camper/staff ratio will be different from that required for a regular camp. More hands and eyes are needed to care for these little ones properly; more laps are needed for comforting and cuddling. Junior counselors may act as aides but they should have had some experience, either as a member of a large family or as babysitters. Many high schools now offer excellent child-care courses through their home economics department—a good resource to tap. Whatever the age it is essential that the people who work with the little ones have a real love for this age—and are selected because it is their first preference. Unfortunately the nursery camp often is the "dumping ground" for the preteens and teens who are related to staff, or whose parents put on pressure with, "She just loves children. I know you will find something for her to do!" and the hapless supervisor finds himself with another camper on his hands!

Place. The site for the nursery camp should be separate—but close. They will love being part of the camp but they need the protection of a fence to keep them from wandering and to protect them from the exciting activities going on "out there." It is fine when the older campers stop to chat with them through the fence; it would not be good to have a group intent on a scavenger hunt rush through their playground, or the outfielder chasing a ball in their midst.

The quality of the indoor space is important for the little ones because it represents security. They need to find their belongings in the same spot, and take their naps in reasonable comfort and quiet.

The play yard must have some shade—and some sun. A large sand box or area is the first requisite, but in addition there should be space for running and digging, and opportunities for pushing, pulling, swinging and sliding, crawling over and under and through, balancing and building.

Ideally they will have their own pool within their own area, but if they are taken to a pool used by older campers, their daily program can sometimes be adjusted so they can use it while the others are at lunch. There are many ways to keep little ones, especially those under three, cool without a pool: a hose with a spray attachment, sprinklers and fountains, water play in wash tubs, and even dish .pans. With a little ingenuity and imagination anything is possible.

Program. The key word in planning program for the nursery is slow. These little ones are hurried enough elsewhere. Before they arrive they may have been hustled through breakfast and on to a bus. They need a comfortable, relaxed environment where they won't hear a lot of "don'ts" and "hurry ups."

Program for them is everything that is going on around them.

Day Camping for Teenagers

The ages from thirteen to sixteen are difficult years for kids *and* their parents, and the summer months add to existing problems of physical and personality changes. Suddenly the eager enthusiastic camper becomes a sophisticated, bored adolescent, too old for "that baby stuff" and too young to hold a real job. At one point this child who changes color as freely as a chameleon is eager and able to accept responsibility, but in the next reverts to a child who still wants to play. It is an uncomfortable time in the process of growing up; a time when the child/adult is easily lured by his peers down the path to dangerous practices, or when a good role model can set his feet firmly on the way to the "good life" of productivity and satisfaction. It is an age when "just hanging around" is the "in" thing to do, but as many a distraught parent knows "hanging around" can lead to danger.

Sometimes a specialty camp will hold their interest. Baseball, riding, sailing, and environmental camps are fine if they are available, and if the parent can afford it. Some day camps attempt to solve this problem with CIT programs.

Counselor-In-Training Program

Ideally this will supply a gradual transition from being a camper to employment as a junior counselor. Planning such a program could follow the same lines as those for the nursery camp.

People. It takes a special kind of person to win the respect and admiration of teenagers. An understanding of the physical changes that are taking place, sympathy for their emotional and social problems, and the ability to listen are requisites.

Program. Ideally this will be balanced with activities for fun and learning experiences. For example, the CIT may need to subjugate his own inclinations while he helps others in the ceramics program, but with the understanding that time will be allowed later for him to "do his own thing."

With each year the balance between work and play will shift and that is why in some camps parents are charged half the usual tuition at first, and this is reduced as responsibilities and work jobs are increased, always with the goal of turning the camper into a junior counselor.

Day Camping for the Whole Family

It is not uncommon for a parent to say with some nostalgia, "I think I will take a leave of absence from my job and come here for the summer." There is little likelihood that there will be day camps for the breadwinners of the family, but a few camps have found a way to share their facilities with families, and at the same time increase income, which will enable them to maintain and improve their property.

Some simply open up the use of the grounds to the families of their campers evenings and weekends, but that incurs problems of supervision, maintenance, and insurance.

One very successful private day camp with unusually fine facilities set up a separate operation, known as the Club, and offered membership priority to their own clientele. The pools, tennis courts, sports equipment, and open fireplaces were all available evenings and weekends to Club members. The hours were limited, and staff included a director, life guards, and maintenance crew who made certain everything was restored to good condition for the next day's campers.

In the 1980s the theme of the White House Conference on Families is "Strengthening the Family." Day camping can make a worthy contribution to this goal.

Inner City Camps

It has long been held that the idea is to take the children off city streets in the summer and give them a week or two in the country—to let them know that the world has trees, ponds, fields, and streams that are clean and in a natural setting. A city has these features, but they have not all been well-kept or respected. In the city parks there are birds, bees, and frogs if only we look.

I learned about a day camp in Hartford, Connecticut, that has reversed the usual process. The camp goes on the assumption that suburban children can gain new perspectives if they are taken to the city. I quote from news articles describing this unusual operation.

Instead of taking children into the wilds to expose them to nature's marvels, this camp aims to expose rural and suburban youngsters to the man-made wonders and blunders of the big city. Dodging traffic, riding elevators, and climbing to the top of a fire engine replace nature hikes, canoe races, and campfire songs. Instead of poison ivy, bee stings, and rope burns, one camper collided head-on with a parking meter, another skinned her knee on the sidewalk, and blisters from long hikes on hot pavement are commonplace.

David, a twelve-year-old boy who normally lives, plays, and goes to school in a quiet suburban town, says he prefers this camp in the city to the quiet, woodsy kind. "There you just see nature," he says, "but in the city you can see everything."

Some of the activities are similar to other day camps, such as swimming and arts and crafts, but they are adjusted to take advantage of the environment. At a morning arts and crafts session the children build cardboard cities and color street maps of Hartford as it was in 1936 and as it looks today. They decorate the trash cans in the city park where they eat their lunches, and when they hike on the city streets, forty-five strong attired in bright yellow T-shirts, they draw smiles and hellos from fellow passers by. When they break into song shoppers smile and some join in.

Trips are planned to cover a wide spectrum of city life every afternoon. There are visits to a film festival, a museum, opera and ballet rehearsals and performances, to a planetarium and aquarium, police and fire stations, the mayor's office, and a post office, as well as a television studio, an office tower, a bank, and the printing plant that printed the camp T-shirts.

They learn about the city communications systems and the various transportation systems.

How do parents feel about sending their children into the city? One mother answered, "When I first mentioned it to my husband he responded incredulously, 'I'm paying tremendous taxes to raise this kid in a rural atmosphere and you want to send him into the city?'" After the child had attended a two-week test session, both parents were so pleased with his city sophistication that they enrolled him for the rest of the season.

"I thought sure he would hear and repeat 'dirty words,'" this mother said, "but it didn't happen, and anyway I decided that since you can't isolate a child from cities forever, they might as well learn to cope at an early age."

Camp Downtown, sponsored by the Hartford YMCA and the Hartford Downtown Council, a business organization, is being eyed by other large cities, and is presently being tried in several.

For further information write to:

> Allen L. Beavers, Jr.
> Hartford YMCA
> 160 Jewell Street
> Hartford, CT 06103

Day Camping for Children with Special Needs

Twenty years ago the idea of bringing children with physical or emotional differences into programs for "normal" children was practically unheard of. In recent years our government has enacted legislation based on the premise that every child is entitled to an education to the limit of his potential, and that, whenever possible, he should be mainstreamed into the existing programs. While this has not been extended into day camping. I want to say from personal experience that it can be done for the mutual benefit of all concerned; those fortunate children who were endowed with all of their physical and mental faculties have much to gain from living and playing with those who are more limited. I offer here some guidelines developed out of experience. I hope that readers will be encouraged to open their doors to these special children, remembering that "everyone is more or less."

Most children accept differences in their stride; often they seem not to notice them. The exceptional child has to earn his way with his peers for they will not coddle or protect him as his family may. Casual acceptance is the greatest gift a special child's peers can offer. On the other hand, a child will show a natural consideration not at all comparable to the maudlin sympathy of an adult.

Staff in a school or camp should be helped in developing the same healthy attitudes. It takes a special kind of courage to let the blind child find his way or the crippled child fall and get up and go on, but these children must test their own limits and find their own patterns for daily living. The adult can watch over their safety without being overly protective.

The decision to accept a child with special needs should be made only after all parties concerned have agreed that the particular situation will benefit the child without seriously detracting from the rights of the other children. In some cases where the child may require more attention than a group counselor can give, it may be necessary to seek a volunteer to help out. This would certainly be a requirement if the child must be lifted or carried.

Probably the most important warning is that the child must come through referral by a professional, with the promise of continued communication and guidance. It is cruel to accept a child and decide later that it was a mistake. These children will experience rejection many times throughout their lives; we should not add to that process.

Even when the greatest care is taken before the child is enrolled, there may be cases when it becomes necessary to let go. It is hard for the adults who have made a personal investment in this life to make that decision, but when that camper has drained the reserves of the counselor the wheels should be set in motion for an alternative plan. Sometimes complete withdrawal is not necessary, but instead the hours can be reduced or additional help provided.

Day Camping for the Elderly

At the other end of the spectrum there has been some experimentation in providing daily programs for the elderly. One such center is a part of the overall camp operation of the Henry Kaufmann Campgrounds, sponsored by the Federation of Jewish Philanthropies. I talked with the executive vice president, Mr. Monte Melamed, and have organized his answers in the same format.

The People

The qualifications are not unlike those I would want for the staff who would work with little children. The staff should be understanding of the physical and emotional needs of this age group; they should truly enjoy being with the elderly and they should be good listeners.

The Place

This is a primary consideration when dealing with our senior citizens, and may well be a stumbling block which stops such a program before it is more than an idea. All physical facilities must be geared to meet physical limitations; this usually means adding ramps, hand rails and bars, handles for grasping, paved walkways, and level ground. There should be as few steps as possible. The terrain that is a challenge to children may be traumatic for the elderly. Quiet, shaded places for just sitting and relaxing with comfortable, sturdy chairs are essential, and dining facilities should be comfortable. Our elder citizens are required to queue up in too many areas of their lives; when they come to camp they should sit at tables in small groups and be served graciously.

The Program

"What do they do?" I asked the director. "Just about everything that children do," was the answer. "They have swimming, dancing, walking, calisthenics, music, and games. Some of the more agile play tennis, volleyball, and shuffleboard. Arts and crafts are popular and we have many a potential "Grandma Moses" in our painting classes. In some aspects of program, such as swimming, we find it best to combine them with the children if it is not too crowded.

"Some of them see the usual camp activities as nothing but children's games. For them we try to bring in informed people who can talk about current events and, in our case, those issues concerning the Jewish people."

"Do you see such programs as proliferating?" I asked. "The need is certainly there," was the answer. "The main problem is one common to all social programs: a lack of funding."

Readers who wish to know more about this program can write to:

Mr. Monte Melamed, Executive Vice President
Henry Kaufmann Camp Grounds
667 Blauvelt Road
Pearl River, NY 10965

Telephone (914) 735-6969 or 2718

chapter
24

Reflections

The thoughts expressed in this book have been collective, representing the opinions and practices of many people and, more specifically, the American Camping Association. These last few paragraphs are strictly the reflections of Grace Mitchell.

I trust that the potential day camp owner will be enlightened but not frightened by the multitudinous details outlined as necessary to successful day camp operation. This is serious business, as is any project having a direct influence on the health, welfare, and happiness of children, but it is a business that will bring deep satisfaction to anyone who is primarily concerned with camper needs and program ideals.

The material has been arranged in the logical sequence followed in setting up a day camp. If the beginning camp director will take it that way, one step at a time, it will not seem so overwhelming. The most successful day camp owners I have known have allowed ample time for investigation, study, and planning before taking the initial step, and then very wisely set a limit on the number of campers they would enroll in the first year. These camps have grown as they were able to expand facilities and their owners have gained experience, but at no time have they reached a state where the tail wagged the dog. As a result they now enjoy an enviable reputation and have been highly successful.

One director tells the story of a taxi driver, engaged to transport campers, who offered this piece of advice. He said, "I don't care what you offer the public, but whatever you promise, give them." Acting on his suggestion the camp director stated very frankly to parents, "We do not pretend to have all the facilities we hope to have eventually, but you may be sure that we shall never be too busy to give time and attention to your child." Parents recognized this as an asset they could not always be sure of in the most expensive camp and, since they were given evidence that the promise was reinforced with sincerity, the camp was successful from the start.

Each day camp director starts out with a ready-made set of beliefs. It is wise to keep an open mind and be willing to change, but it is also important to back up convictions with courage if necessary. One director says, "I know that our program is too highly organized. We should be doing more real camping, but Mr. Smith insists that we teach his son to play baseball." Another says, "I cannot conduct a program that is contrary to my belief in what is right for children. I will have to show Mr. Smith that what we have to offer his boy is good." Actually each camp director must decide at the outset whether he is going to run his camp for the benefit of children or to please parents, remembering that "he who tries to please everyone pleases no one."

The director of a well-established day camp will be less likely to get into a rut or become too complacent if he will make an effort to visit another day camp each year. This is not easy in the midst of the busy camping season, but usually pays rich dividends to the visitor, who is sure to examine his own camp with new perspective after each visit. The Standards implementation program of the American Camping Association has been largely carried out by volunteer visitors—experienced camp directors trained in the techniques of visitation.

It has been my privilege to visit many fine day camps in this way, and I frankly admit that the benefits to my own camp exceeded the contribution I may have made to others.

I saw many excellent programs, but I did observe, more than once, what I considered poor use of existing facilities. Opportunities for genuine camping experiences were overlooked while children were engaged in traditional activities. More than once I saw the entire population of a large camp all swimming at the same time while all other program areas were idle. Program could have been staggered so that camper groups could have been small, and maximum use made of all the facilities all of the time.

While he is looking at the program the day camp director should bear in mind that it is not essential for every camper to be doing something all the time. The nicest gift we can give to some children is an opportunity to be still and do nothing; the finest thing we can teach them is to take time to stop, look, and listen. Day camp can be an oasis in the midst of a world where pressure and haste prevail.

In addition to constant appraisal of facilities and program, the day camp director should have a continuing plan for development and improvement. If the day arrives when he cannot think of another way to make his camp a better place for children it is time for him to retire. Of the many resources available to help him, the first is the American Camping Association. Membership in this national organization, the only one devoted to professional camping interests, will give him access to written materials, a subscription to *Camping Magazine*, and an opportunity to attend conventions or meetings where he can share ideas with experienced camping leaders. In addition, he can always write to the national headquarters for help with specific problems.

In most Sections of the American Camping Association there are Day Camp Committees to plan special programs and services for day camp members, and some local groups have round table discussions where they share information. Although one would suppose that ethics need not be mentioned in connection with people responsible for the guidance of children, misunderstandings and unfortunate competitive practices exist occasionally, and a round table discussion is often an effective means of straightening out such incidents.

As a further aid to professional growth the day camp director will want to develop and maintain a good library.

We have included a few of our own favorites at the beginning of this book but in addition we suggest that the reader write to the American Camping Association and the National Recreation Association for their bibliographies.

Other youth-serving agencies have also developed materials that are available to camping leaders, usually at a minimal cost. The addresses of these and sources of pamphlets are given in the Appendix.

In conclusion, I would like to offer encouragement to anyone who is considering starting a day camp. Of the many and varied experiences I have had in the past half-century of my life the best years were those devoted to day camping. Someone has said, "It is as hard to separate love of your work from love of the people you work with as it is to separate the sun from the sunshine." Camping people are good people dedicated to the cause of children, generous with their help and fun to be with. You couldn't join a better society!

In the last two decades we have seen an increase in social and economic ills. Rebellion against moral and ethical traditions, violence, child abuse, and an increase in the divorce rate, leading to a breakdown of the traditional family structure, have rattled the security of our children. I have watched many of them return to camp each summer as if they were clutching the center post in the midst of a spinning world. Camp was the one place where they could find things staying the same. I like to believe we gave some of them the emotional strength to cope—and survive.

Within the past year I sat beside a pleasant-faced woman on a plane who said, "You are Mrs. Mitchell. You wouldn't remember me but I sent two children to your day camp." To her amazement when she told me her name I said, "Oh yes, Richard and Linda—how are they?" (Camping people are like that!) "Linda is in her last year of graduate school," she replied, "and Richard is married and has two children. I hear him telling them about when he went to camp and I think 'Every child should grow up with memories like that!'"

This story expresses the feelings of pride and satisfaction I enjoy in my own memories of day camping, and for whatever I may have contributed to thousands of children. There is no greater reward!

Appendix
ACA, Standards, and Accreditation

The American Camping Association (ACA) is a nationwide, non-profit, non-sectarian organization of people interested in organized camping for children and adults. Members include nearly 6,000 camp directors, camp owners, camp staff members, educators, clergymen, and others associated with the operation of camps.

The purpose of the American Camping Association is to assure the highest professional practices and administration and extension of the unique experience of organized camping. To achieve this purpose, the Association has three primary goals:

1. To maintain contact with contemporary societal forces as related to camping and to develop appropriate response and action,
2. To enhance the quality of the organized camping experience,
3. To interpret the value of organized camping to the public.

The program of the Association is administered through 32 Sections covering all 50 states and several foreign countries. Section, Regional, and national officers are elected by the membership and serve without pay. The financial support of the organization comes primarily from the dues of its members. Other support comes from convention fees, the sale of publications, and foundation grants.

The American Camping Association serves as consultant and advisor to many state and federal agencies related to the field of camping and to colleges and universities in the field of outdoor education and camping.

The Standards Program

The purpose of the Standards program is to assist administrators in the provision of a quality camp experience for participating campers.

In a camp that meets the Standards and is accredited, the program endeavors to provide each person with the opportunity to increase his/her development toward a fulfilling, productive life in a healthy and safe outdoor environment.

Standards represent desirable practices basic to quality programs. By meeting 14 specific required Standards and at least 75 percent of applicable Standards in each of four operational categories—site, administration, personnel, and program—a camp, whether owned by an organization, institution, agency, or individual, may become an accredited camp. These requirements are considered minimum or baseline. Few camps receive accreditation by meeting the minimum; the majority receive accreditation with compliance of 90 percent or more.

The book *ACA Camp Standards with Interpretations for Accreditation of Organized Camps* contains a comprehensive description of the Standards. A simple listing of Standards is also available entitled *ACA Condensed Standards for Organized Camps*. Either may be purchased from the ACA Publications Service.

For further information on Standards or Accredited Camps look for the American Camping Association in the White Pages of your telephone book, or write or call: The American Camping Association, Bradford Woods, Martinsville, IN 46151-7902; Phone: (317) 342-8456.

In 1956 Day Camp Standards were adopted for use with the then four-year-old camp Standards program of the American Camping Association. By 1965, following four years of work, ACA Camp Standards were consolidated, recognizing the extensive commonality in the operation of all types of camps. Though the instruments have been refined since that time to reflect diversity in specialized programs meeting specialized needs, the current approach to Camp Accreditation is still through a consolidated set of Standards.

ACA recognizes the need for quality in all camps and makes available Standards materials to anyone. ACA members may have their camps visited and accredited at no charge, but nonmembers pay for the service. The accrediting process is a self-policing action by the members and one of the marks of a profession. Nationally trained and certified "visitors" experienced in camping make an on-site visitation at least every three years to evaluate a camp's compliance with the Standards. Although the visitors do check off compliance with Standards, they are not inspectors as such but rather work with the camp personnel in helping them to conduct a quality operation. The visitor's function is educative.

The scoring is processed through an evaluation system in the national office. Based on this scoring report, the local ACA Section Board of Directors approves the accreditation of camps under its jurisdiction. A National Standards Board monitors the application of the Standards and endeavors to keep them current and viable. However, the Standards program is administered through the 32 local ACA Sections. Several hundred well-qualified ACA members volunteer their time for implementation of the Standards.

In addition to the regular full camp accreditation, the ACA provides for site approval only. A site that has been approved means that the operation meets those Standards specific to sites only. These Standards are concerned with facilities, site layout and management of the natural environment, and administrative practices related to a specific site and operation. Organizations and groups renting such sites know that certain basic environmental and operational requirements have been met.

Accreditation Process

Accreditation is the end result of an orderly procedure involving the camp, the ACA national office, the ACA Section Standards committee, and the Section Board.

The "visitor" is the person who makes the actual on-site "visitation." Camp visitors are ACA members who are experienced in camping and are certified by the Association after satisfactorily completing an official visitor training program.

When there are two or more visitors conducting the visit, one person, usually the most experienced, is designated the lead visitor.

Procedures for Accreditation—New Camps

Specific procedures are carried out by the American Camping Association, both at the national and at the Section level, during the accreditation process. These are designated as "ACA-Steps." In order to complete this process, specific steps, each called a "Camp-Step" are followed by the camp director or the camp representative of the camp seeking accreditation.

Camp-Step 1: A camp representative writes to the national office, American Camping Association, Bradford Woods, Martinsville, IN 46151-7902, indicating interest in camp owner/director membership in the ACA or nonmember accreditation information.

ACA-Step 1: The national office returns a Camp Application for Accreditation/Annual Accreditation/Reaccreditation/Site Approval/Reapproval and other information. An order form for the Standards book will be included so the camp may purchase a copy of this important guide and make early preparations for the Standards visit.

Camp-Step 2: The camp representative, board, director, et al, review the materials received from the national ACA and return the completed applications for Camp Accreditation with appropriate membership form or nonmember fee.

Preparation for the camp visit commences after the signing of the Statement of Compliance. All four statements should be studied by the applying camp with additional attention given to the Prerequisites for Accreditation Standards. The Standards should also be closely examined and efforts initiated to work toward complying with those the camp does not already meet. Using the Standards as a guideline will be helpful in camp administration.

ACA-Step 2: After the Application for Accreditation is returned, the national office informs the Section Standards Chairman through the camp Standards report of the camp's desire for accreditation. From this point through the entire process of accreditation, the local Section makes the visit and recommends classification.

ACA-Step 3: A specific priority schedule for visitation is established. All new camps are given priority category #1. The Section Standards representative contacts the camp and invites the camp director to attend a Section Camp Directors Standards Orientation Session.

Camp-Step 3: If the on-site director of camp is not the same person who is administratively in charge and/or making the visit arrangements, then the person making the visiting arrangements must confirm that the on-site director not only has and understands the Statement of Compliance and the Prerequisites for Accreditation Standards but also is being kept fully informed of the visitation arrangements. The on-site director attends the Director Orientation Session.

ACA-Step 4: The Section sends further visitation information to the camp representative, who processes all designated materials within established deadlines and is the main contact with the Section. The information includes:

a. Listing of written materials needed to complete visit;
b. Approximate date of visit, visitors assigned, and visitation arrangements;
c. Copy of letter sent to visitor(s) assigned—this designates lead visitor—and may include a general description of a typical visit;
d. Statement that the stockholders, camp committee, camp chairman, agency board, or interested persons related to camp are welcome to participate in the visit.

The assigned lead visitor makes final arrangements for the visitation with the camp representative.

Camp-Step 4: The camp representative confirms the visitation date with the lead visitor and further prepares for the accreditation visit. He collects required written documents, informs other appropriate persons related to the camp of the visitation date and requests their presence if so desired, and completes other arrangement details.

ACA-Step 5: The accreditation visit occurs.

ACA-Step 6: The visitor and camp director complete and sign the comment form and score sheet. The lead visitor of the Section sends the original scoring sheet to the ACA national office for processing. A second copy is sent to the Section Standards chairman, a third copy is given to the camp director, and the visitor keeps a fourth copy.

ACA-Step 7: The national office sends the results of the visit (score) to the Section Standards committee. The committee reviews each camp's scoring form and comment form and makes recommendations for each camp's classification; accredited, provisional, or not eligible.

ACA-Step 8: The Standards committee presents its recommendations to the Section Board (usually at the first meeting in the fall) which votes on the recommendations and notifies the national office of its decisions.

The Accreditation decision is made by the Section Board of Directors based upon the recommendation of the Section Standards committee, which bases its recommendation upon the Standards visitation score percentages, knowledge of the camp, and visitor(s) recommendations.

ACA-Step 9: Section Board transmits action in writing to:

a. Each camp and responsible persons,
b. Other responsible groups as determined necessary by each Section.

Authority to Accredit

The American Camping Association Camp Standards program is a national program based upon the integrity of the local Section as the implementing agency within the association structure. As such, the Sections conduct visitations and approve accreditation for a camp that has met the prerequisite Standards and minimum score percentages or reject the accreditation for a camp that has not done so.

On the other hand, the ACA Camp Standards program is nationally established. Changes in the Standards are the prerogative of the Council of Delegates through the National Board of Directors. The administration of the Standards program has been delegated to the National Standards Board. Furthermore, Sections are an arm of the national body according to the ACA bylaws, and in order to maintain the integrity of the ACA Standards program, the Sections do not have the authority to waive either the established prerequisite Standards or the specified minimum score percentages for compliance.

If a Section Board deems that it is highly desirable to waive one or more of the minimum score percentages, such request may be made to the National Standards Board according to the procedures set forth by that board.

As distinguished from the foregoing, the Section Board may adjust inaccurate responses to the Standards that resulted from clerical or procedural errors or misinterpretations. Such adjustments may be initiated either by the authorized Section personnel or by the camp through the established procedure for review.

Adopted by ACA Council of Delegates
March 1978

5251086

Photos in this book were submitted by the following camps: Brown Ledge Camp, VT; Camp of the Quoowant, DE; Chinnock, CA; Circle M Day Camp, IL; Deerkill Day Camp, NY; Four Winds & Westward-Ho, WA; Gold Arrow Camp, CA; Jewish Community Center Day Camp, IN; Nebagamon, WI; Winona Lake Camp, IN; and YMCA Camp Orkila, WA.